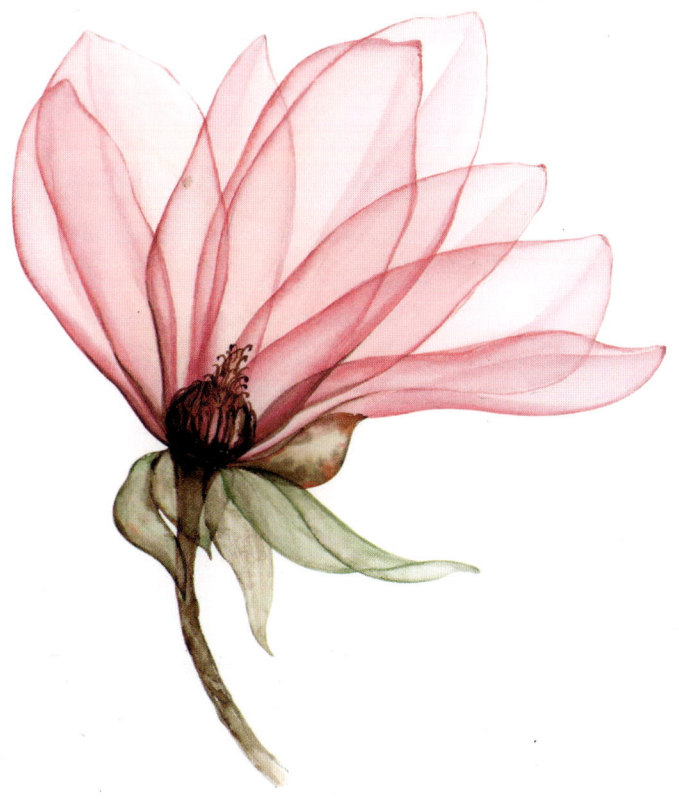

OLGA KOELSCH

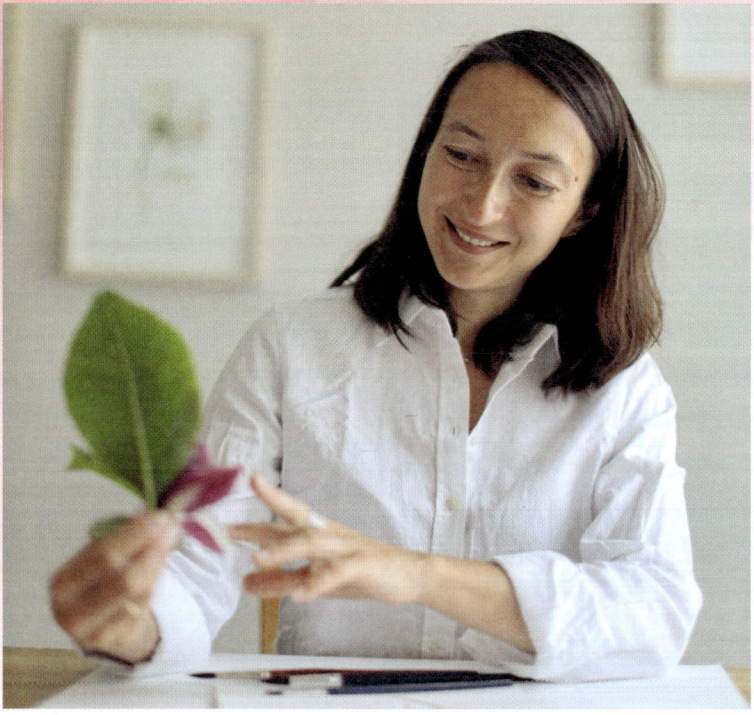

Olga is a self-taught watercolour artist, pattern designer and botanical illustrator. She originally pursued a freelance art career in botanical illustration, after working in marketing for several years, but craved more expression and freedom in painting. Olga began to blend her knowledge of botany with modern watercolour techniques, creating stunning transparent flower bouquets that have now become her signature work.

As well as designing for and collaborating with clothing and stationery brands, Olga loves sharing her knowledge and experience in watercolour. She started a YouTube channel to offer painting lessons; she also has a hugely popular Instagram page where you could have a sneak peek at her process, find inspiration and connect with other artists.

Olga lives in Bergen, Norway, with her husband and two sons.

www.olgakoelsch.com
@ @olga.koelsch
▶ @olgakoelsch
♪ @olgakoelsch
www.creativemarket.com/olga.koelsch

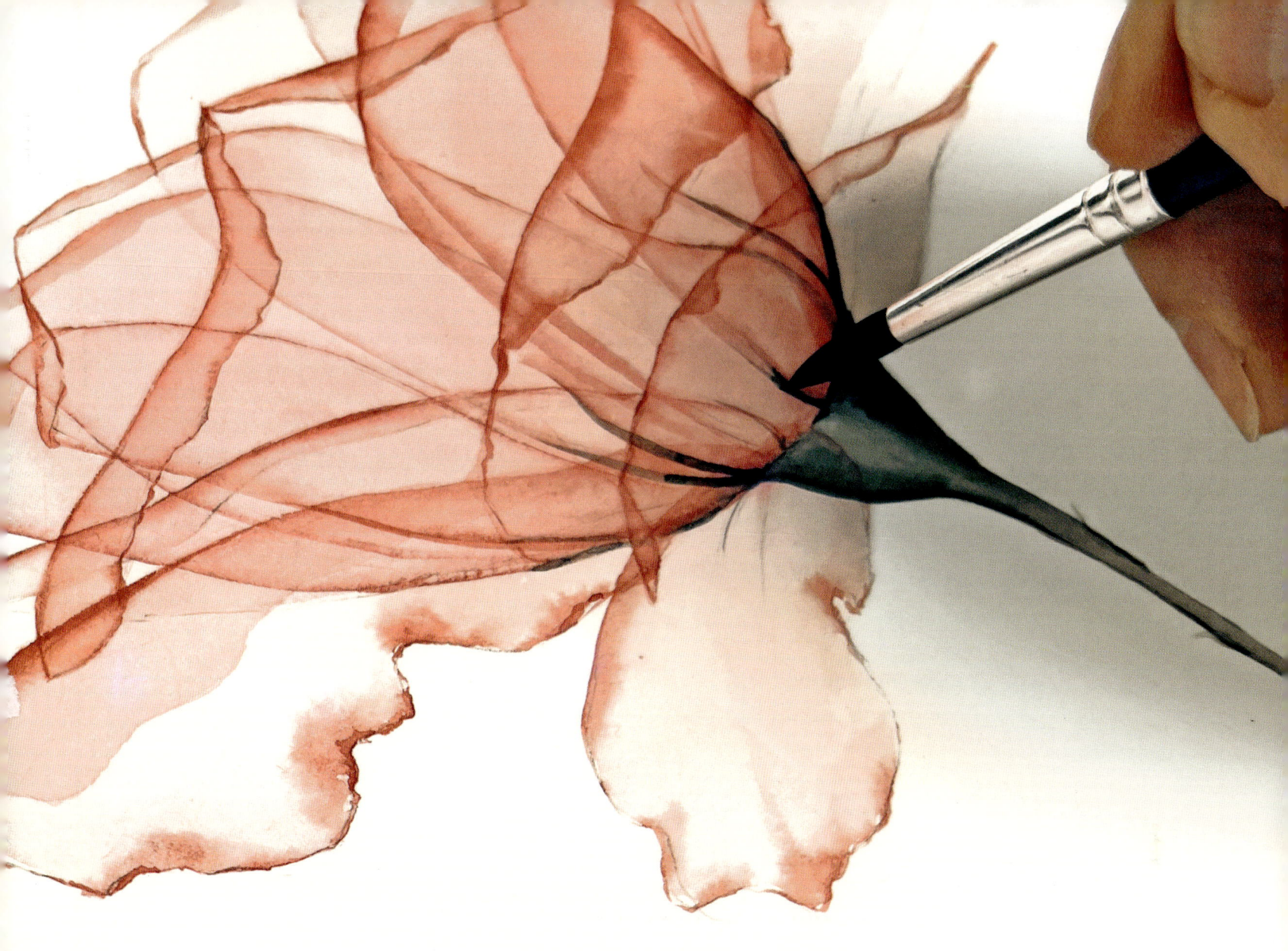

How to Paint
TRANSPARENT
Watercolour
FLOWERS

First published in 2024
Search Press Limited
Wellwood, North Farm Road,
Tunbridge Wells, Kent TN2 3DR

4 5 6 7 8 9 10

ISBN: 978-1-80092-147-4
ebook ISBN: 978-1-80093-131-2

Bookmarked Hub
Extra copies of the outlines are also available to download free from the
Bookmarked Hub. Search for this book by title or ISBN: the files can be found under 'Book
Extras'. Membership of the Bookmarked online community is free.
www.bookmarkedhub.com

Publishers' notes
The Publishers and author can accept no responsibility for any consequences arising from
the information, advice or instructions given in this publication.

For errata, please visit our website (www.searchpress.com) or the Bookmarked Hub
(www.bookmarkedhub.com).

GPSR information can be found at www.searchpress.com
Printed in China, RD082025

About the author
– www.olgakoelsch.com
– ⦿ @olga.koelsch
– ▶ @olgakoelsch
– ♪ @olgakoelsch
– www.creativemarket.com/olga.koelsch

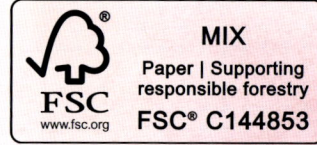

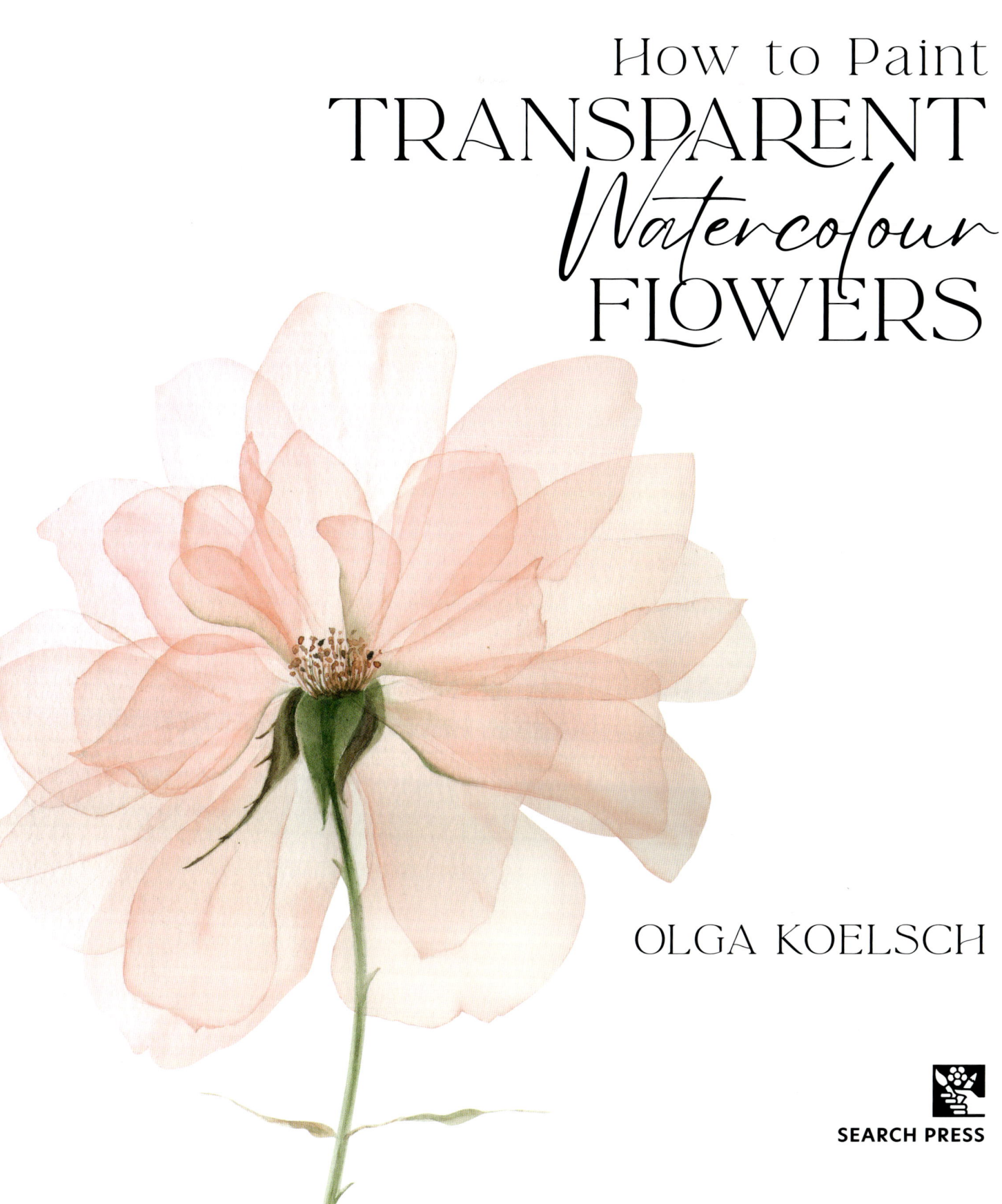

How to Paint
TRANSPARENT *Watercolour* FLOWERS

OLGA KOELSCH

SEARCH PRESS

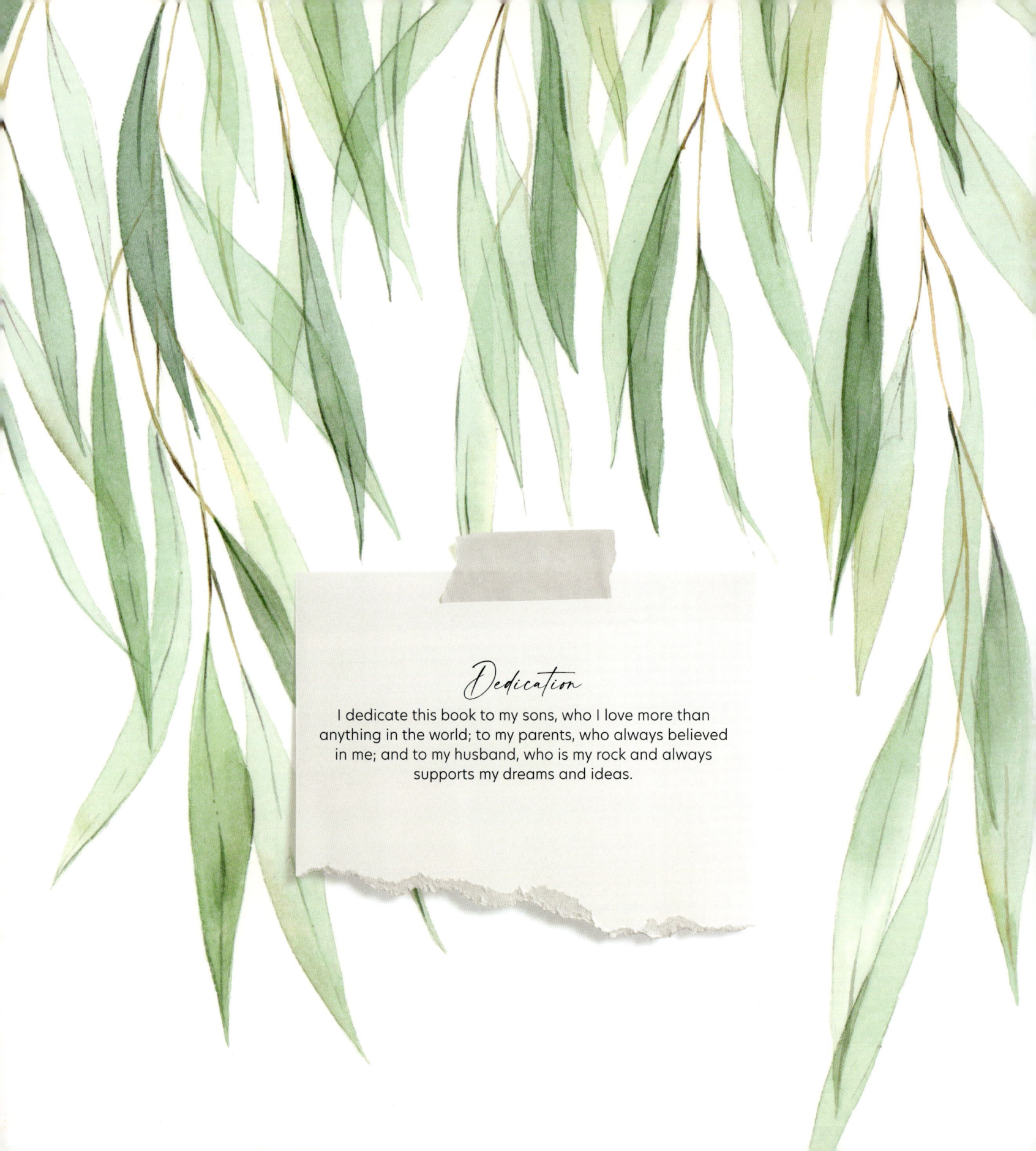

Dedication

I dedicate this book to my sons, who I love more than anything in the world; to my parents, who always believed in me; and to my husband, who is my rock and always supports my dreams and ideas.

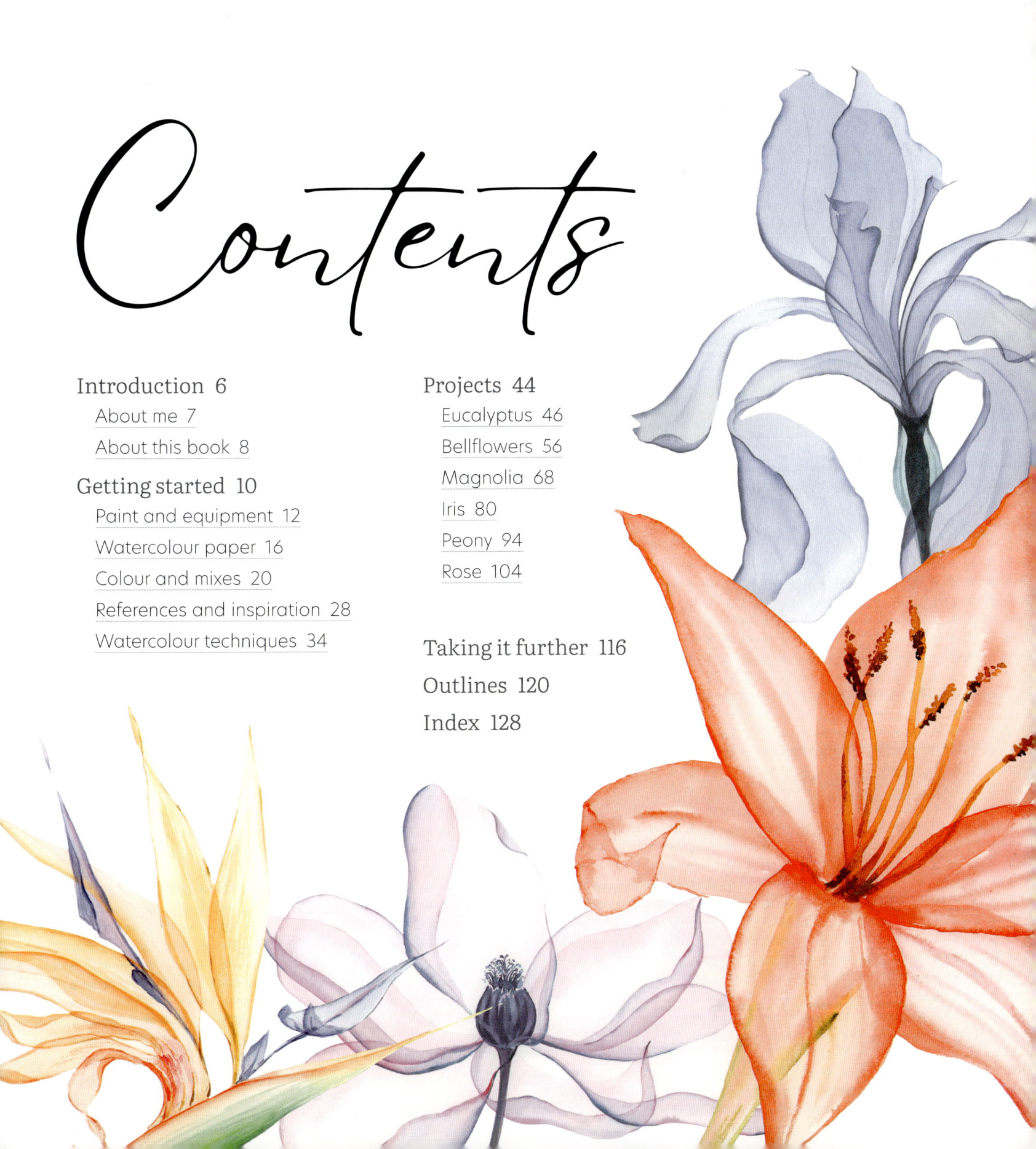

Contents

Introduction

Hello, dear friend – I am very glad to see you here! You might be looking for inspiration on bookshelves in an art store or have got this book as a present – or we might have already met each other across social media. Regardless of the path that brought you here, I'm truly delighted that you've picked up this book. It feels very special for me, as it marks a stage in my art journey where I can share my knowledge with others, and perhaps inspire those who are just starting out or feeling stuck as I was years ago.

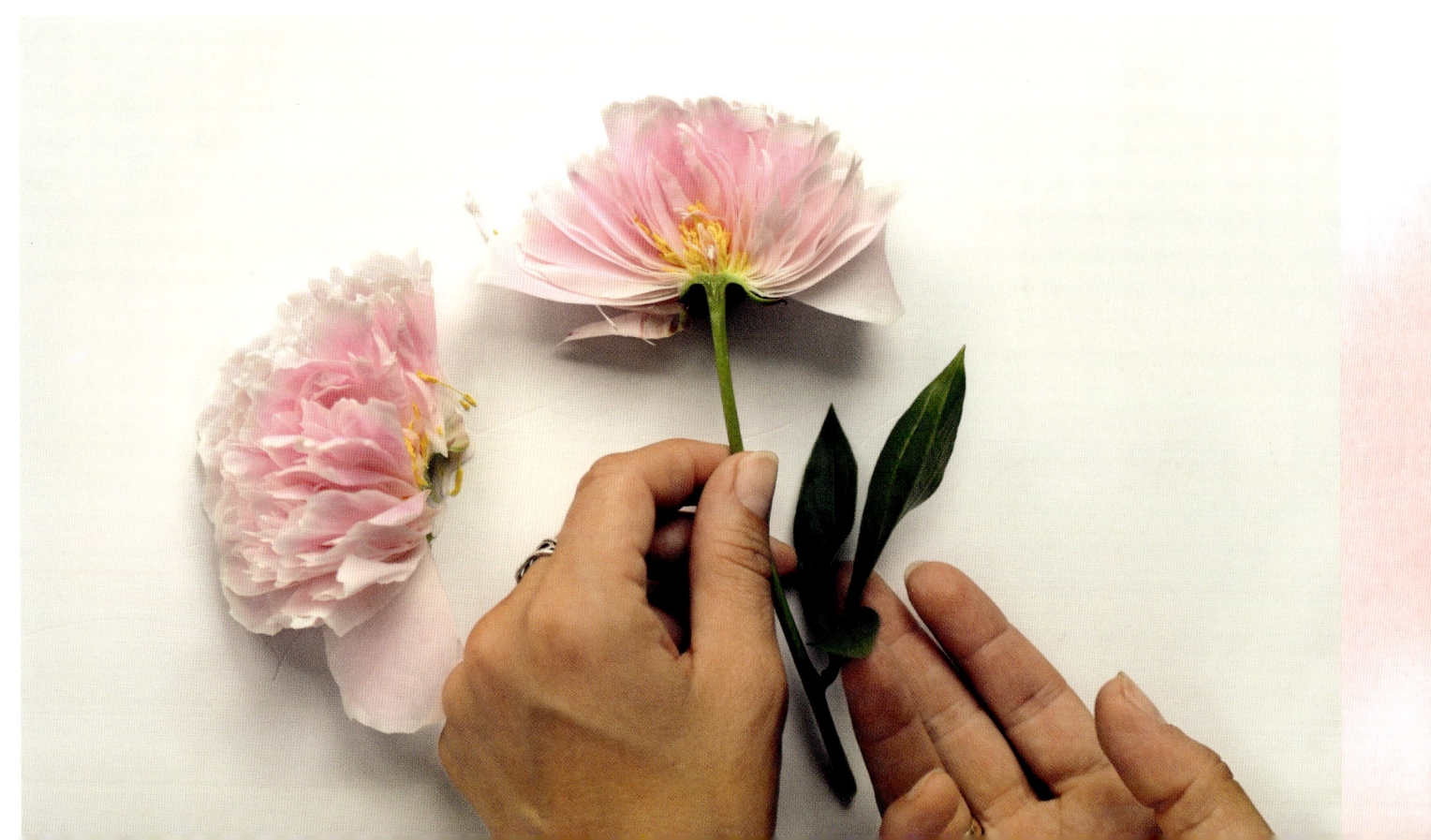

About me

What began as a healing escape after a work day has transformed into a small business. If I had told myself 10 years ago that I would be making a living by painting flowers, it would have sounded like a joke.

I'd been in marketing for over 15 years, working for companies with no connection to art. But after a long working day, and then an hour's commute on the metro, I would come home and paint with watercolours, just for myself. My curiosity led me to explore various topics, from landscapes to still life to fashion illustration. Yet, every time, I circled back to painting flowers. These were the subjects where I found my peace of mind and made a special connection to art. My aspiration was to master botanical illustration in watercolours. I studied the books of Billy Showell, which helped elevate my skills in a very short period of time.

Sometimes, our life changes direction in ways we can't imagine. Back to back, I moved to Norway, met my husband and became a mother of two boys. That was a really busy time. Like many immigrants, I faced challenges such as learning a new language, adapting to a new culture, making connections and friends, and searching for a job.

In this new life, painting became my constant and source of stability. I was painting nearly every day, and sharing my art on Instagram. The support and encouraging feedback I received helped me to keep pushing forward, and then I got my first clients who wanted to commission my illustrations.

After the birth of my second boy, in 2017, I decided to give myself a year to explore the idea of becoming a freelance artist. By then the idea of becoming a full-time artist and surface pattern designer began to take shape – it seemed like an exciting path that promised flexibility and creative fulfilment. When I first established myself as a freelance artist, working from a home studio (which was merely a small desk back then), I felt quite nervous. However, with the support and encouragement of my husband, along with my own persistence, everything fell into place and my efforts paid off.

For some time my art was tightly connected to traditional botanical illustration – the kind where you paint one life-like, highly-detailed flower for weeks. I was mastering techniques for painting them, and even knew the Latin names of flowers. I gained more and more clients, and participated in key global exhibitions for botanical illustration.

Although, for a while, I cherished painting flowers in this traditional way, I reached a point in my artistic journey where I felt quite disconnected and got 'stuck'. I wanted to explore alternative ways to portray flowers, ways that were looser in style and allowed watercolours to flow as they liked. It was then that I researched and discovered modern watercolour techniques, which offered much more freedom and expression. My intention was then to find a personal style that bridged the worlds between traditional botanical illustration and the spontaneity of loose watercolour techniques.

I started to experiment a lot with drawing styles, references, paints, paper and colours. I can still remember the day when I was browsing the internet for inspiration and stumbled upon Albert Koetsier's mesmerizing X-ray photographs of flowers. The flowers looked so fragile and intricate, and their delicate beauty seemed to be enhanced through X-ray photography! I began to wonder how I could paint flowers with watercolour in a similar way.

My experience in botanical illustration was a great help, but I wanted to increase lightness, ease, and freedom in the painting process. Step by step, the transparent technique became one of my favourite approaches to watercolour, and eventually a signature style. I am absolutely in love with this painting method, and I am looking forward to sharing my passion with you.

About this book

I've had many questions over the years asking whether one needs experience to paint transparent flowers, or if artists already experienced in watercolours may uncover something new with the techniques I use.

The answer is the same for both: it's not about experience, it's about your attitude. Art is a skill that can continuously be refined. There are always new things to learn and different perspectives to embrace.

This book fits all skill levels. As you navigate through it, you will explore different projects that use the transparent technique in different ways, so you can learn various approaches and tricks. You will get reference photographs; outlines, if you need help with your initial sketches; and explanations for every step. My mission was to reveal my tips and tricks for painting life-like flowers without getting into complex details. By learning my approach, you will be able to understand the process of painting transparent flowers in watercolour, and eventually create your own unique pictures.

I encourage you to start painting immediately and put the theory into action. I believe that the key to success is consistency and putting theory immediately into practice – it trains your hand, sharpens your artistic skills and moves your progress forward. I recommend painting little and often: this makes it easier to build practice time into your busy life, and painting in small steps allows you to take a step back and have a fresh look at your artwork. I've found that the transparent technique offers you the freedom to pause at almost any moment and come back whenever it is convenient.

I also encourage you to share your artworks with others, to support each other, and to grow more confident in sharing your creations publicly.

I can't wait to see what you will achieve – the beautiful flowers you will be able to paint, techniques you will learn from me, and the inspiration you will get with reading this book!

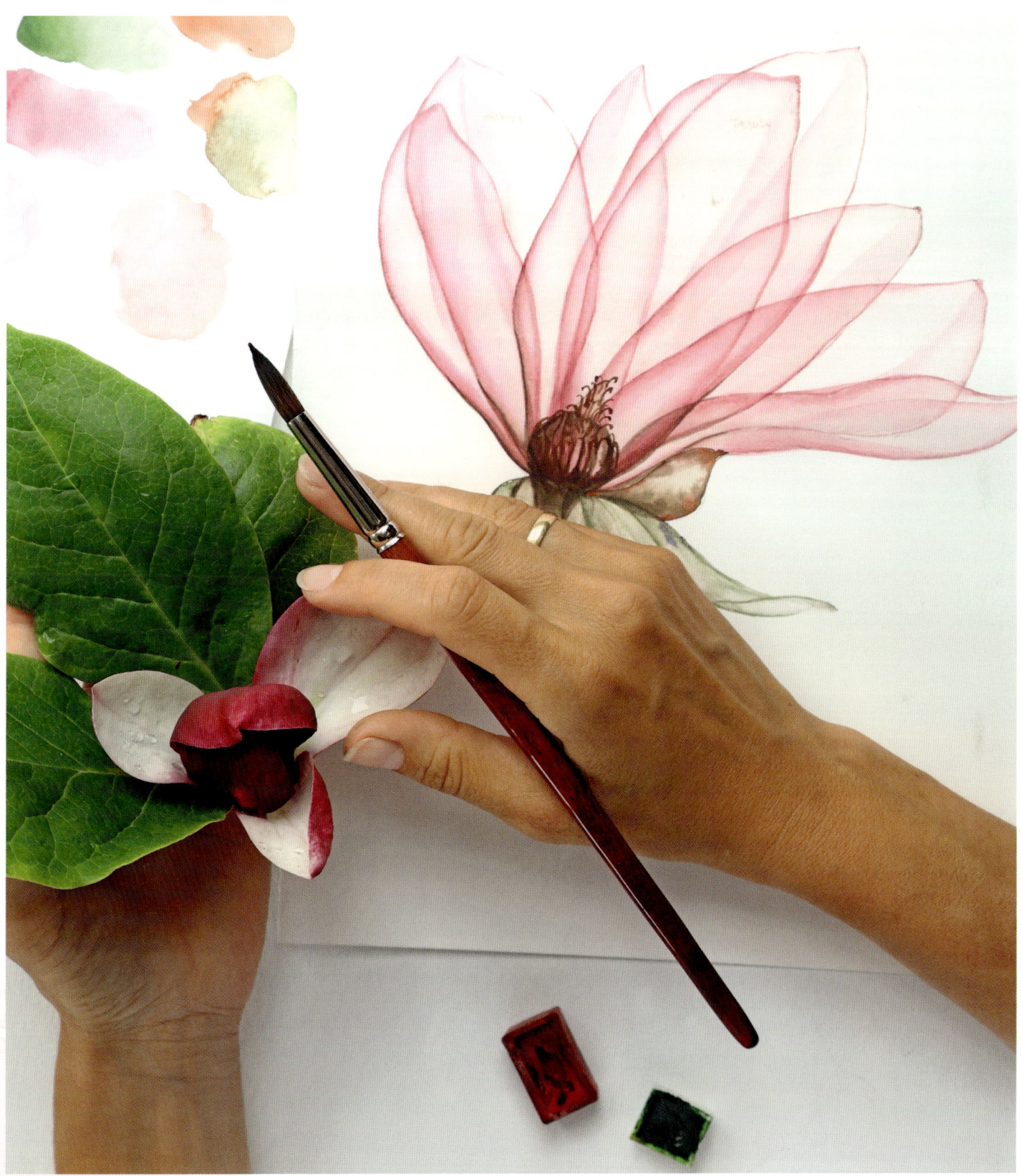

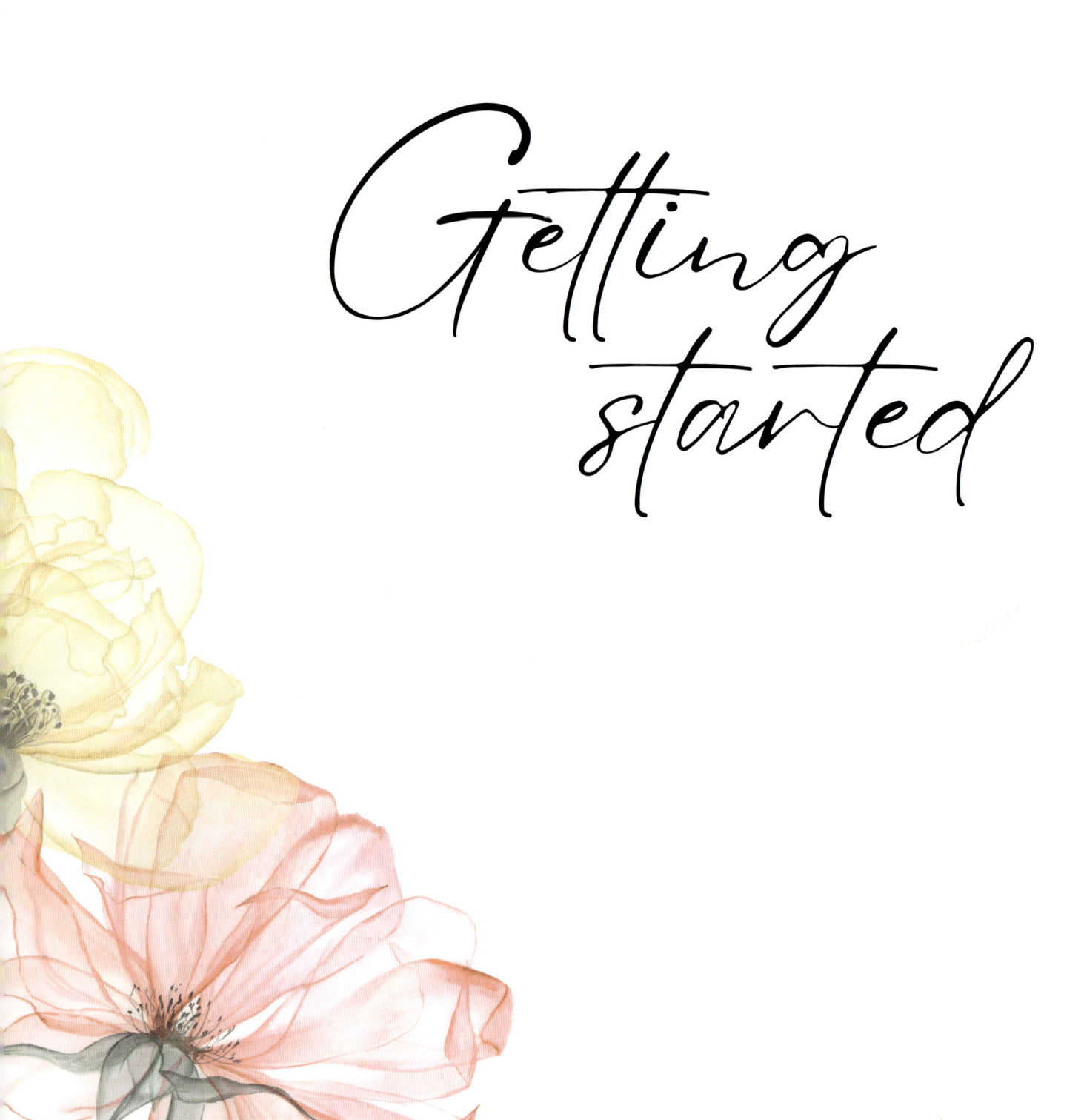

Getting started

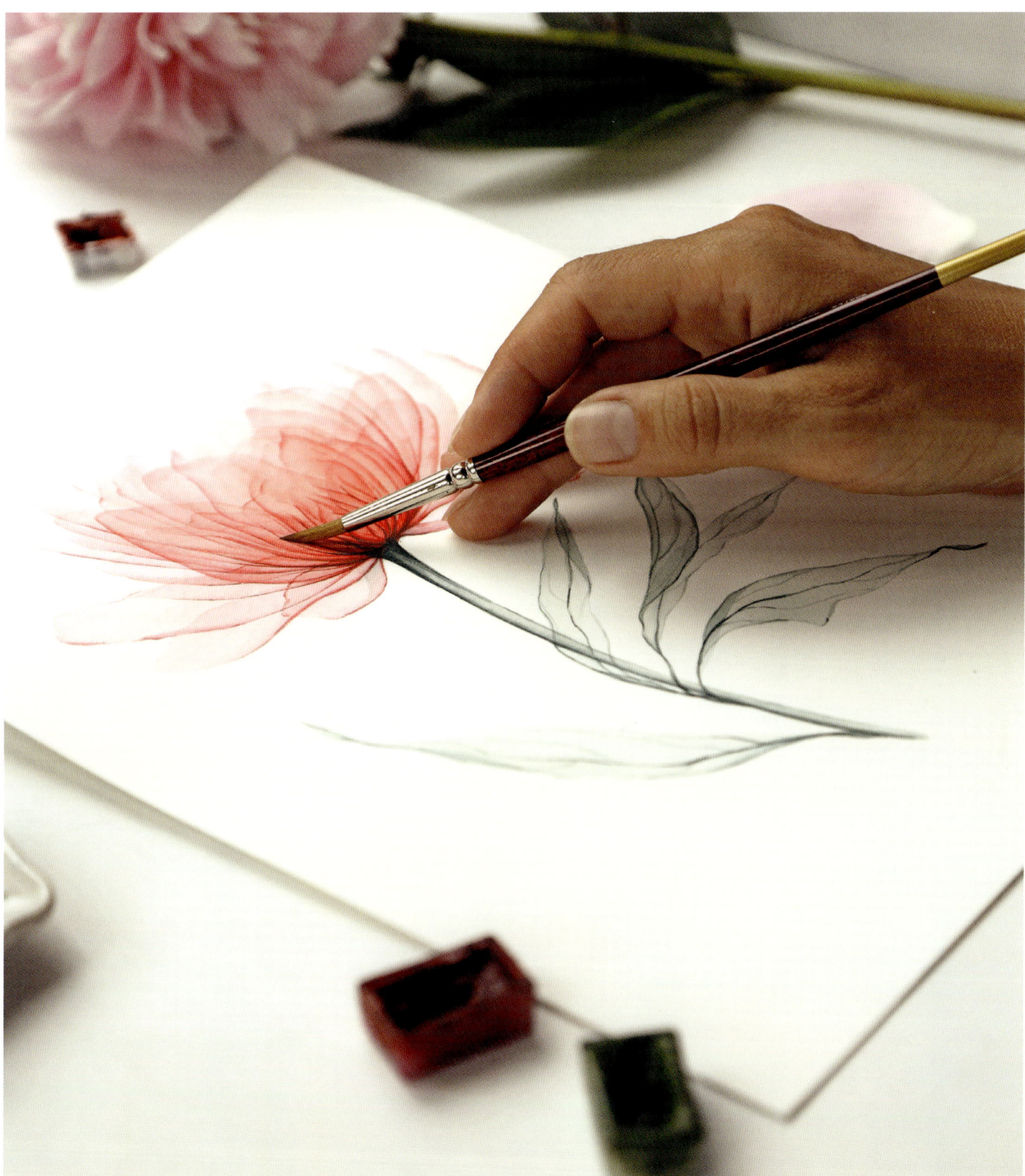

Paint and equipment

Choosing the right art materials can be overwhelming, with numerous options, brands and tools available. It's tempting to buy a wide range of painting supplies without knowing how to use them effectively. I'll show you the basic and most important materials you'll need to achieve your first results and simply enjoy painting. Picking the right supplies at the start will help you to enjoy the process and love the results.

To start with any watercolour painting, you'll require three essential supplies: watercolour paper, paint brushes and paints. As you progress, learn and explore this technique, you'll gain a better understanding of which additional supplies you need to add to your basic kit.

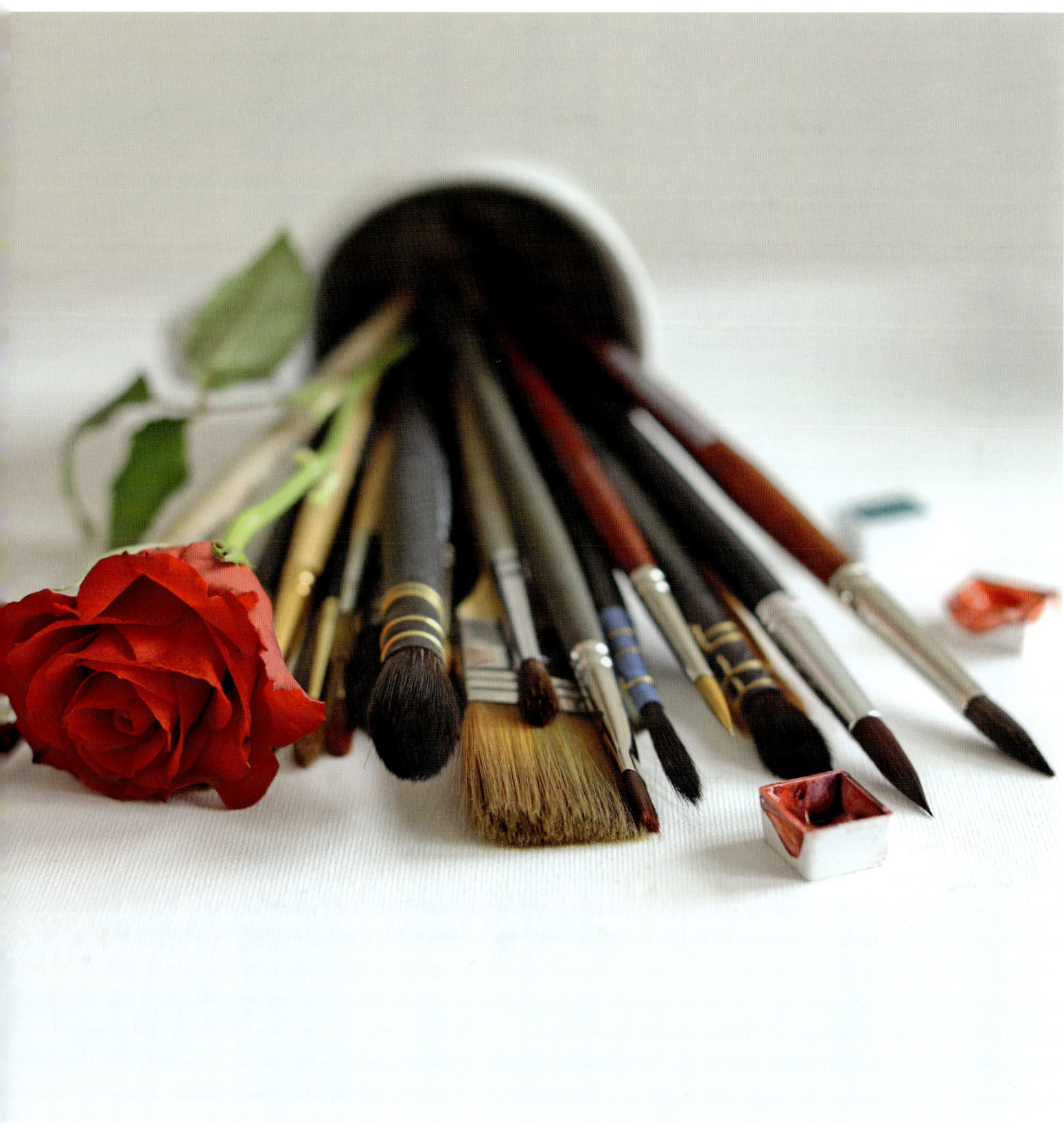

Watercolour paints

I prefer a limited colour palette for each painting as it allows you to focus on the finest details and the beautiful inner structures of the flowers.

There is an ongoing debate about whether watercolour paints in pans or tubes are better. However, for gentle floral paintings that use the transparent technique, I find watercolour pans are the most practical choice: as you shall discover later, we paint mostly with very diluted mixes, and just a small amount of paint is needed; pans allow you to pick up the amount you like. With tubes, it's easy to squeeze out too much paint.

For transparent techniques, it's crucial to avoid opaque watercolour paints. Most paint-making brands indicate whether a paint is transparent, opaque, or semi-opaque. Look for the symbol 'T', 'Transparency/Opacity: T' or a white square on the paint packaging.

Brushes

Brushes are very important. Do you need a good brush? Absolutely! A good brush almost 'paints by itself'. Do you need an expensive brush? Not necessarily. For transparent painting, which combines traditional botanical illustration and loose techniques, the most important aspect is having a brush with a fine tip. Fine tips not only allow you to paint delicate details, but also give you better control of outlines and create crisp edges for the petals.

In my painting technique, I usually use two synthetic brushes of slightly different sizes. My favourite sizes are the no. 4 and no. 6. In addition, I recommend having a soft, round no. 10 sable brush for creating broad washes. This type of brush doesn't damage the surface of watercolour paper, and allows you to apply a lot of layers on top of each other.

Extras

Here are a few additional items that will be helpful in your painting process:

- **Ceramic palette:** A ceramic palette with several deep wells is the best for mixing colours. Sometimes this type of palette is referred to as 'flower-shaped' or 'daisy'.

- **Mechanical pencil:** I prefer using a 0.3 or 0.5 mechanical pencil for drawing, as these create stable, fine lines and don't need frequent sharpening.

- **Kneaded putty eraser:** A putty eraser is incredibly useful for removing pencil lines without damaging the paper surface. It absorbs the pencil marks, leaving behind very light traces that are sufficient for painting.

- **Soft white eraser:** Once your painting is halfway finished, you may want to remove pencil marks to get a better sense of the picture. While a kneaded putty eraser can't remove pencil marks from beneath the paint layers, a good soft white eraser can gently erase pencil marks, even from surfaces coated with watercolour. Never use coloured erasers, as they may leave marks on your paper.

- **Kitchen paper or cloth:** This is an absolute must-have tool to ensure better water-control. Use it to remove excess water from your brush during painting.

- **Small jars, for water:** Having small jars of water to hand is helpful for diluting dried paint mixes and softening your paints in the palette.

- **Masking/paper tape:** This helps to fix the watercolour paper to your painting desk or window (see page 36) without damaging it.

- **Hairdryer:** If you feel confident noting when a paint is starting to dry nicely, you can speed up the drying process between stages with a hairdryer. It's important not to dry the work too early, as the looseness of the paint may mean the colour flows in the wrong direction.

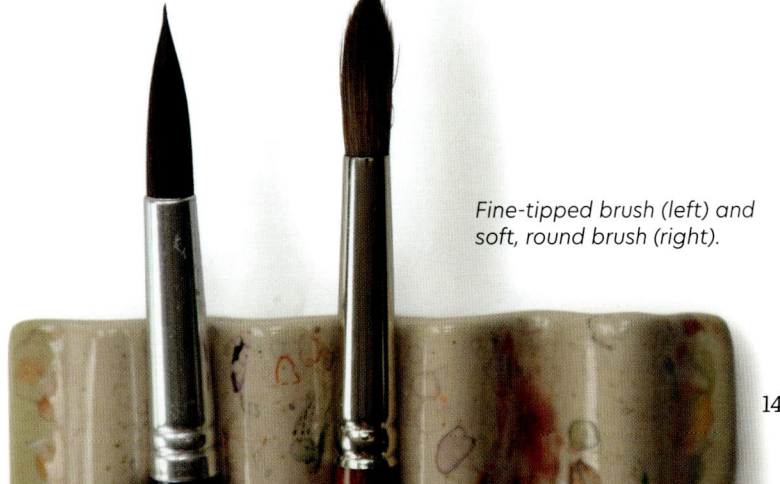

Fine-tipped brush (left) and soft, round brush (right).

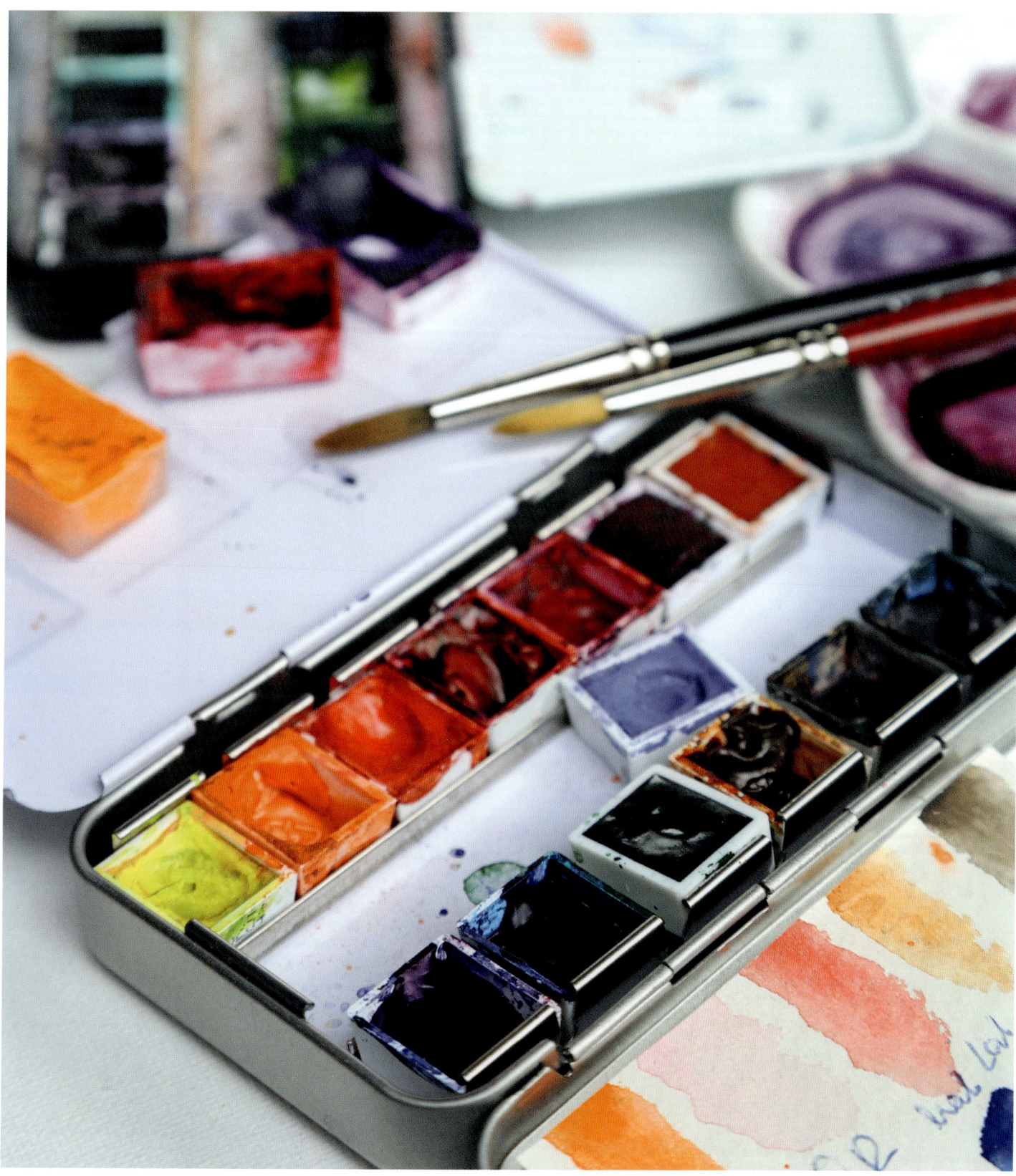

Watercolour paper

With the transparent technique, we will mostly be painting on a plain white or off-white background. That way, the shape of the flowers really stands out. When it comes to paper, there are essentially three key factors to consider, and each of these elements can significantly impact your painting experience.

Material

Watercolour paper is available in two main materials: cotton, wood pulp, or a blend of the two.

- **100% cotton paper** is the best paper, in my opinion, because of its absorbency and even colour distribution.

- Most beginner watercolour papers are made either purely from **wood pulp** or a wood-pulp/cotton blend. While this helps keep costs down, it can result in issues with colour absorption, especially for larger or multiple washes. They are great for practising brush strokes and colour combinations, and for creating loose paintings with a maximum of two layers.

- In my opinion, **mixed-type** papers are a false economy, since they are priced similarly to 100% cotton papers but offer a quality similar to wood pulp.

Texture

This refers to the characteristics of a paper's surface, whether it's smooth, slightly textured, or heavily textured. There are three main types to consider:

- **Hot-pressed paper (known also as 'smooth paper'):** This is smooth watercolour paper that has been 'ironed' flat. It is ideal for detailed work, from traditional botanical illustrations to transparent techniques. Hot-pressed paper is also great for showcasing gradients, as the smooth surface allows the paints and water to mix softly.

- **Cold-pressed paper (known also as 'fine grain paper'):** This paper has a slightly bumpy or grooved texture that has been pressed flat but not ironed. This type of paper is excellent for water control, making it ideal for beginners. The slight texture allows for even absorption of paint and water into the fibres, providing more control – particularly when working wet on wet.

- **Rough paper:** Rough watercolour paper has the most defined texture and is often used for abstract or impressionistic paintings. Its highly absorbent surface adds character to the final artwork, but is not suitable for fine detail work.

Weight

The weight of watercolour paper refers to its thickness or absorbency. Here are three common weight options:

- **200gsm (100lb):** This is the minimum weight recommended for watercolour painting. Any lower and the paper will not absorb water properly, resulting in waves and rolls on the surface. This weight only allows you to paint a single layer in a loose technique.

- **300gsm (140lb):** Considered the standard weight for watercolour paper, this weight is suitable for most techniques and purposes.

- **640gsm (300lb):** If you prefer a paper that can handle more water and, in turn, allow you to compose larger paintings without the paper warping or buckling, this paper could be a good fit.

What to choose?

To sum it up – for transparent techniques, having good-quality watercolour paper with the right texture and weight is crucial. Look for 100% cotton paper with a hot-pressed (smooth) texture. I've experimented with various paper types for this technique, and nothing works better than 100% cotton paper, either satin or hot-pressed, weighing 300gsm (140lb).

I would avoid cold-pressed paper with rough textures, as it doesn't allow for fine, delicate details. Non-cotton paper weighing 200gsm (100lb) also limits the number of layers you can use and your ability to create smooth gradients and washes.

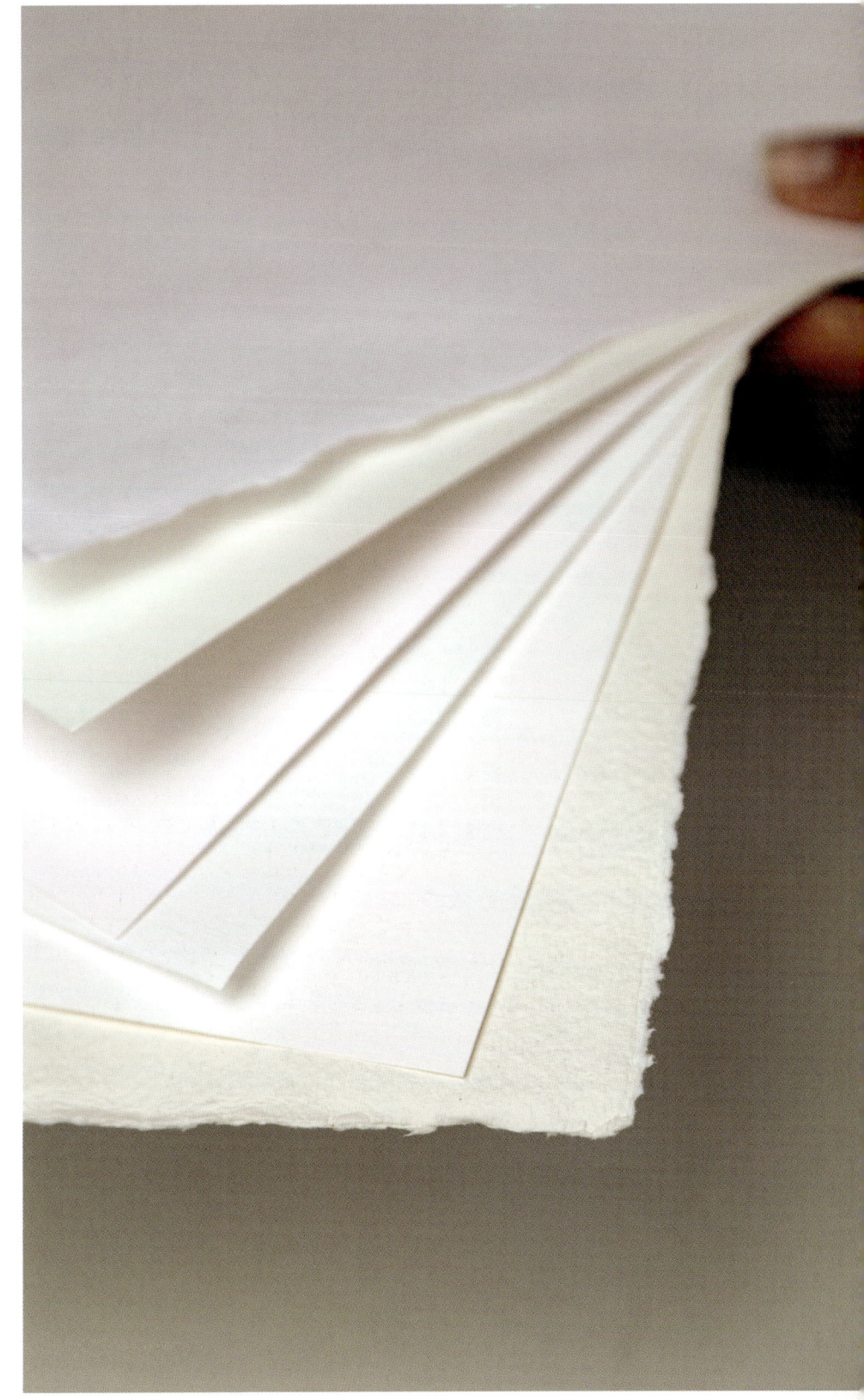

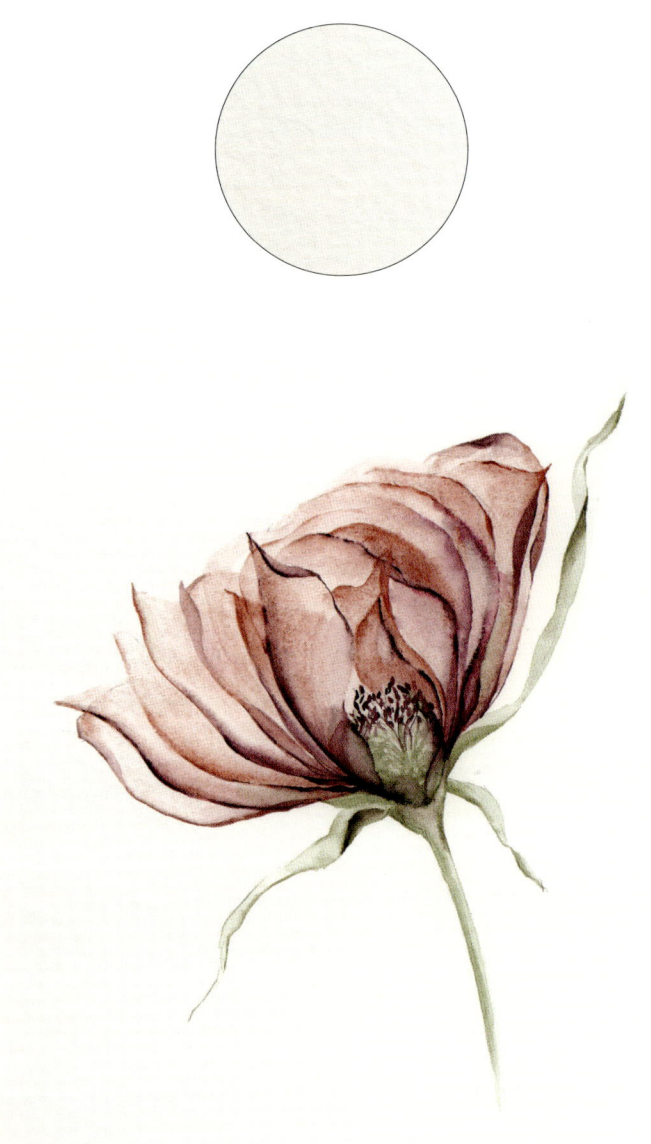

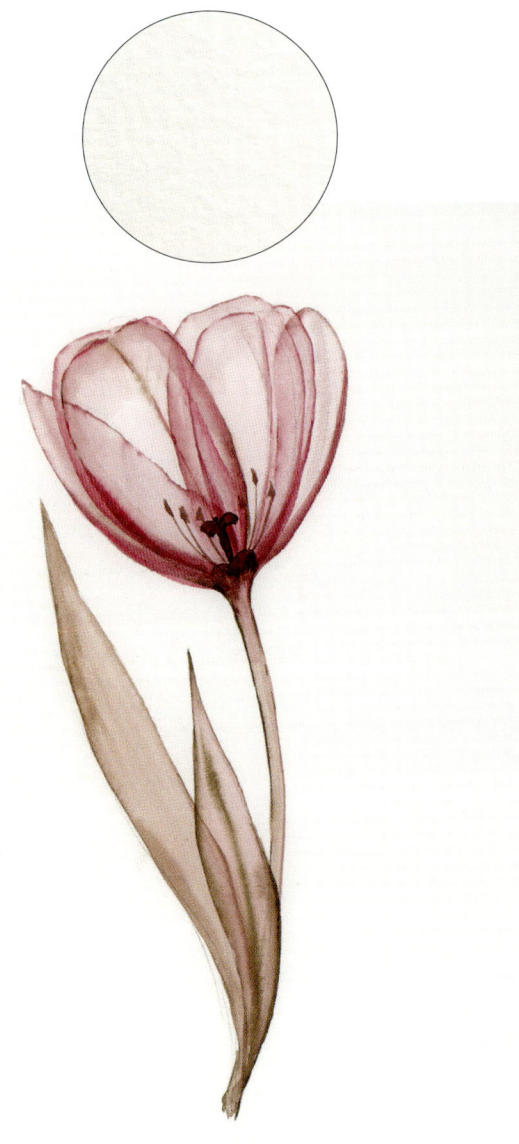

Pink rose painted on cold-pressed paper

You can see the rough texture of the paper coming through in the petals, and how unevenly the colours are distributed. Furthermore, the outlines and details are not very crisp. Nevertheless, I like the 'vintage' quality of this picture.

Tulip painted on 200gsm (100lb) wood-pulp paper

I had some difficulties applying multiple layers of paint to the painting, as this type of paper is very sensitive to lots of water and wet paint, and can be worn down with too many wet brush strokes. I managed to achieve the transparency effect by outlining the petals with the wet-on-dry technique (see page 39), and simply skipped the glazing of some of the petals.

You could use this paper for practising brush strokes and to paint in a more free-hand style (see the magnolia, in the right-hand painting opposite).

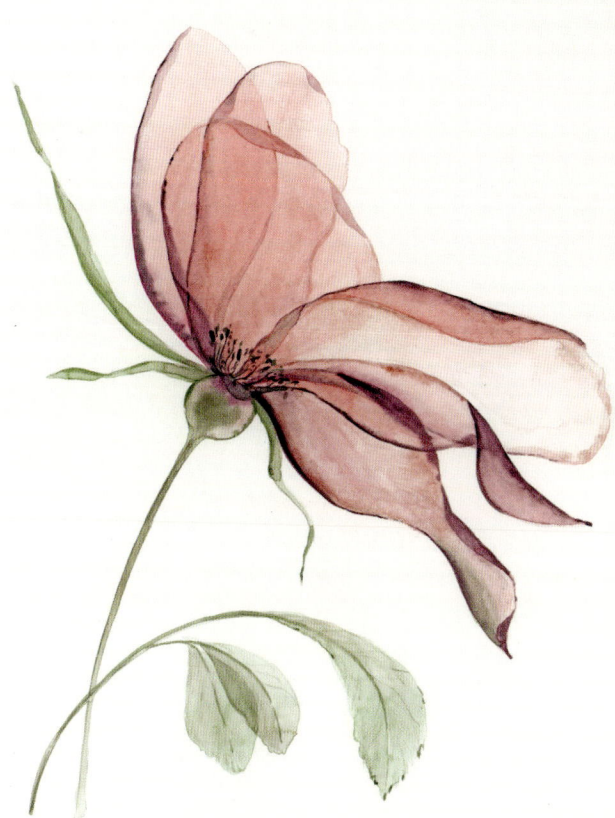

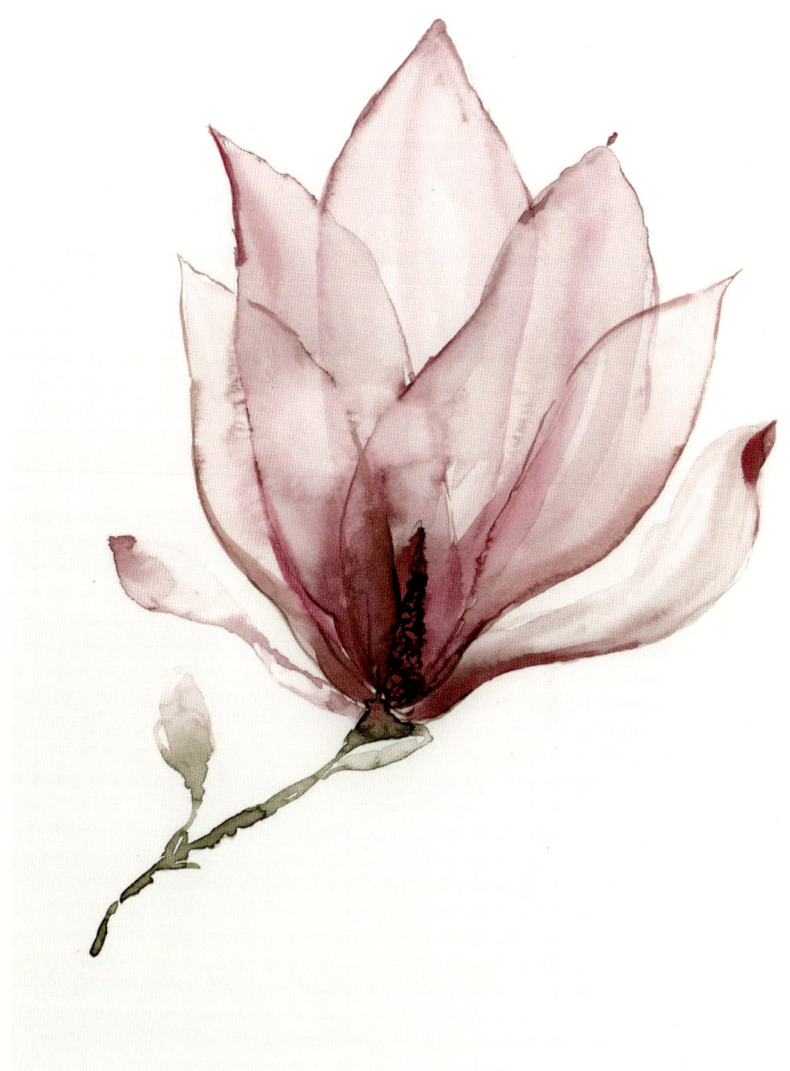

Dog rose (above) and magnolia (right) painted on hot-pressed 25% cotton paper

I think this was the most challenging combination of paper qualities. Although the texture of this paper is very smooth, because of the small percentage of cotton, the paints do not sink into the small recesses in the paper, and are easily washed out with subsequent glazing layers – required in the dog rose above. This type of paper is much better for a quicker, looser technique that involves just one layer of paint, such as the magnolia, right.

Colours and mixes

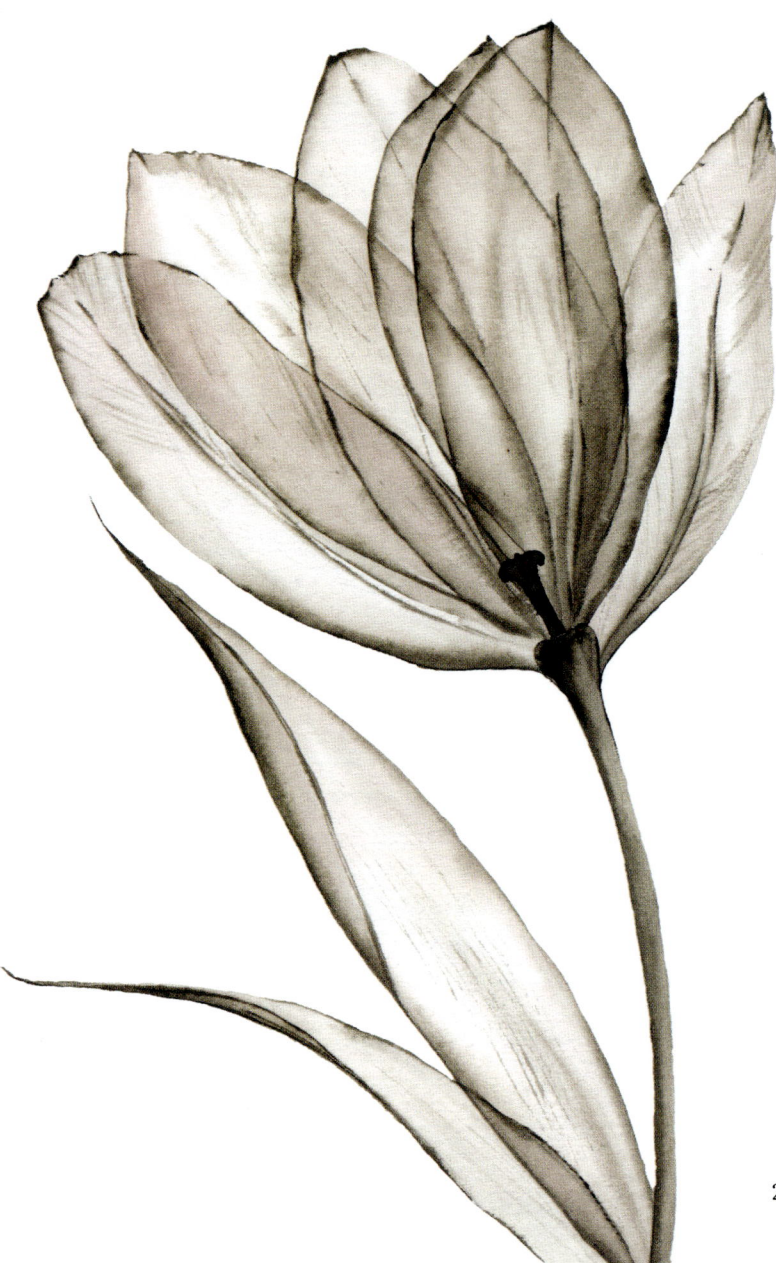

The transparent technique involves applying multiple layers of paint, with a focus on lines and contrasts. This means it is mostly about creating contrasts rather than a rich variety of colours so, typically, I use only two colour mixes in one painting: one for the flowers and one for the greenery (stem and leaves).

Like most artists, I love checking out new materials and paints. However, especially if you're new to watercolours, I would recommend restricting yourself to a limited colour palette. With a limited palette, you get to know your colours better and become more confident with mixing. When practising, you could even try painting with just one colour, so you can focus more on technique and reduce the stress of colour mixing. With just one colour, you can create very stylish and modern illustrations. For example, with monochrome painting, you use only darker colours like blacks, earthy tones (see the flower, left) or blues (see opposite).

Once you master your basic colours, you can add more variety. Experimenting will help you become very flexible and confident with colours.

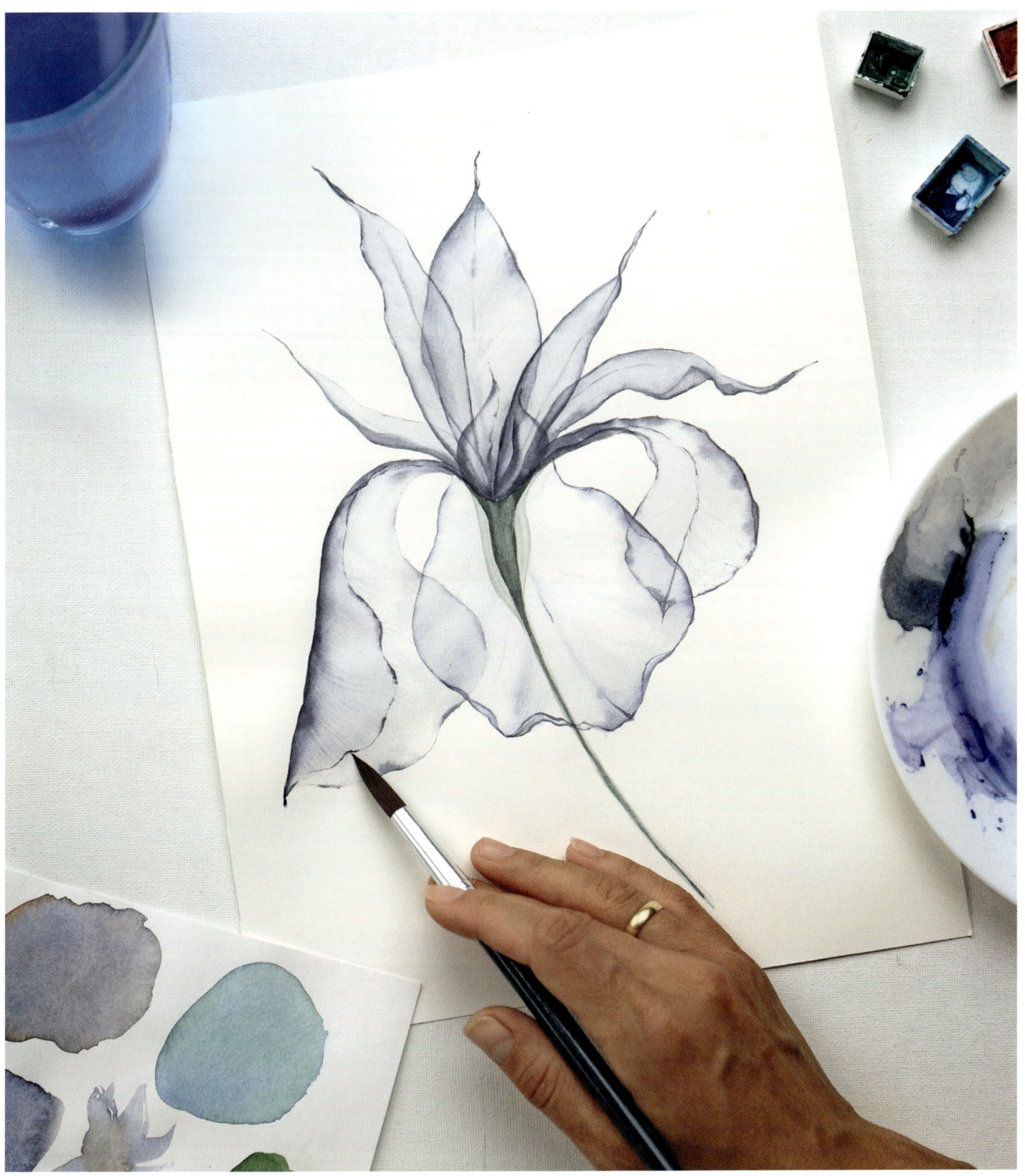

Basic palette

I used a limited number of colours for my work, and often use the following shades:
- Cadmium Yellow
- Quinacridone Rose
- Madder Lake Deep
- Burnt Sienna
- Ultramarine Blue
- Sepia
- Phthalo Green
- Payne's Gray.

If I had to choose just three colours, they would be Quinacridone Rose, Burnt Sienna, and Phthalo Green. Occasionally, I enjoy using two 'fancy' colours: Pyrrolle Orange and Olive Green.

Often I lean towards a more dusty, 'vintage' palette, which is why I often use Burnt Sienna in mixes. In Fig. 1, the bottom colours are almost the same as the top pure colours, just with a hint of Burnt Sienna.

Fig. 1

PURE COLOURS

Quinacridone Rose   *Madder Lake Deep*   *Phthalo Green*

'DUSTY' VERSIONS

 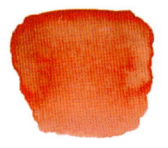 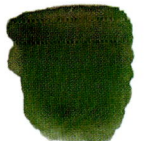

Quinacridone Rose + Burnt Sienna   *Madder Lake Deep + Burnt Sienna*   *Phthalo Green + Burnt Sienna*

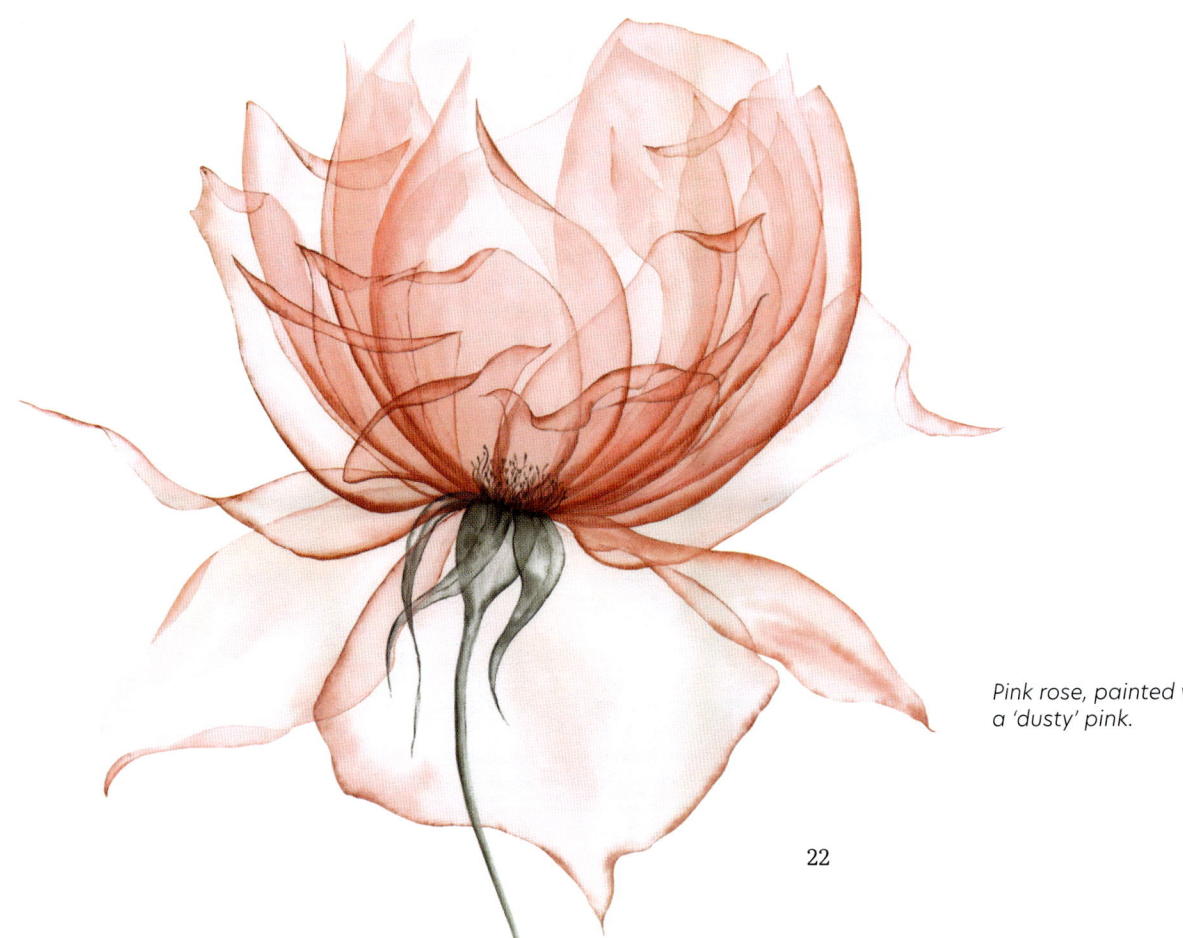

Pink rose, painted with a 'dusty' pink.

Creating contrasts

I would like to emphasize the importance of understanding contrasts, especially for the transparent technique. Nice contrasts are what catches our eyes at first glance, and they add depth and dynamics to the painting. Below, and on pages 24, 25 and 27, you'll find the key types of contrasts.

Temperature contrast

When you begin to learn to paint, terms like 'cold red' and 'warm blue' can be quite confusing as we usually never think of red as a cold colour or blue as a warm one. Nevertheless, the warm/cold difference becomes apparent when they are compared to each other.

Let's take colours from the basic palette and add a hint of blue to one side, then yellow or red to the other. Now, you can see that the same hue becomes warmer or colder (see Fig. 2).

Fig. 2

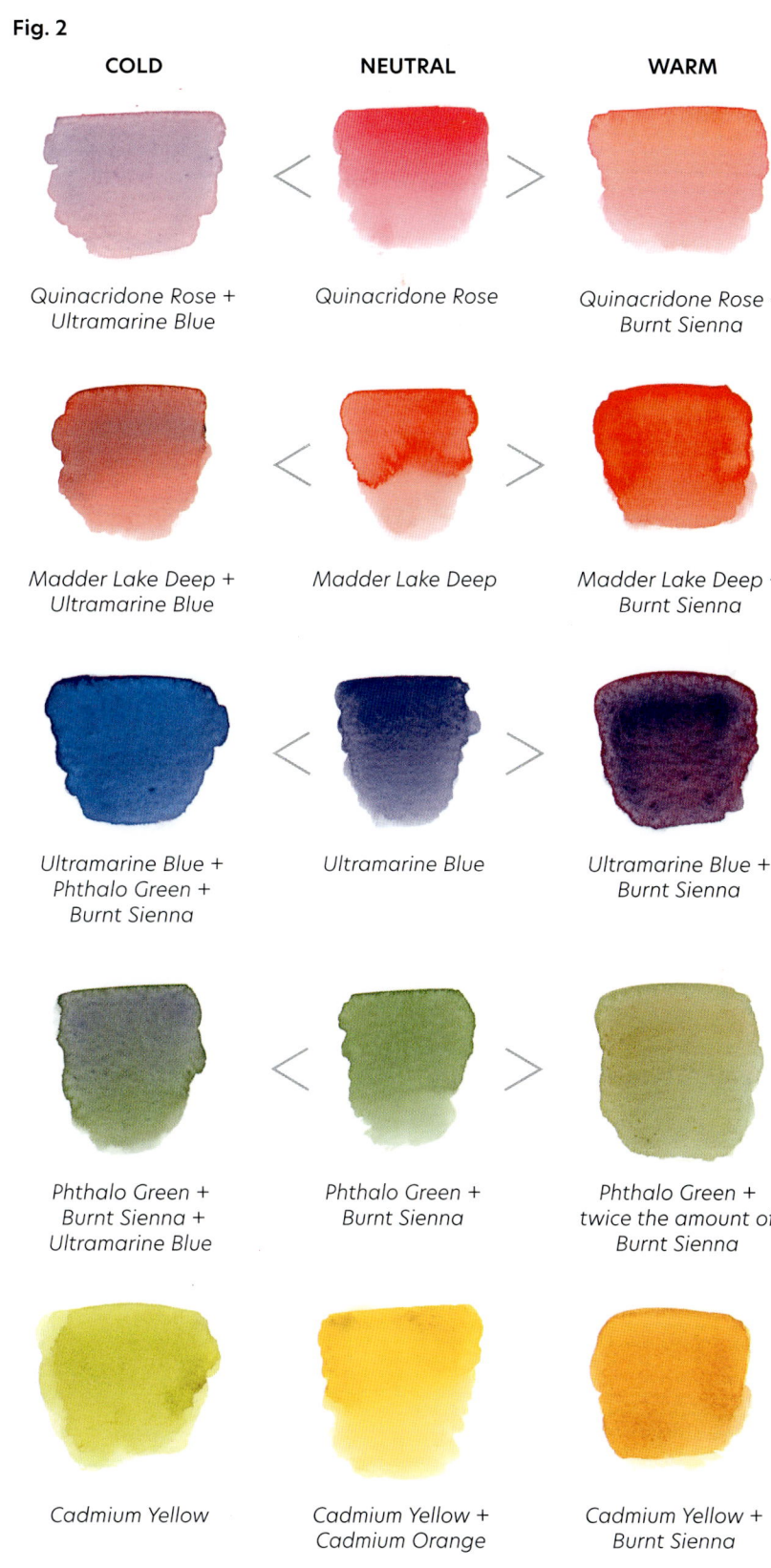

COLD	NEUTRAL	WARM
Quinacridone Rose + Ultramarine Blue	Quinacridone Rose	Quinacridone Rose + Burnt Sienna
Madder Lake Deep + Ultramarine Blue	Madder Lake Deep	Madder Lake Deep + Burnt Sienna
Ultramarine Blue + Phthalo Green + Burnt Sienna	Ultramarine Blue	Ultramarine Blue + Burnt Sienna
Phthalo Green + Burnt Sienna + Ultramarine Blue	Phthalo Green + Burnt Sienna	Phthalo Green + twice the amount of Burnt Sienna
Cadmium Yellow	Cadmium Yellow + Cadmium Orange	Cadmium Yellow + Burnt Sienna

Fig. 3

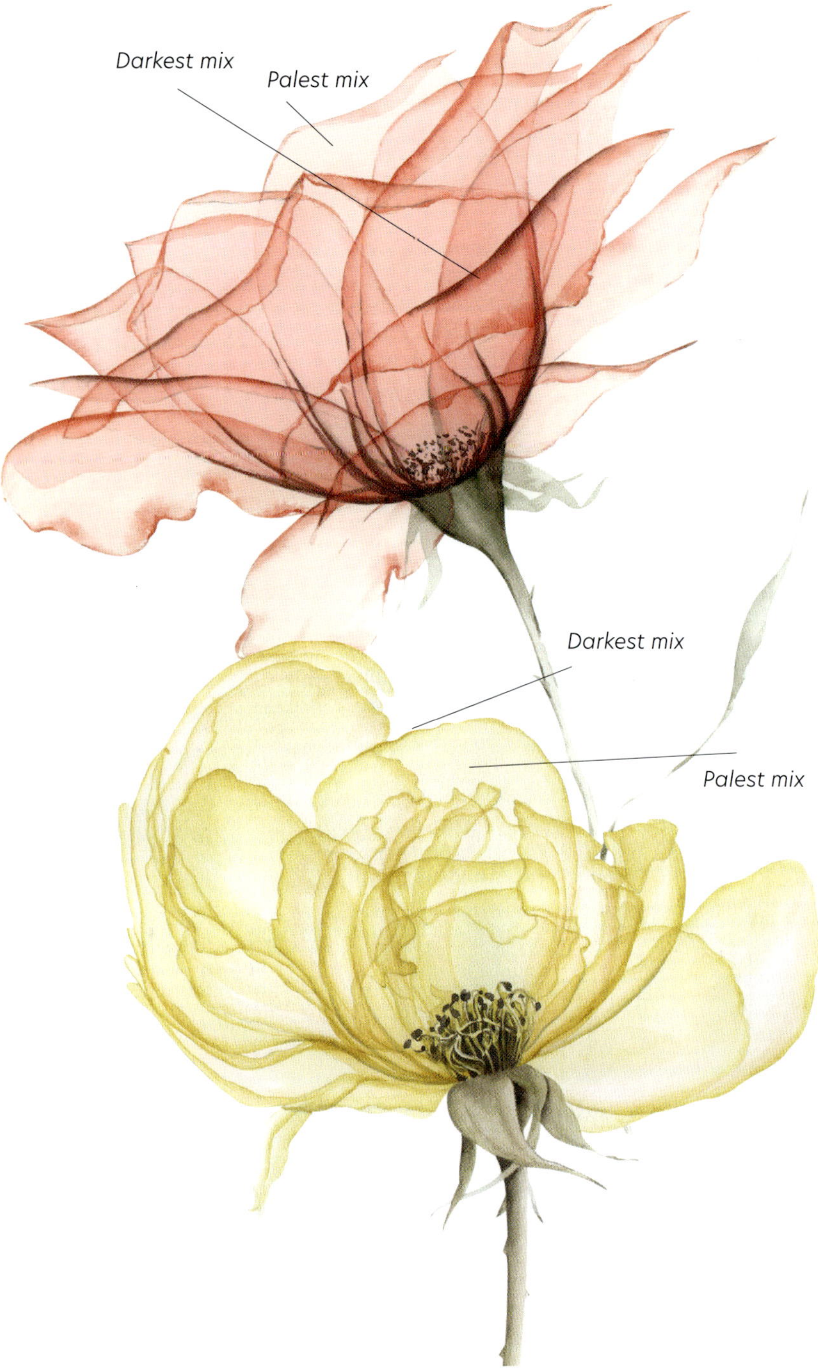

Darkest mix

Palest mix

Darkest mix

Palest mix

Value contrast

This is the main contrast we need to keep in mind when painting transparent flowers. It's simply the combination of light and dark tones of a single colour that create the volume and the transparent effect (see Fig. 3).

To practise it, take pure paint directly from a pan, add it to a palette then gradually dilute it with clean water until you have a very pale colour and a watery mix. In Fig. 4, the left-hand ends of the gradients are the 'pure' mixes that are then diluted appropriately to create different values. In the techniques and projects I describe the pure colours as the 'dark mixes', and their diluted versions as the 'pale mixes'.

The darker the colour, the bigger the contrast between its darkest and lightest shades. That's why painting yellow flowers with the transparent technique is the biggest challenge – since it is a pale colour, it has a lower contrast.

Fig. 4

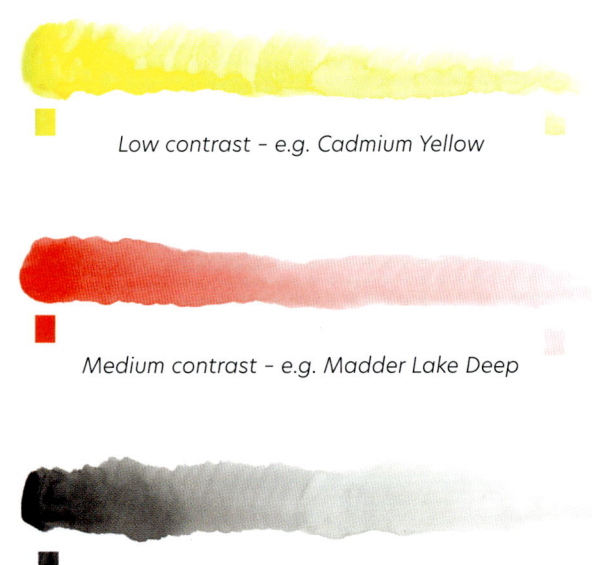

Low contrast – e.g. Cadmium Yellow

Medium contrast – e.g. Madder Lake Deep

High contrast – e.g. Payne's Gray

Hue contrast

This is the contrast between two colours on opposite sides of the colour wheel. These are called **complementary colours**. (See Fig 5.)

When we paint red roses on green stems, the contrast is pretty evident. But how do you maintain the contrast when the petal colour is not completely red, but is slightly colder or warmer in hue (see page 23)?

Firstly, I recommend practising mixing different shades of green. If we add a hint of either a cold or a warmer colour to the green mix, we can shift the colour of the green to create an ideal hue contrast for the petals. For example, the green can become more bluish and cold in hue, better emphasizing orange-yellow flowers, or become more olive or brown in shade, creating a beautiful contrasting match for blue blooms. See Fig. 6 for a variety of greens.

Fig. 5

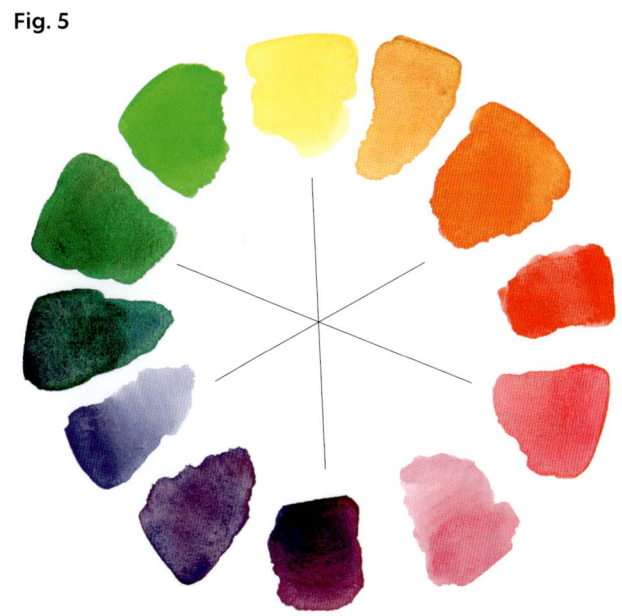

Fig. 6

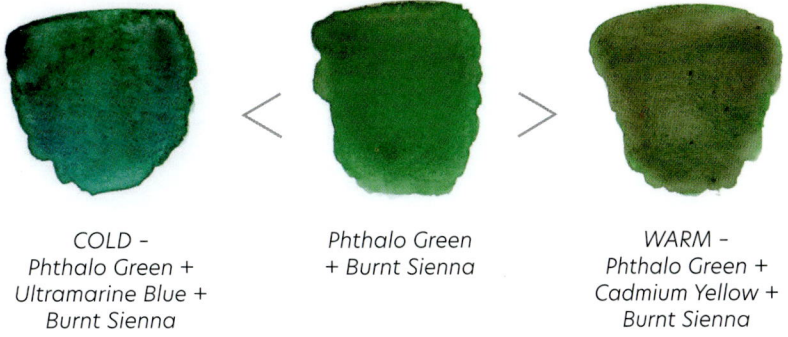

PURE GREENS

COLD –
Phthalo Green +
Ultramarine Blue

Phthalo Green

WARM –
Phthalo Green +
Cadmium Yellow

NEUTRAL GREENS – adding Burnt Sienna

COLD –
Phthalo Green +
Ultramarine Blue +
Burnt Sienna

Phthalo Green
+ Burnt Sienna

WARM –
Phthalo Green +
Cadmium Yellow +
Burnt Sienna

Conclusion and exercises

To sum it up, for the best appearance, we need:

- temperature contrast

- value contrast

- hue contrast.

Let's take a look at some examples!

Say we choose Madder Lake Deep as our flower-petal colour, which is what I've done for the flower in Fig. 7. It belongs to the red group and has a warm tone, so the best contrast for its greenery (i.e. the stem and leaves) will be a green group that has a cold tone. One of my favourite cold green mixes is Phthalo Green and Ultramarine Blue with a hint of Burnt Sienna (see the bottom-left swatch in Fig. 6 on page 25), so I used this for the greenery. Compare the colours in Fig. 8 – a colder colour was used for the flower petals, so was contrasted with a warmer green for the stem and leaves.

I have prepared some of my favourite contrast mixes in Fig. 9. I recommend that you test your palette in this way and have your own samples in front of you.

Please remember that our colour choices are very individual and define our style. That's why, if your basic palette and preferences are different from mine, you can absolutely create beautiful and unique artworks. Just remember to consider contrasts!

Fig. 7

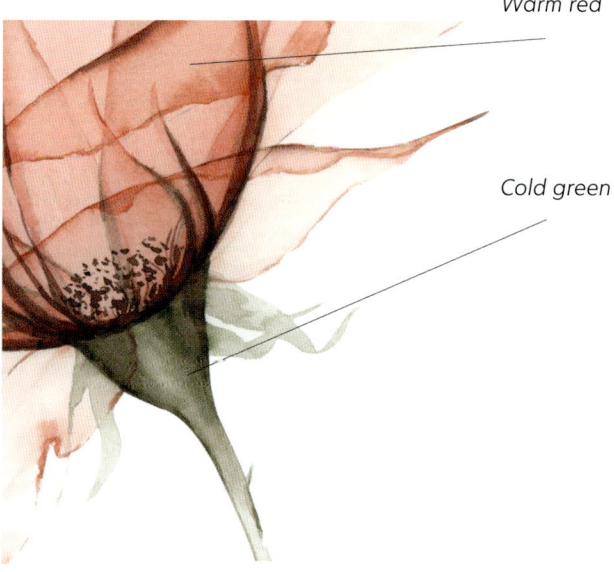

Warm red

Cold green

Fig. 8

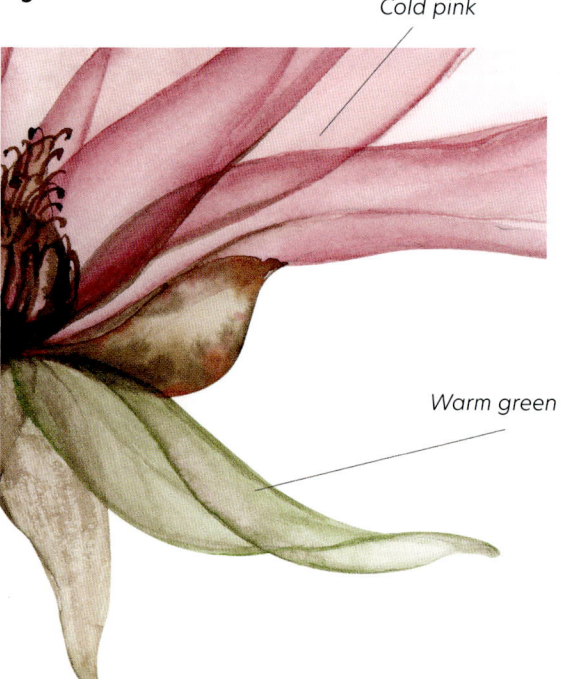

Cold pink

Warm green

Tips

- Payne's Gray can be used on its own in monochrome paintings but also as a 'mixer' to add dark tones, richer shades and contrasts to your main colour.
- Instead of painting huge colour charts of swatches and mixing everything with everything, I would recommend practising painting colour charts within one hue (see Fig. 6 on page 25).

26

Fig. 9

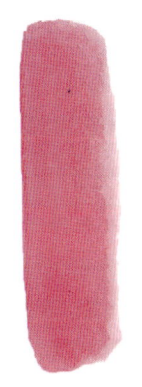 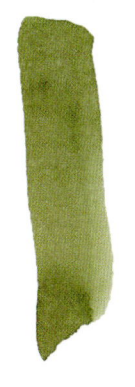 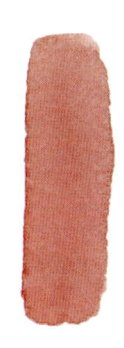 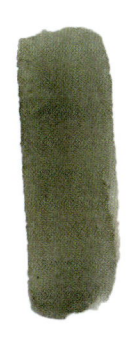 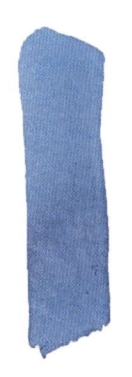 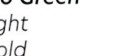 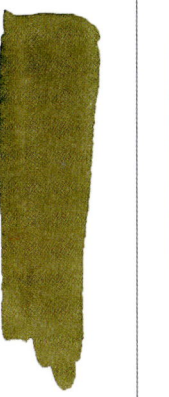 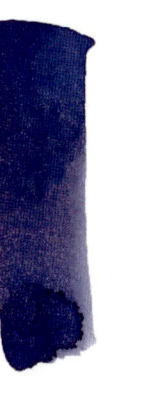

Quinacridone Rose
- *light*
- *cold*

Olive Green
- *dark*
- *warm*

Madder Lake Deep
- *dark*
- *warm*

Sage Green
- *dark*
- *cold*

Ultramarine Blue + Phthalo Green
- *light*
- *cold*

Olive Green
- *dark*
- *warm*

Ultramarine Blue
- *dark*
- *cold*

Olive Green
- *light*
- *warm*

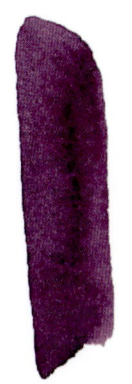 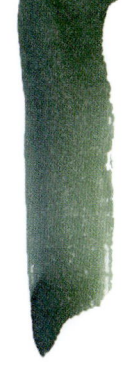  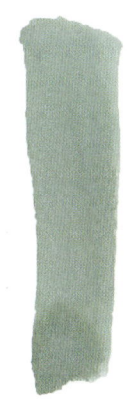 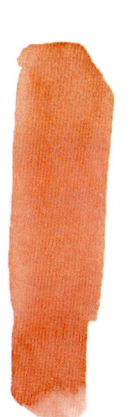 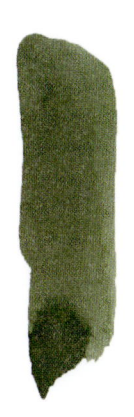 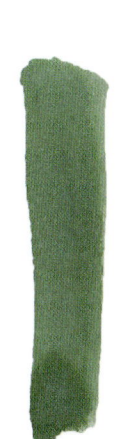

Ultramarine Blue + Quinacridone Rose
- *dark*
- *warm*

Phthalo Green + Ultramarine Blue + Payne's Grey
- *dark*
- *cold*

Cadmium Yellow
- *light*
- *warm*

Light Emerald Green
- *light*
- *cold*

Winsor Red or Alizarin Crimson + Cadmium Orange
- *light*
- *warm*

Sage Green
- *dark*
- *cold*

Cadmium Orange or Pyrrole Orange
- *light*
- *warm*

Sage Green
- *dark*
- *cold*

References and inspiration

Painting from references (either photographs or live flowers) is very important. We all know what a tulip looks like. But often when we are painting from memory, we tend to omit details and interesting features. This means you could end up with all your flowers looking pretty similar to one another.

When we are painting from references, we discover so many pretty details like the way a petal folds, unique vein details and spots of colour which will make each of our paintings different and eye-catching. When using references, especially live flowers, we have a chance to explore nature much better – to have a look inside a flower and observe its inner structure, which always add a special touch and value to our work.

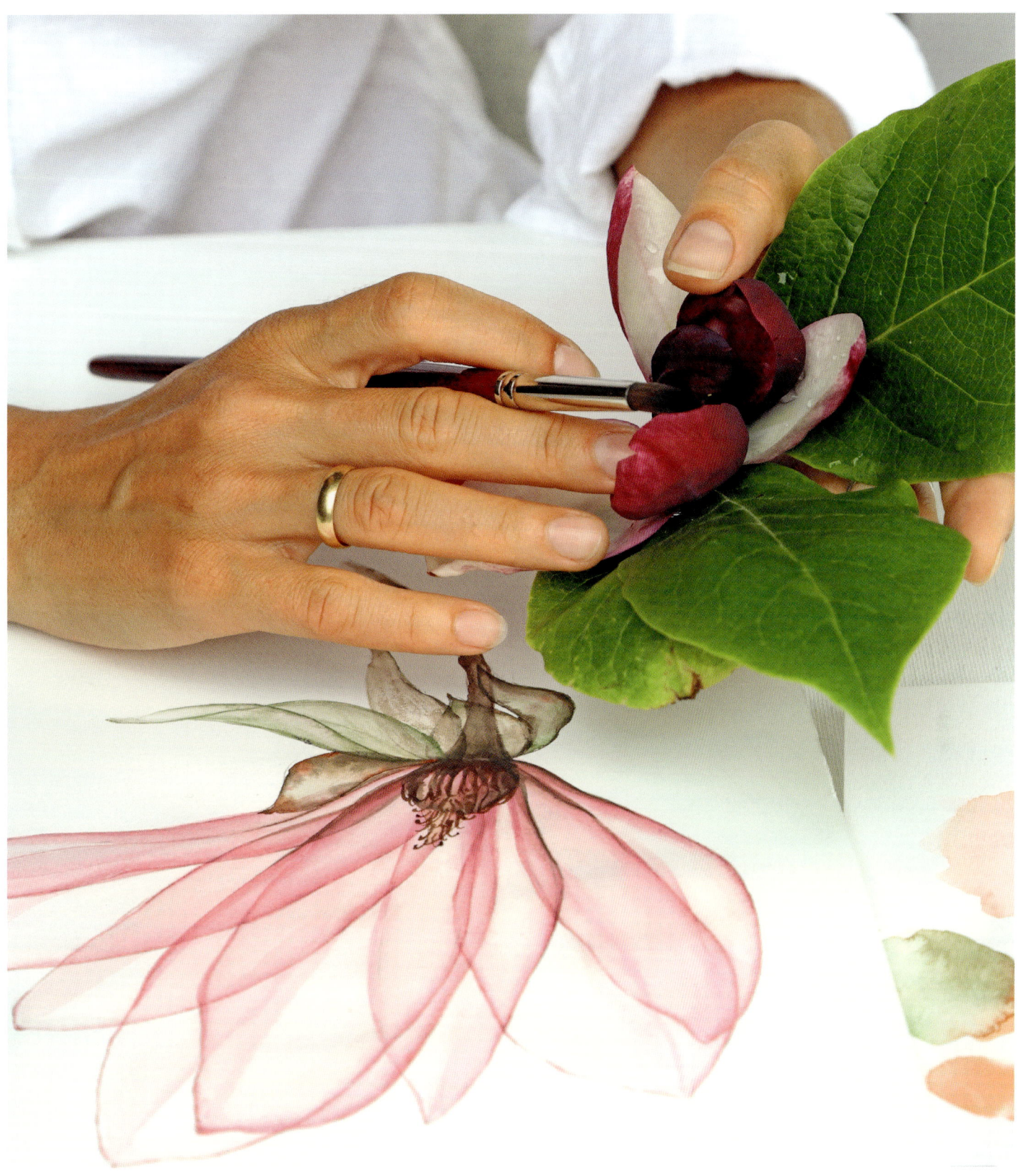

Where to get inspiration and references?

Often we have plenty of pictures on our phones, or bookmarked or saved on pages or boards online, to use as the main inspiration and reference material for our artworks. But what images do we use when we want to show off the inner structure of flowers, to achieve the transparent technique?

For building a flower structure, I usually follow a few simple steps.

STEP 1: CAPTURING THE KEY FLOWER SHAPES AND PETALS

The easiest way to do this is with photographs. They are perfect for capturing the main shape of a flower, understanding its colours, and getting a grasp of the key elements and forms. I prefer using my own pictures. Fortunately, the place where I live in Norway has amazing public gardens that are full of inspiration, even if the flowers only bloom for a super short period of time!

When you're taking pictures, especially if the flowers are all bunched up together, make sure to focus your camera on just one bloom. On smartphones, simply tap the screen where the flower is to get it to focus.

While you're taking pictures, go ahead and explore the flower if you can. Look inside and snap some shots of the petals, stigma and pistil. Count the petals when possible, too, and check out how they attach to the stem.

If I need to paint something exotic but it's not the right season to take pictures, I use websites like Pixabay or Unsplash. They have lots of royalty-free content that one can use for references. Make sure to use these for references and inspiration only; never directly copy the artwork.

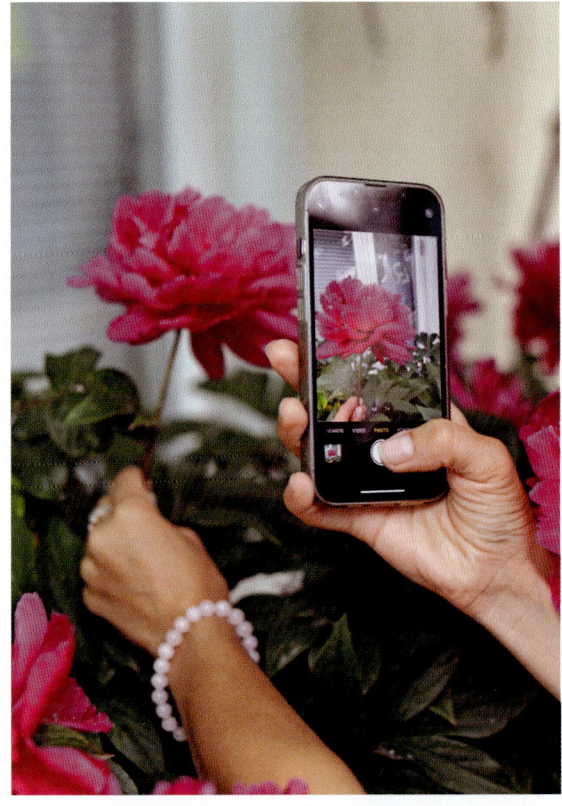

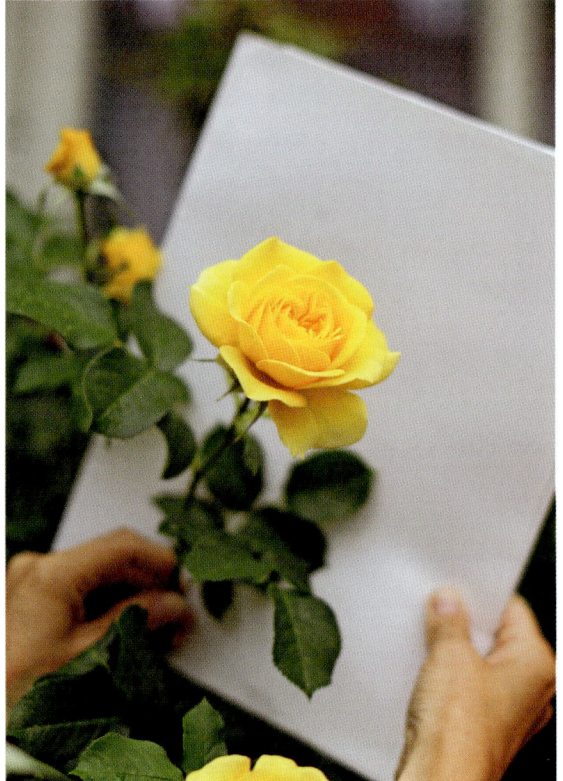

Tip

When photographing flowers with a busy background, grab a piece of white paper or a white paper folder and put it behind the flowers. It's like a pretend cut-out, separating the bloom from the background without actually cutting it.

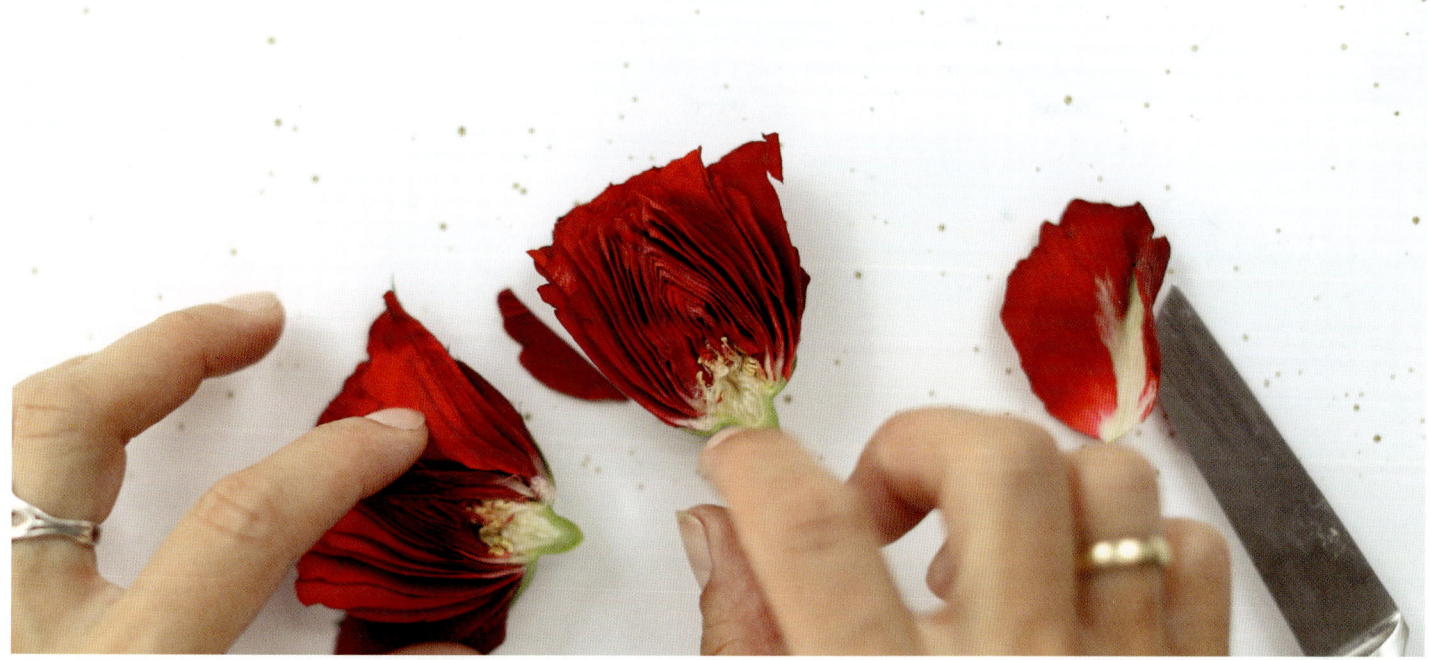

STEP 2: CAPTURING THE INNER PARTS OF FLOWERS

When it comes to to the fun part of re-creating the inner part of a flower, there are a couple of options.

- You can **explore traditional botanical illustrations** (see the example, right) because they usually show the flower structure with great precision. These can be found in specialist botanical books, or you can simply search online by typing the flower's name then 'flower structure' into the search field to find scientific illustrations.

- Another fun approach is simply to **cut a flower in half**. This method works wonders, especially for multi-petalled flowers like roses (see the photograph above). By cutting a real flower, you can closely examine its intricate details and capture them in your artwork. It allows you to observe the delicate layers of petals, the graceful curves, and the subtle variations in colour.

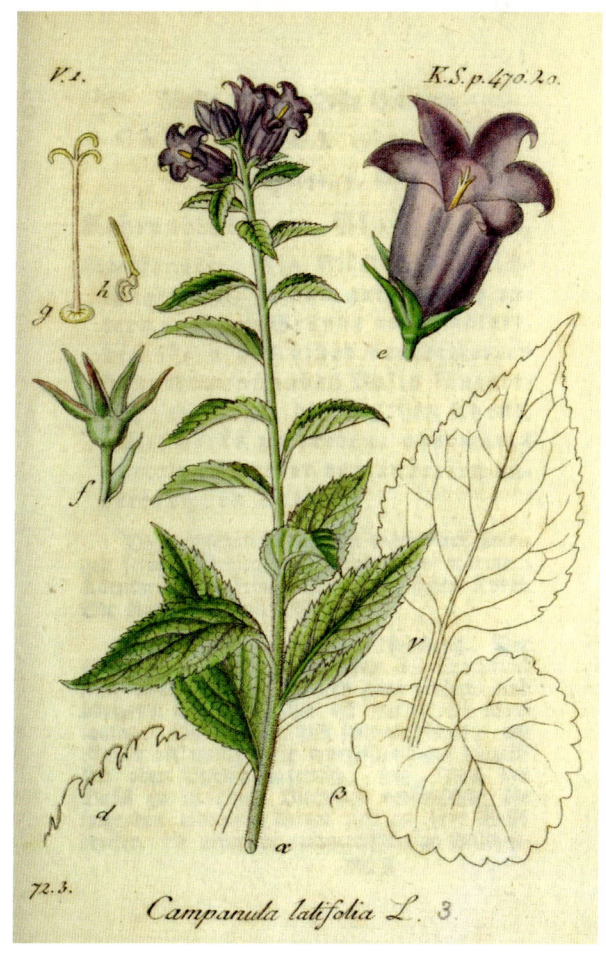

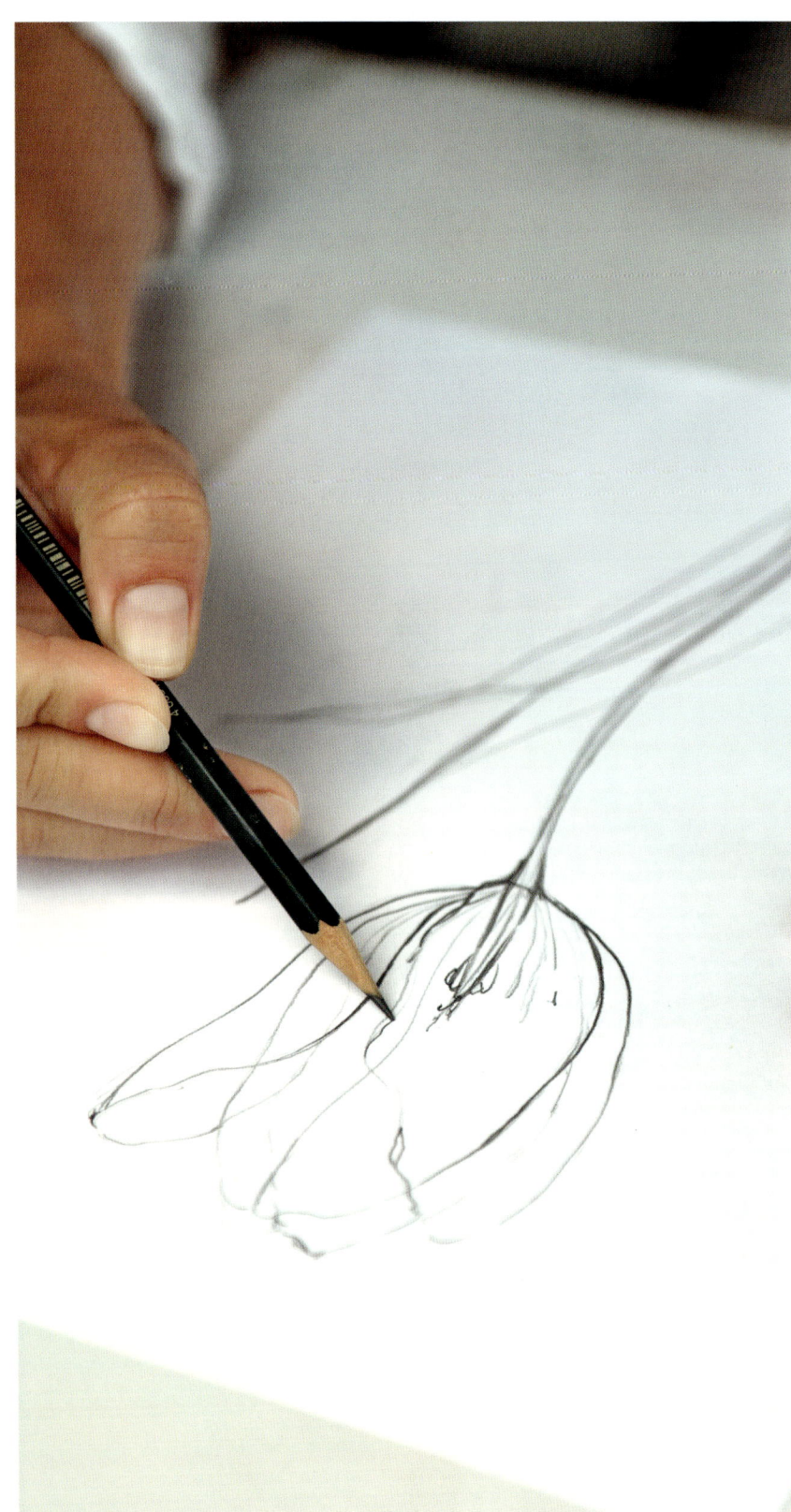

STEP 3: CREATING A DRAWING TO MERGE DIFFERENT SOURCES

Now, here comes the slightly tricky part, but also the key to achieving the transparent effect: we need to bring both the outer and inner parts together in one image.

In addition to the front petals, we should suggest the 'invisible' lines for the back petals in our drawing. Once that's done, we can place the pistil and stamens according to our references, be they scientific illustrations found online or in books, or our own pictures of the inner structure.

I know this stage might sound a bit complicated, but trust me: after trying it a couple of times, it becomes a very creative and enjoyable part of the process!

Remember, also, that this technique is all about impression and modern style – you don't need to create a traditional, completely accurate botanical illustration. So, don't be afraid to exaggerate some elements, add dynamic curves, and put your personal touch on it. That said, adding life-like, recognizable details where possible will give your artwork that 'wow' factor.

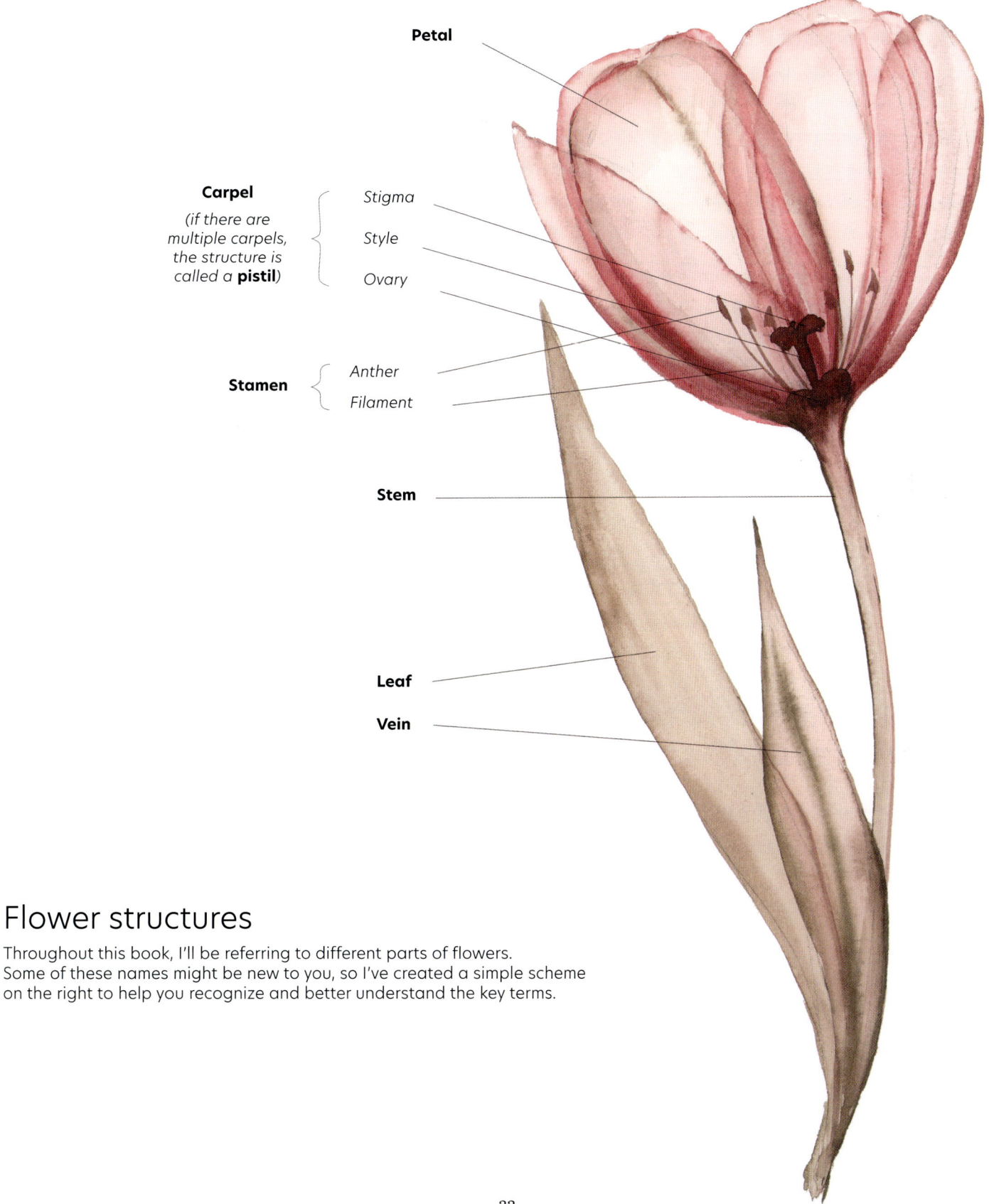

Petal

Carpel

*(if there are multiple carpels, the structure is called a **pistil**)*

Stigma

Style

Ovary

Stamen

Anther

Filament

Stem

Leaf

Vein

Flower structures

Throughout this book, I'll be referring to different parts of flowers.
Some of these names might be new to you, so I've created a simple scheme
on the right to help you recognize and better understand the key terms.

Watercolour techniques

The transparent technique requires a lot of patience and time.
On the other hand, it is a very meditative process that allows you to paint
at your own pace, with the possibility to step back, make corrections and
appreciate each step of the process.

Overleaf, you'll learn the key skills to get you started with painting
transparent flowers, explored by painting a simple tulip. Then, in the
projects, you'll see how I use these methods in different ways to achieve
a range of effects.

If you wish to practise the techniques on the same flower, the traceable
outline for the tulip can be found at the back of the book, on page 121.

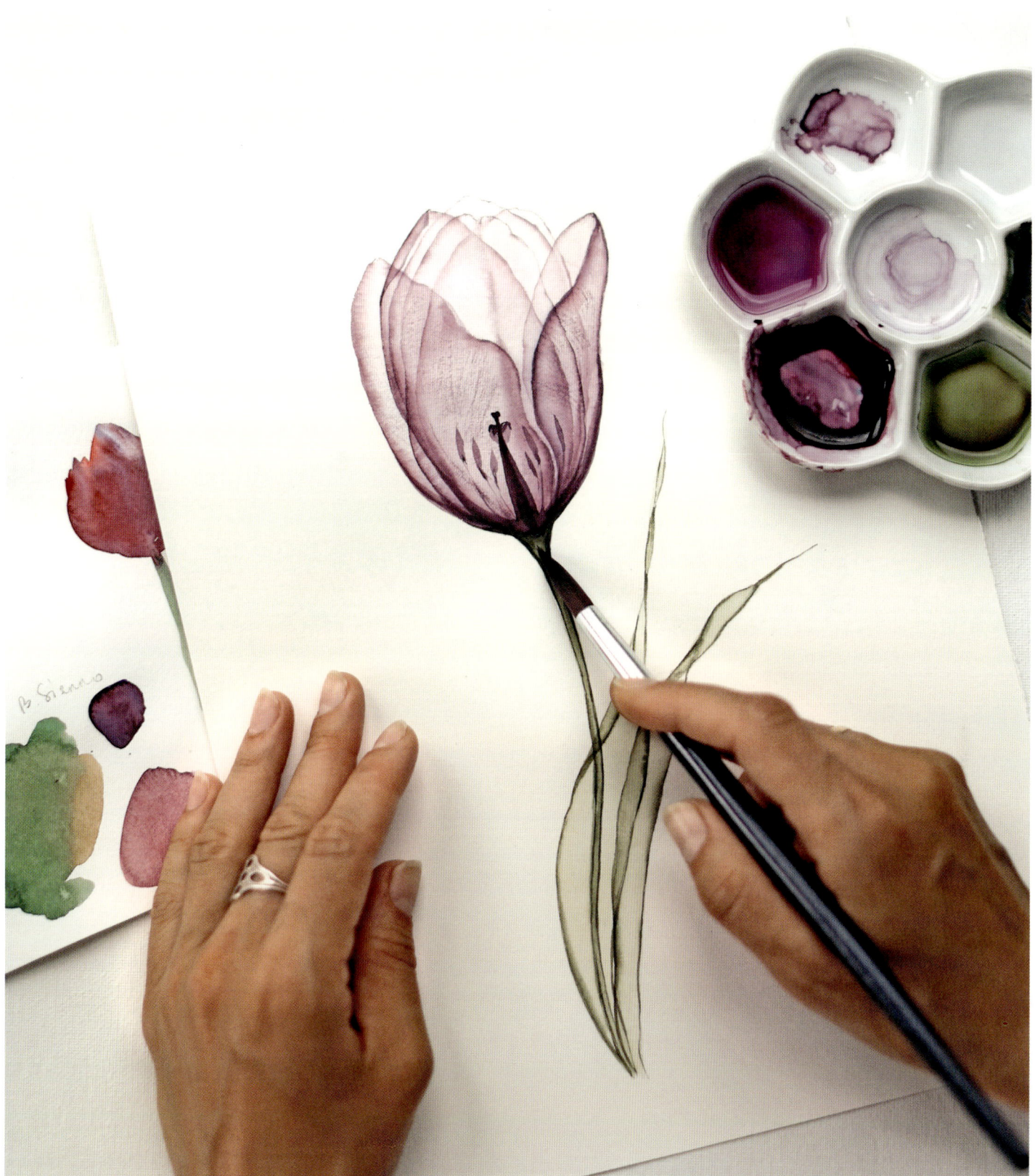

How to transfer the flower outlines onto a painting surface

At the beginning of your transparent-flower journey, I recommend that you trace the complete drawing of your chosen flower, which you will find on pages 120–127.

Usually, I avoid drawing all the petals in the beginning, to let my flowers 'grow' in the course of the painting process and to avoid making the drawing too messy. I focus on the basic flower structure and on a few of the most evident and bigger petals.

If you wish to follow a similar process, first transfer the basic flower structure with the largest and most prominent petals. Then, after a few painting steps, transfer the next group of petals. This will help you stay organized and ensure that you don't get lost in all the lines. I've done this with the peony project, on pages 97 and 99.

There are few ways to transfer outlines. You could use special light boxes or light pads, carbon paper or special tracing paper. I like to keep it simple, and transfer all my drawings with the help of a window on a bright sunny day. Photocopy your chosen flower outline, stick it to the window with paper tape, place your watercolour paper directly on top and then transfer the outlines with a pencil.

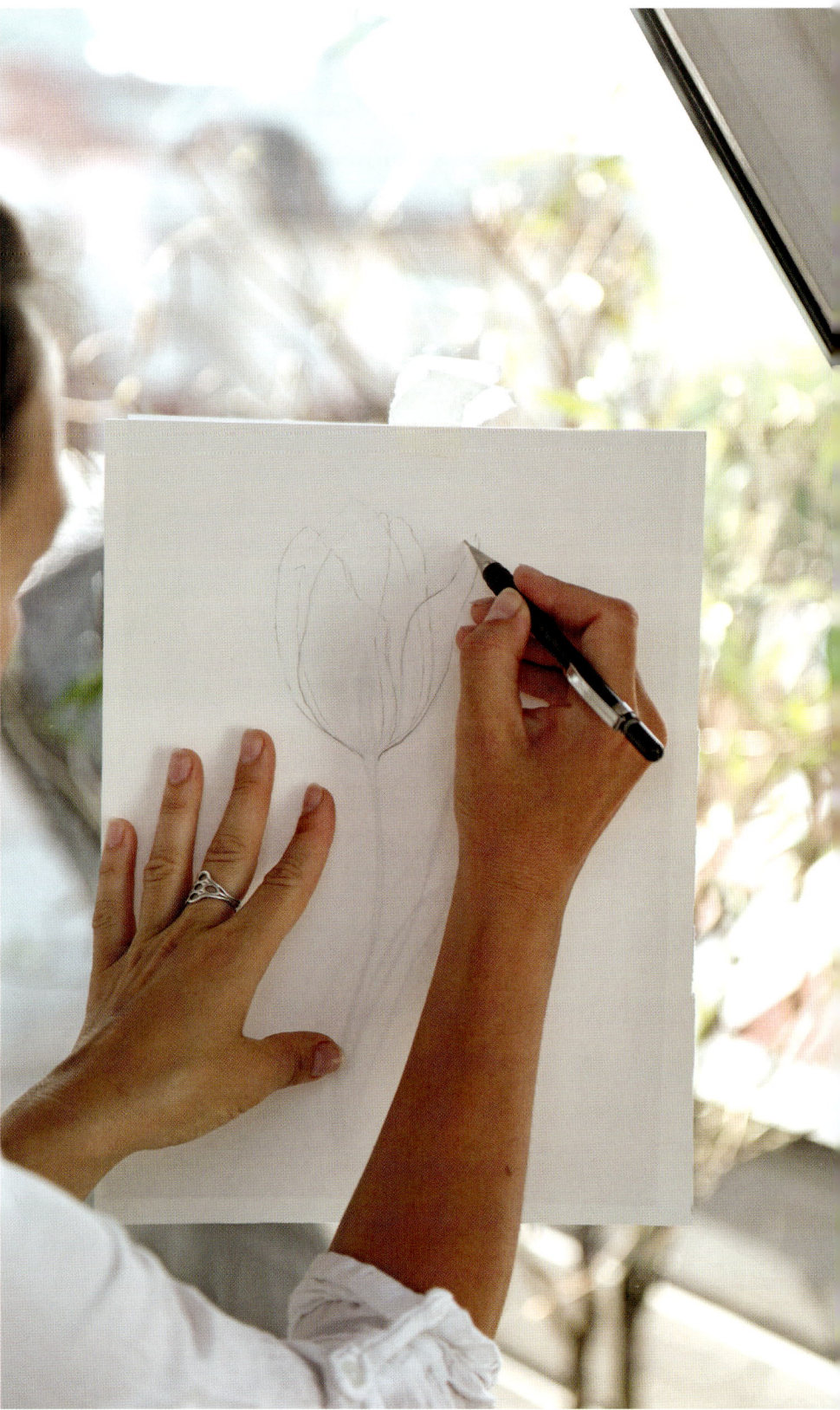

Basic watercolour techniques

Knowing and mastering the basic techniques gives you the freedom to paint with confidence, and to experiment through the process of creating a painting too. For these reasons, it's worth giving yourself a bit of time just to practise the key techniques.

WASH AND GLAZE

When you start to learn about watercolour painting, often you come across terms like 'watercolour wash' and 'watercolour glaze'. What are the applications for both, and what are their differences?

A watercolour **wash** refers to a layer of diluted colour that is applied over a relatively large area of a painting. It is often used to create backgrounds or to establish the base colour for petals and other elements (**A**). A wash is particularly effective at creating smooth and flowing backgrounds for flowers in traditional watercolour artworks.

A watercolour **glaze** refers to the application of multiple layers of diluted paint or clean water on top of each other. Glazing is mainly used to paint a specific element, like a petal, rather than a large area. In transparent painting we use glazing because it allows us to layer paint, creating beautiful graduation and translucent effects in watercolour.

When using the glazing technique, first you paint a shape onto untouched paper or a painted element with a very diluted paint mix; then you allow it to dry completely (**B**). After the painting is dry, you paint a new shape over the top of the previous colour (**C**).

It is very important to let the previous layer dry completely before painting another one on the top! It's also crucial to avoid creating puddles at the second stage of glazing. To remove excess water, simply dab your brush on kitchen paper then touch the semi-dry brush on the puddle to soak up the excess water (**D**).

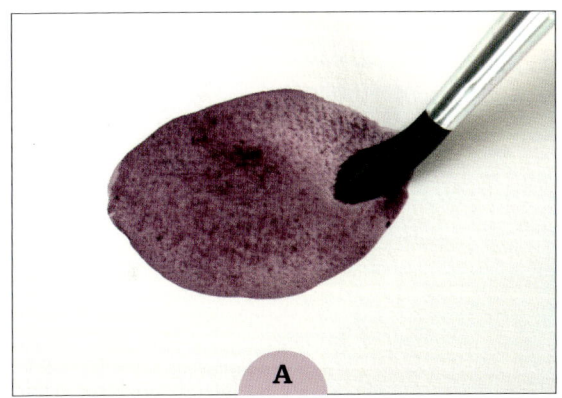

A

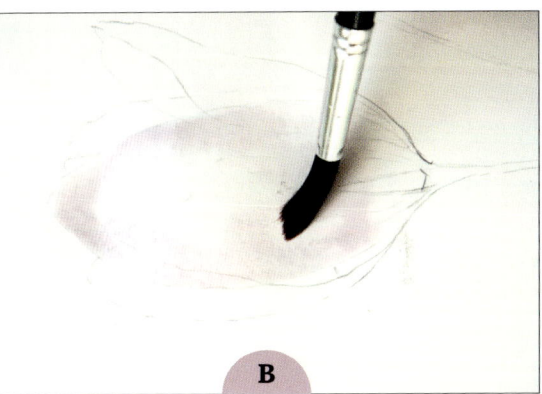

B

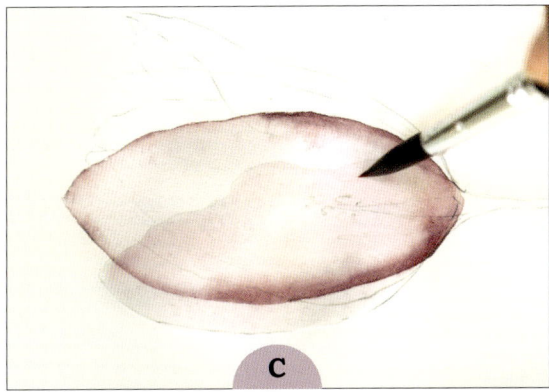

C

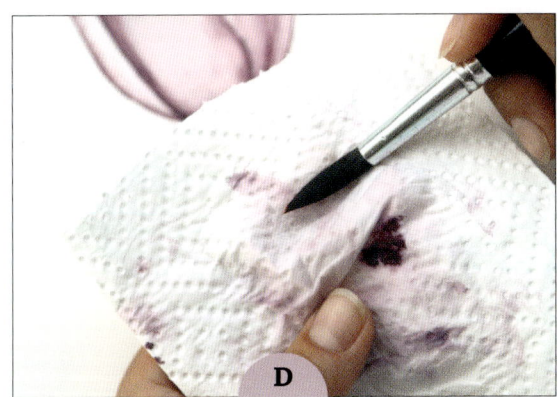

D

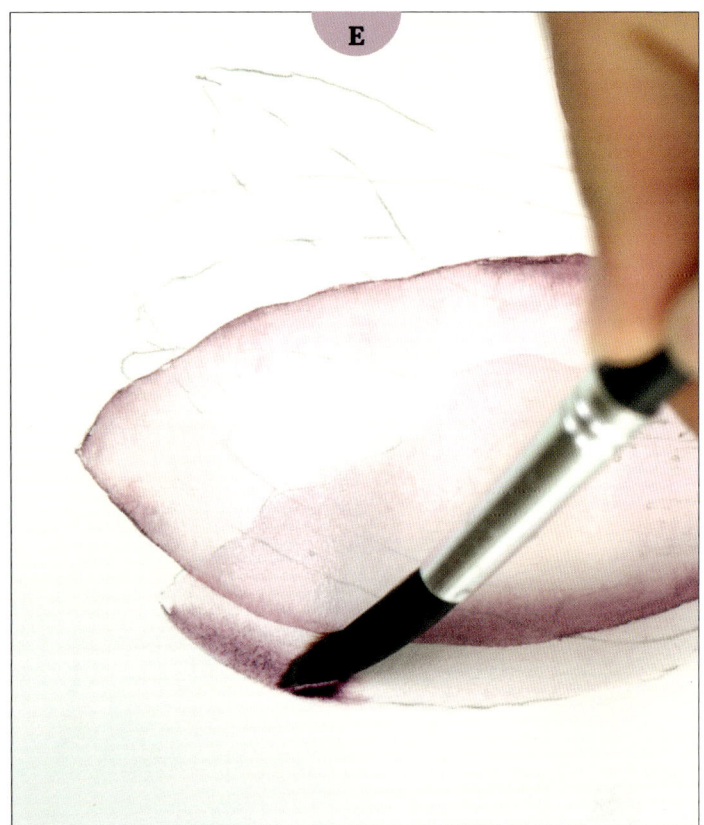

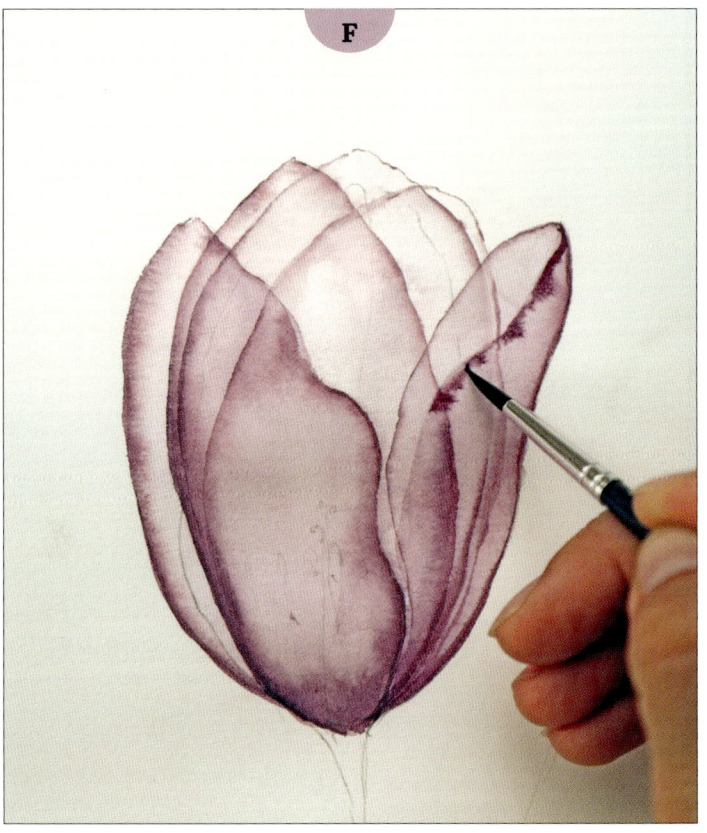

WET-IN-WET

This is a technique that is exactly how it sounds: wet paint is applied to a wet surface. Usually diluted paint is used, and the wet surface will be either pre-moistened paper or a layer of paint on the paper that is still wet (**E**).

The wet surface allows the colours to blend and merge together in a soft and fluid manner. This technique is often used to create subtle gradients, smooth transitions between different mixes, and atmospheric effects in painting petals or leaves.

DRY-IN-WET

The dry-in-wet technique involves applying a relatively dry paint onto a wet surface, creating a crisp effect that's often ideal for outlines. Dry paint is pure colour taken straight from the pan or tube, or a mix of colours on your palette picked up with just enough water on the brush.

To use the dry-in-wet technique, you first wet a specific area on the paper with water. Then, while the surface is still wet, you apply relatively thick paint to it (**F**). The wetness of the surface allows the paint to interact with the water, creating interesting blending effects and producing a softer transition between colours.

This method offers a balance between total control and spontaneity, and in turn creates vibrant and dynamic artworks.

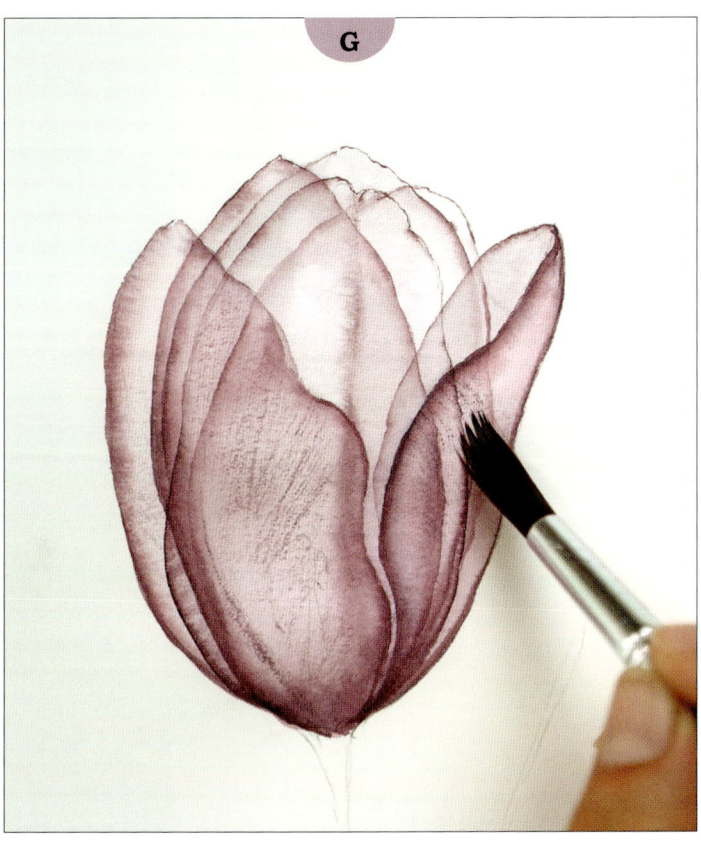

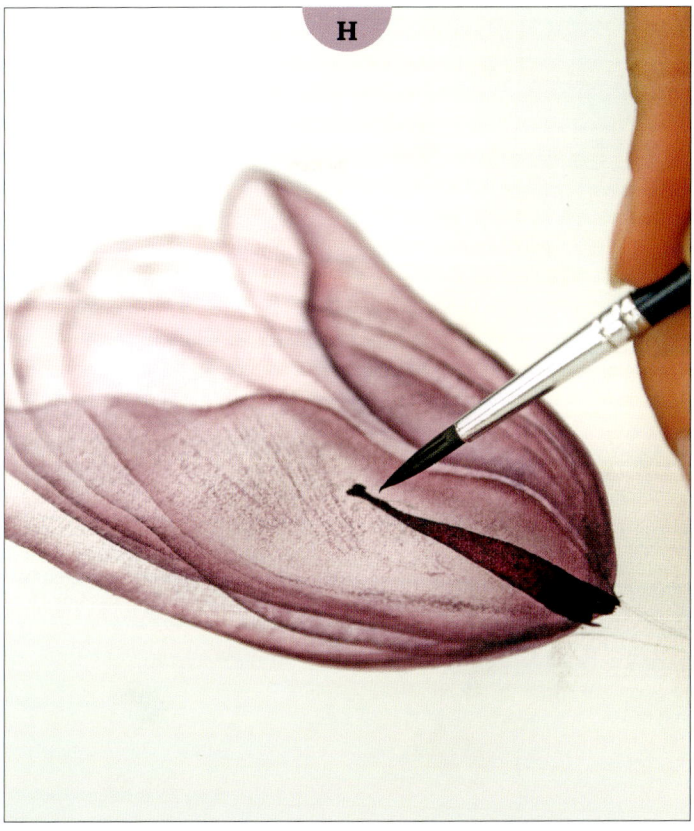

DRY-ON-DRY

Also known as the dry-brush technique, this method involves picking up a minimal amount of paint on a slightly damp brush then quickly stroking it across a dry surface (**G**).

This technique is particularly useful for depicting subtle details such as tiny petal or leaf veins.

WET-ON-DRY

For this technique, wet paint is applied to a dry surface, which can be either dry paper or an area of previously dried paint.

First, apply a layer of paint and allow it to dry. Once the bottom layer is completely dry, you can then apply wet paint on top of it (**H**), creating distinct and defined brush strokes or details.

I usually use this technique for adding bold crisp outlines or fine details without excessive blending.

Transparent watercolour techniques

Now let's bring all the basic techniques into practice and explore how to use them to paint transparent flowers.

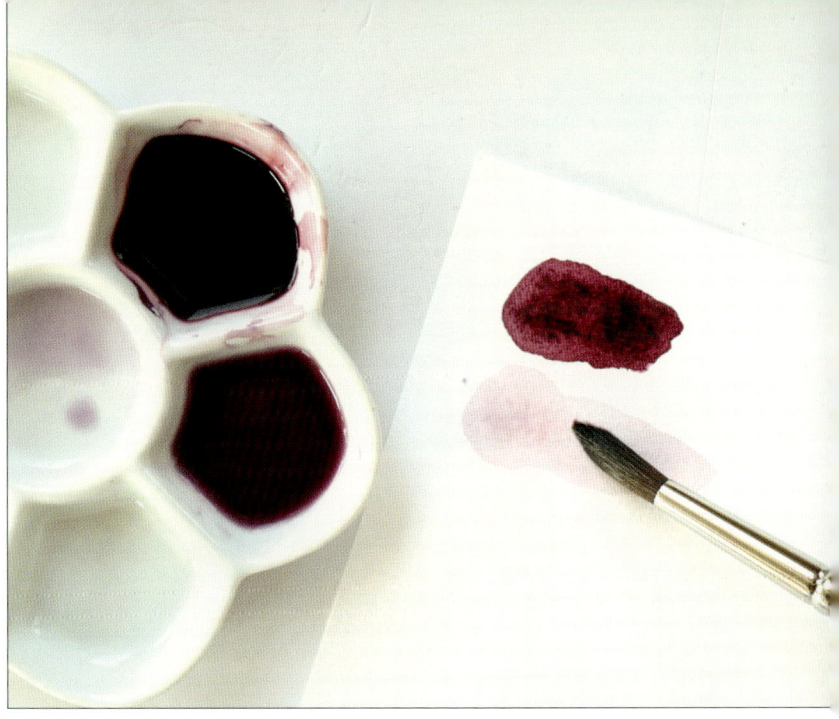

ACHIEVING DIFFERENT CONCENTRATIONS OF PAINT

Essentially, transparent painting uses multiple layers of diluted colours. The main principle is to create a tonal contrast within one petal.

To achieve that effect, in advance prepare two mixes of the same colour – one dark (thick paint with a little water added) and one very diluted (lots of water added to the mix to make it loose). Remember, in watercolour it is easier to make your painting darker than the other way round. I recommend using palettes with several deep wells so you can prepare enough mixes and dilutions of the same colour.

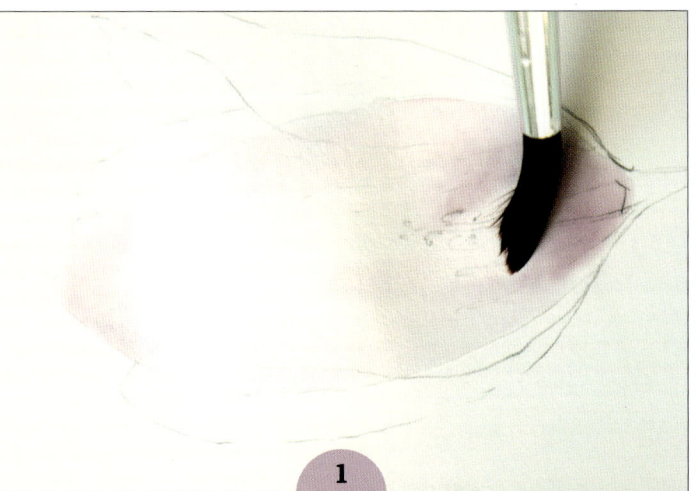

THE MAIN APPROACH

To paint petals and leaves with the transparent effect, combine wet-in-wet with dry-in-wet. The main area of the petal is painted wet-in-wet then the outlines are painted dry-in-wet.

I recommend using two brushes at the same time – one for the diluted mix to paint in the main petal area, and another, smaller brush for the bold mix to paint in the outlines.

1 Glaze the petal with a very diluted mix using a no. 6 round brush, distributing the mix evenly on the paper with no puddles.

2 While the glaze is still wet, run the bold mix along the edges of the petal with the tip of a no. 4 round brush. As you do this, soften the dark colour with a clean, damp brush, moving from the top to bottom of the petal.

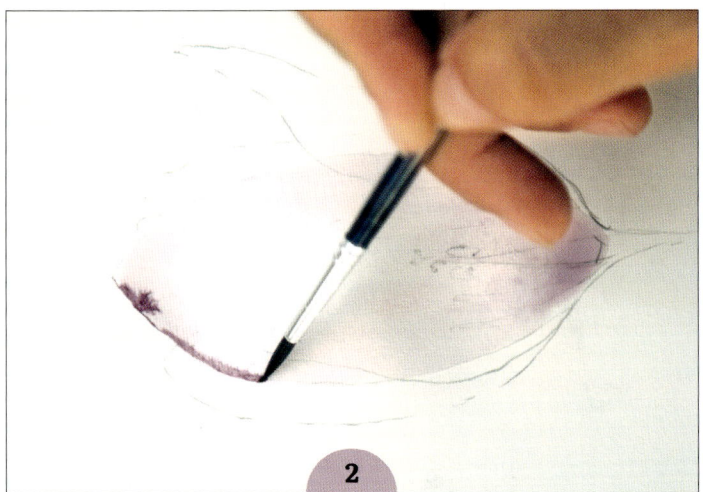

PAINTING GRADIENTS

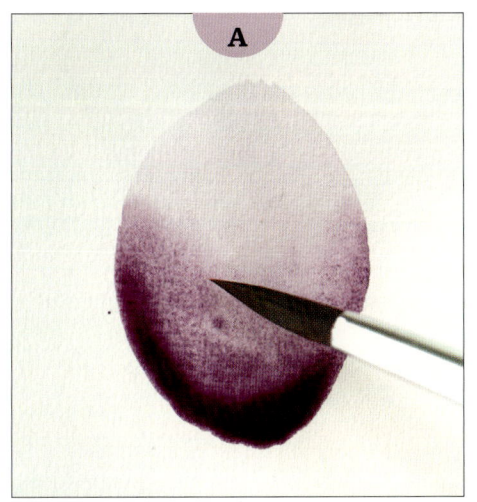

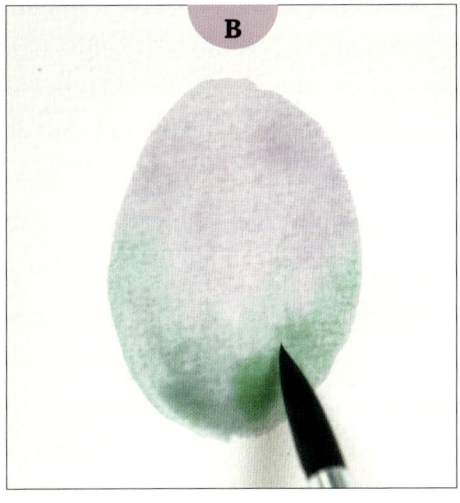

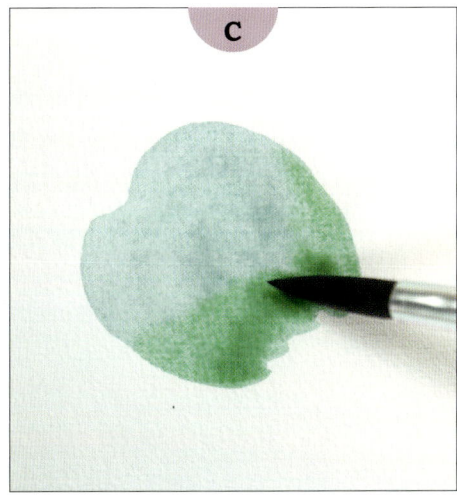

Value (light to dark)

Usually petals have very delicate fine tips and a much thicker bottom area where they are attached to the stem. To show this, you need to paint petals with a gradient.

Glaze the petal with a very diluted mix using a no. 6 round brush. Distribute the mix evenly on the paper with no puddles, as seen in step 1 opposite. While the paint is still wet, add a bit of the dark mix in the bottom area of the petals. Distribute the darker mix from the bottom upwards, stopping around the middle area, then soften the middle 'line' with a clean, damp brush (**A**).

Hue (colour)

In the same way as the single-colour (value) gradient, you could paint with a two-colour gradient when you want to show a variety of petals hues.

For petals (B): Glaze the area with the main diluted colour. Touch in the second colour where necessary then gently blend them with a no. 6 round brush.

For leaves (C): To add depth to the leaf, apply a small amount of the darker mix to the bottom part with the no. 6 round brush.

OVERLAPPING AREAS WITH THE GLAZING TECHNIQUE

Before painting overlapping areas, make sure that the paper is completely dry. You could either wait until it dries out by itself or use a hairdryer to speed up the process.

Using a no. 6 round brush, glaze an overlapping area with a very diluted mix. If there are many intersections between the petals or leaves, it's best to paint one part at a time and allow each layer to dry completely before moving on to the next. This stops the colours from bleeding into each other.

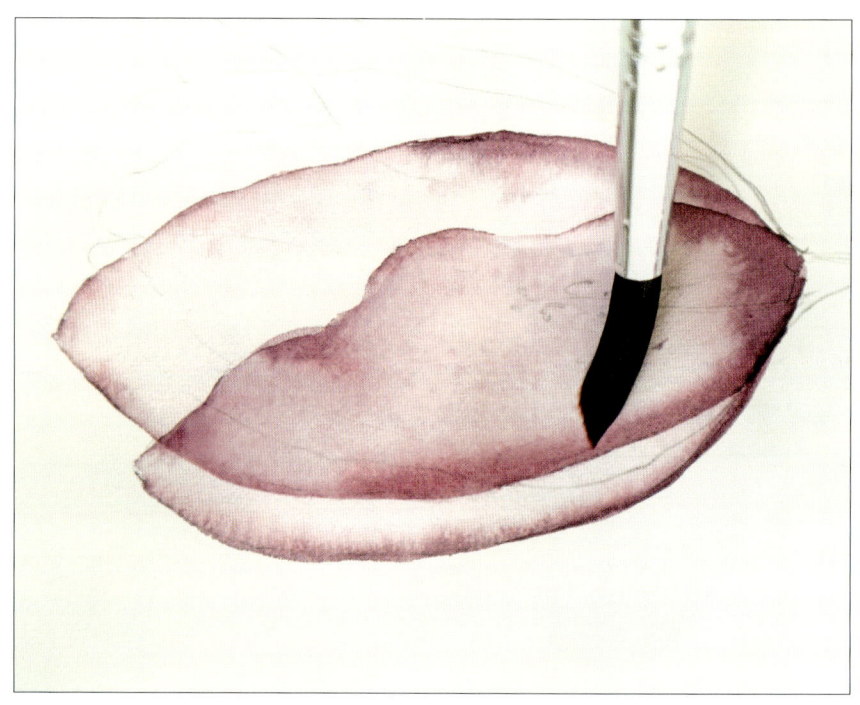

EMPHASIZING TRANSPARENCY

In order to accentuate transparent effects in watercolour flowers, you need to create more contrast between the lighter surfaces of the petals and their edges, including the areas which we usually can't see.

After working a glaze, with the tip of a no. 6 round brush, add a bold but watery mix along the edges of the petals while the glaze is still wet. Soften the darker colour with a clean, damp no. 4 round brush, working from the inner side of the shape.

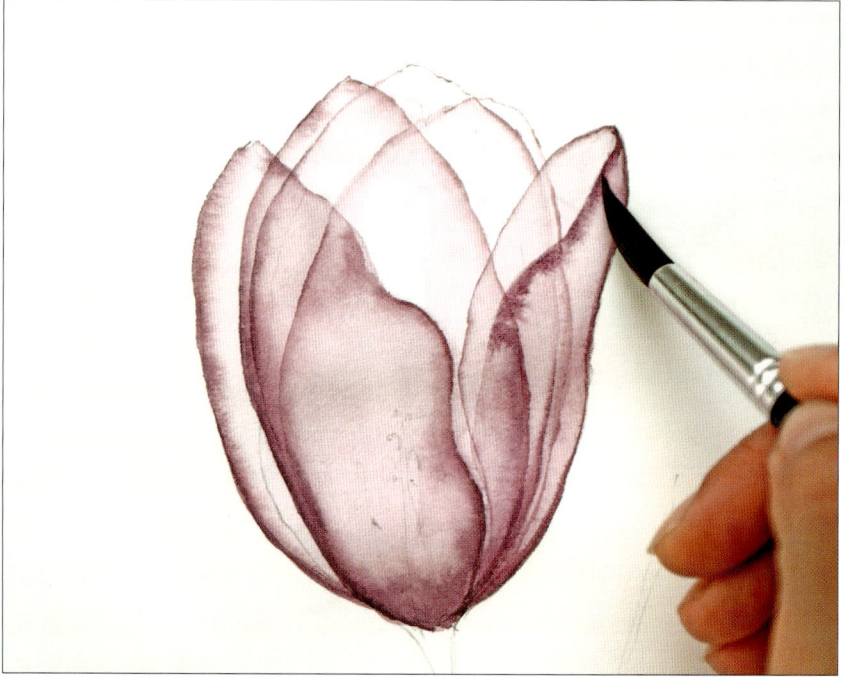

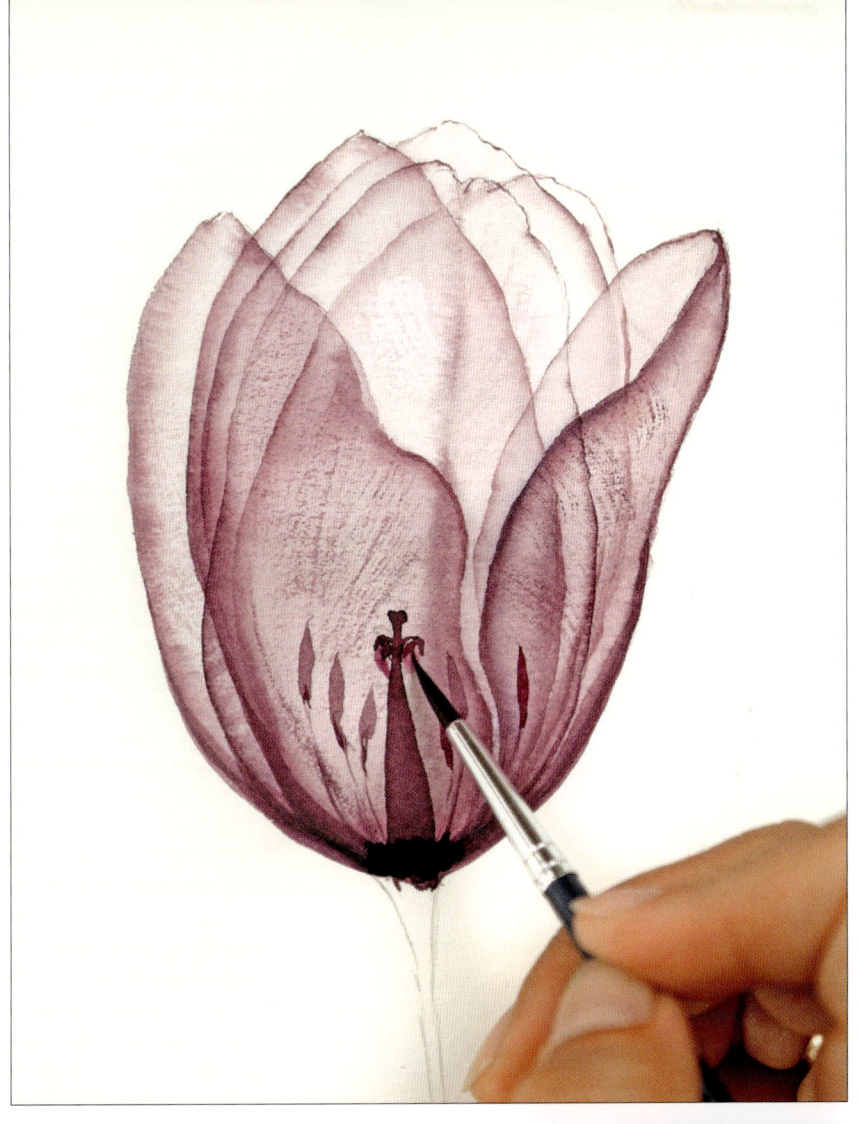

PAINTING DETAILS DRY-ON-DRY

For painting veins and other details, use a no. 4 round brush with a very fine tip.

For veins: With just the tip of the brush, pick up a diluted mix and paint a line, applying a little bit of pressure at the very bottom. Side veins can be mapped out in a similar way, albeit with the lines starting from the central vein rather than the bottom of the leaf or petal.

For inner flower details: With a no. 4 round brush, pick up a diluted mix and paint a silhouette of the carpels or pistils from top to bottom. If you wish, you may find it easier to draw the general shape initially, then paint it in. With the tip of the brush and a slightly stronger mix, paint in details such as the stigma(s) and ovary. Note that you don't need to re-create the details completely; imagine you are painting silhouettes – the essential shapes but not every minute detail.

For the stems: With a no. 4 round brush, pick up a diluted green mix and paint the stem from top to bottom. There's no need to paint the whole stem in one go: move down slowly, grab more of the mix when necessary and gradually add new brush strokes so as to keep the stem colour as consistent as possible.

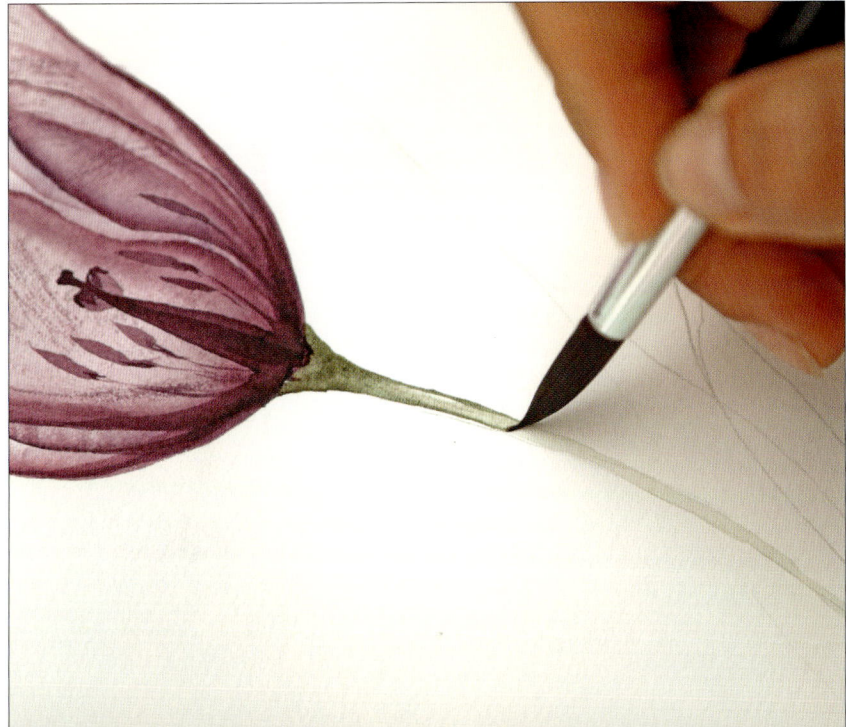

Projects

Now I am inviting you to dive into painting your own flowers. On the following pages you will find six different projects that I have organized to flow from the easiest to the more complex.

In each project we will be exploring something new along with a fresh challenge, such as creating gradients, adding extra colours and increasing the amount of petals. Each project is broken down into small steps, enabling you to paint at your own pace.

For the best results, at first I recommend you paint one picture following my instructions step-by-step and the same reference images – and, if necessary, using the corresponding outline at the back of the book. For your second attempt, I encourage you to paint the same plant but use your own references, applying everything you've learnt into your unique artwork.

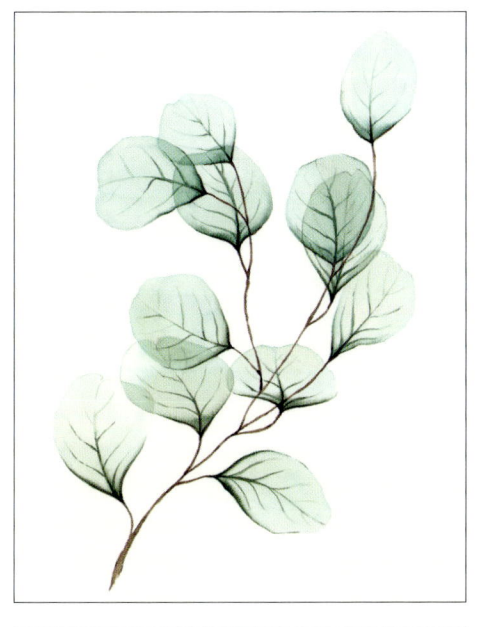
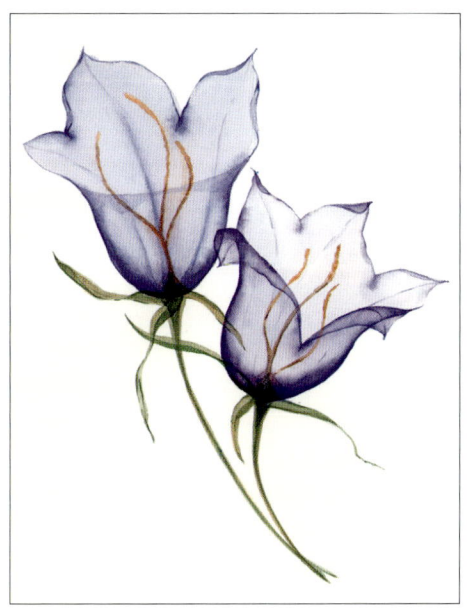
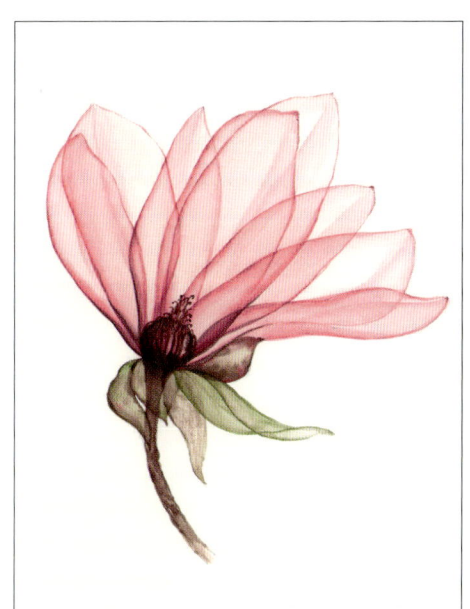
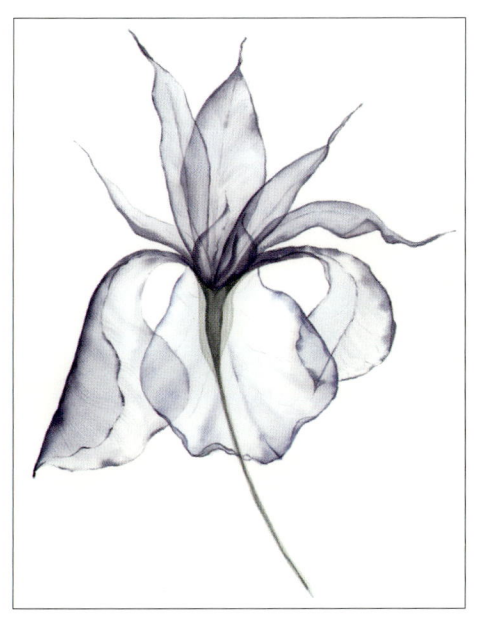
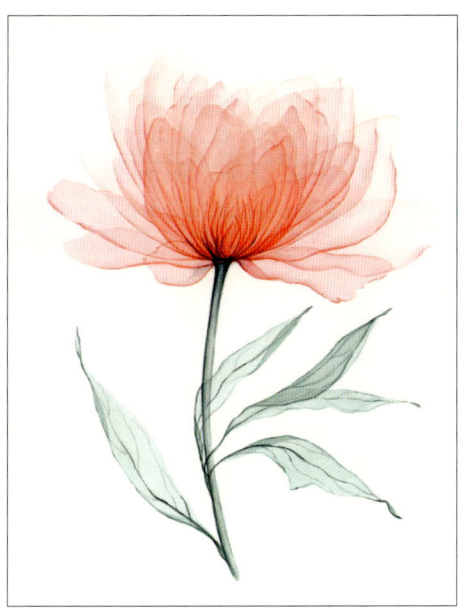
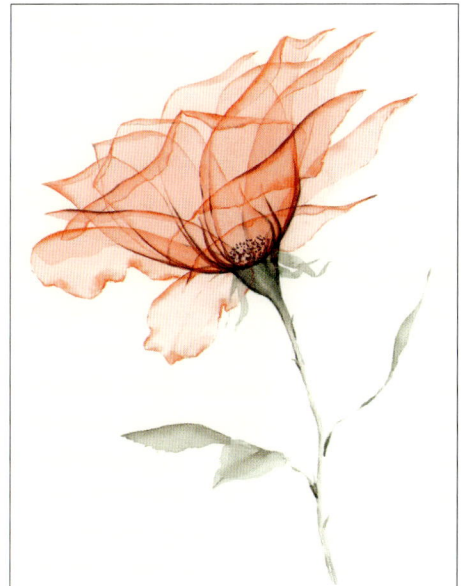

Project One:

Eucalyptus

Greenery, painted or in life, can add a great deal of beauty to our interiors. Painting greenery has become increasingly popular, as it can make for a stunning piece of wall art on its own or be combined with florals for a complete composition. I have decided to take a cucalyptus branch as an example, but the steps I will be sharing can be applied to painting other types of green plants as well.

The top leaves of the eucalyptus branch are in direct sunlight, which gives them a cooler tone. As you move down the branch the leaves are mostly in the shade, and therefore become warmer in colour.

Through painting eucalyptus I will show you how to add gradient and different shades in your painting.

You will need

WATERCOLOUR PAINTS:
Phthalo Green, Ultramarine Blue, Burnt Sienna

MATERIALS AND TOOLS:
22 x 30cm (8½ x 12in) sheet of hot-pressed paper; sharp (or mechanical) HB pencil; putty eraser and soft white eraser; kitchen paper or cloth; no. 4 and no. 6 round synthetic brushes with very fine tips

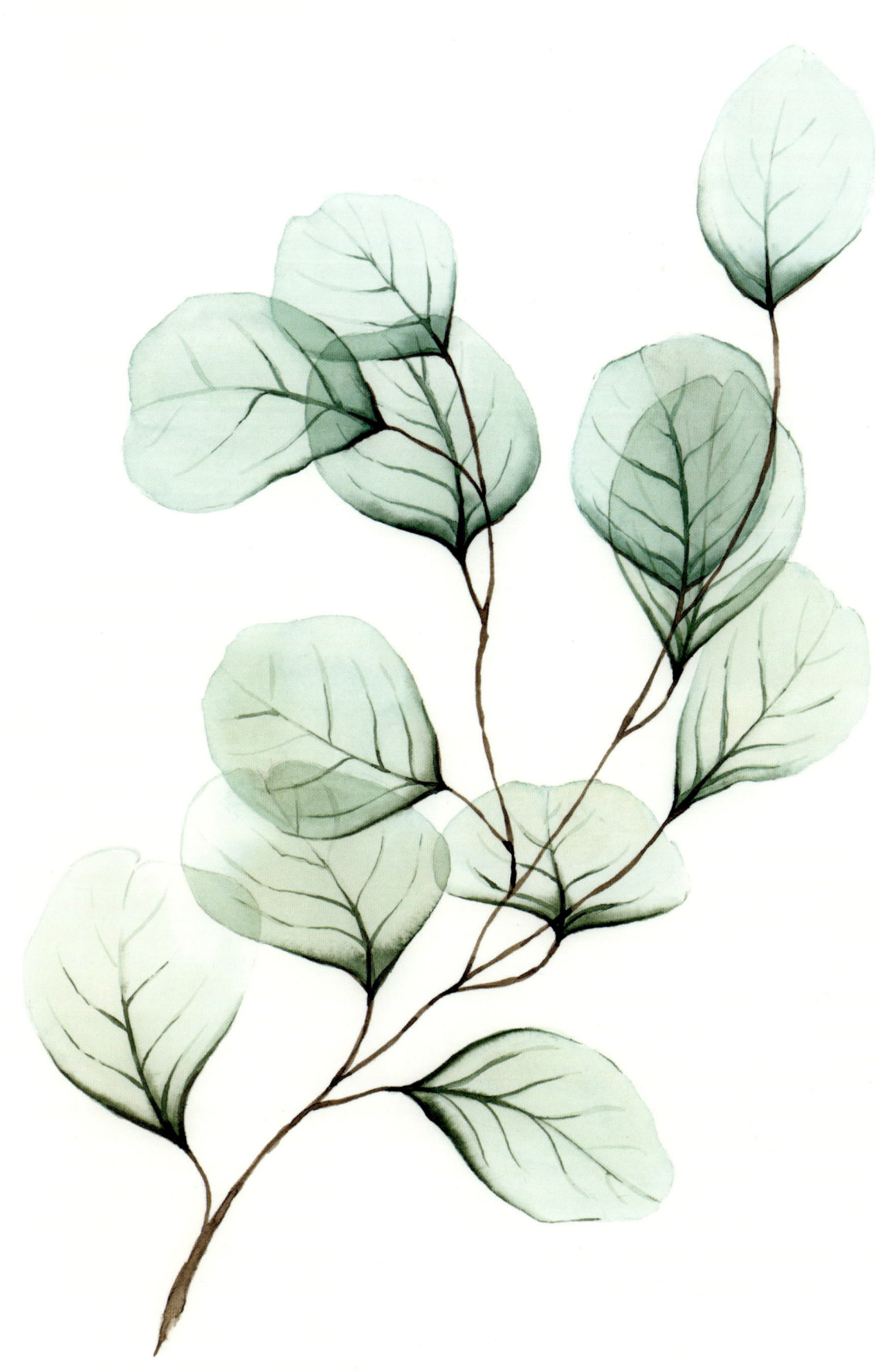

Basic mixes

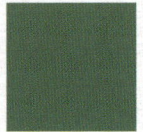
DARK COLD GREEN
Phthalo Green,
Ultramarine Blue and
Burnt Sienna

DARK WARM GREEN
Phthalo Green, Burnt
Sienna and a hint of
Ultramarine Blue

BROWN
Ultramarine Blue and
Burnt Sienna

LIGHT COLD GREEN
As detailed above,
but very diluted

LIGHT WARM GREEN
As detailed above,
but very diluted

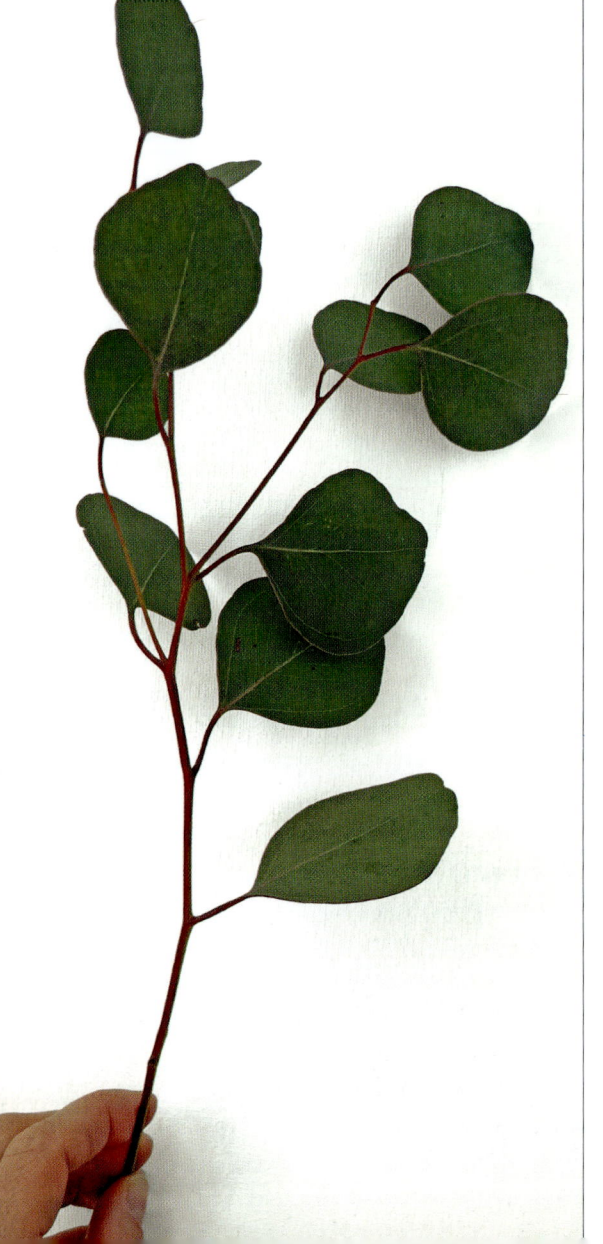

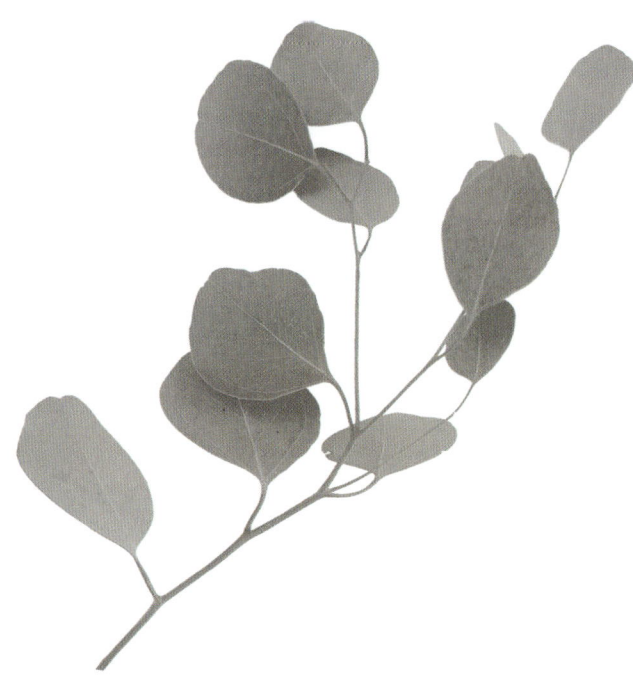

Reference photographs

Typically, eucalyptus leaves have a thinner texture at the top and a denser texture at the bottom where they attach to the branch. When painting leaves, it's important to keep this in mind: leave the top areas light and transparent, and add more weight and details to the bottom part of the leaves.

Sometimes it helps to turn the reference photograph black and white to see details and contrasts better. Focusing on the structure and details in the plant, rather than the correct hue, improves the understanding of the transparent technique. Most photo-editing apps, including ones on your phone, allow you to turn photographs black and white very easily. And remember: you can always paint a project just in one colour, which would make the finished painting very modern and stylish! (See page 20 for an example of this.)

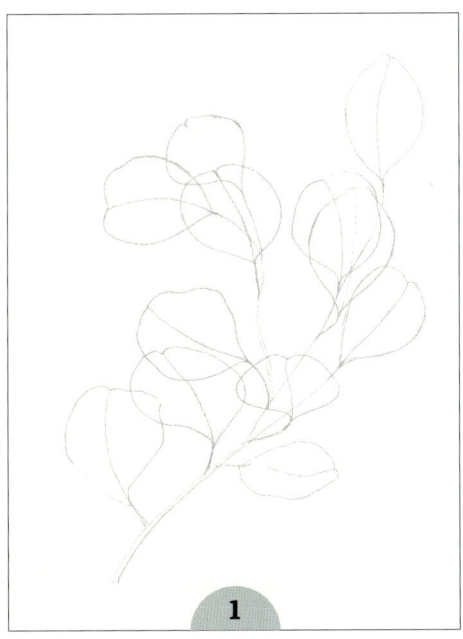

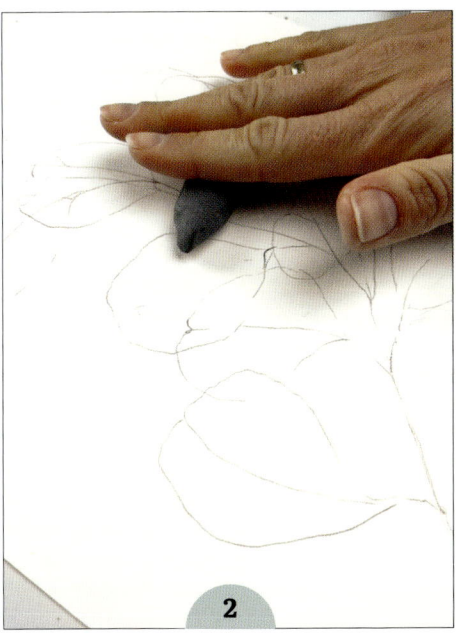

1 Drawing the branch. Using the outline on page 122 or the photo reference opposite, draw the eucalyptus branch.

2 Softening the outline. Once you are happy with the drawing, rub back the lines with a putty eraser, leaving a faint outline.

3 Mixing the paints. Make up the four green mixes, referring to the swatches and their details opposite. Start with the two darker mixes then, once you are happy with the hues, take a drop of each mixture, place them in separate wells in the palette and dilute each with a large amount of water to create the lighter mixes.

Tip

To create a smooth transition between the cool and warm greens, first mentally divide the branch into three sections. You will paint the top section with a cooler green mix, the middle section with a mix of both cool and warm greens, and the bottom section with a warmer green mix.

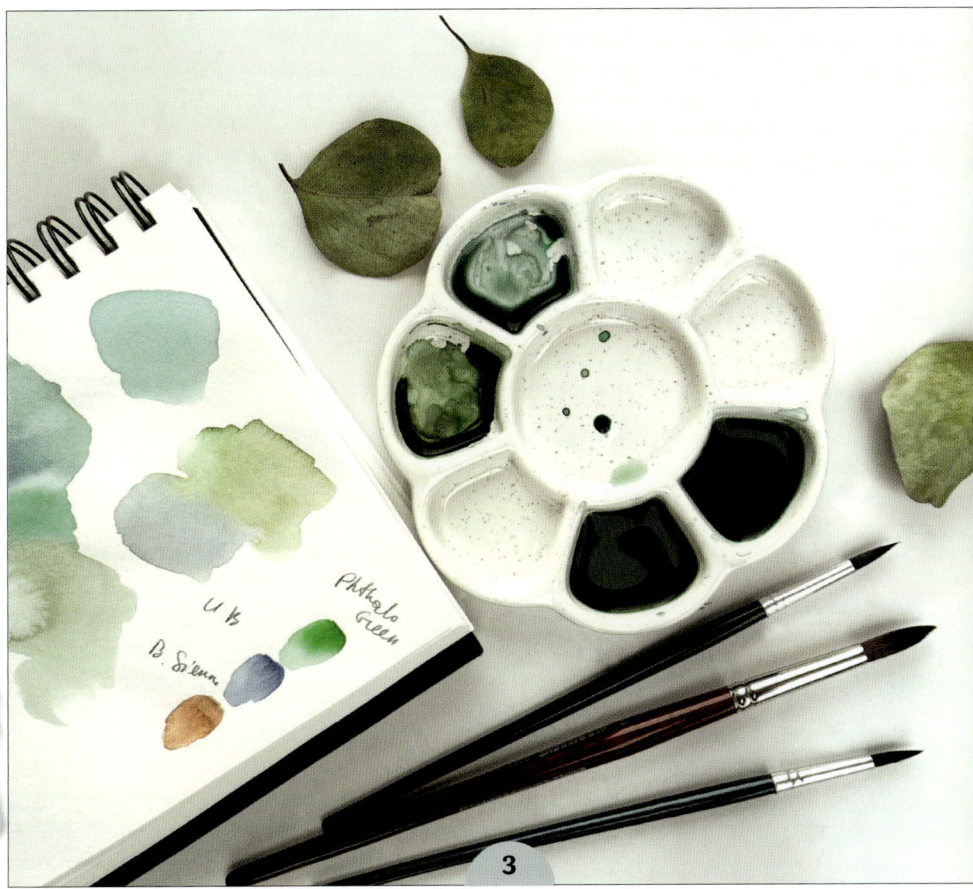

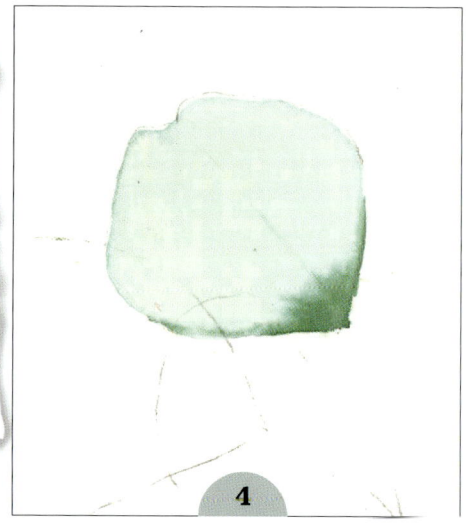

4

First layer of leaves: top section. Using the no. 6 brush, wet the top leaf then glaze it with the light cold green mix. Then touch a drop of the dark cold green mix to the bottom point of the leaf while the paper is still wet and distribute the colour upwards with a clean, damp brush.

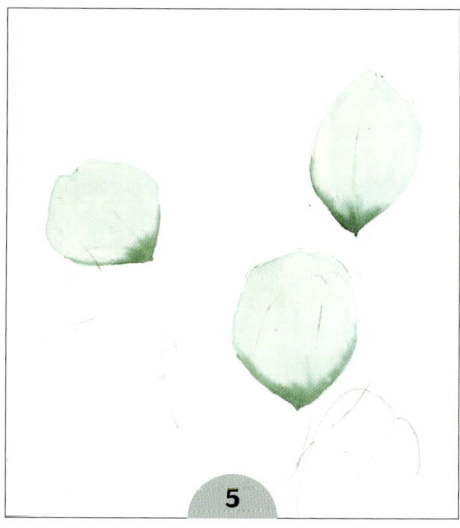

5

First layer of leaves: top section continued. Paint all the top leaves (that don't overlap other leaves) in the same way.

6 First layer of leaves: middle section. Inside each of the middle leaves, we need to have a gradient of colour – cold green to warm green – to help create a neat transition in the painting, from the top leaves with cooler tones to the bottom leaves with warmer tones (see the tip on page 49). Using the no. 6 brush, wet the top of one middle leaf then glaze it with the light cold green mix. Along the bottom edge of the wet paint, touch in the light warm green and distribute this downwards to the bottom of the leaf (**6a**). To add depth to the leaf, apply a small amount of dark warm green at the bottom, then gently distribute this upwards (**6b**). Repeat for the other middle leaf (the one that doesn't overlap another leaf).

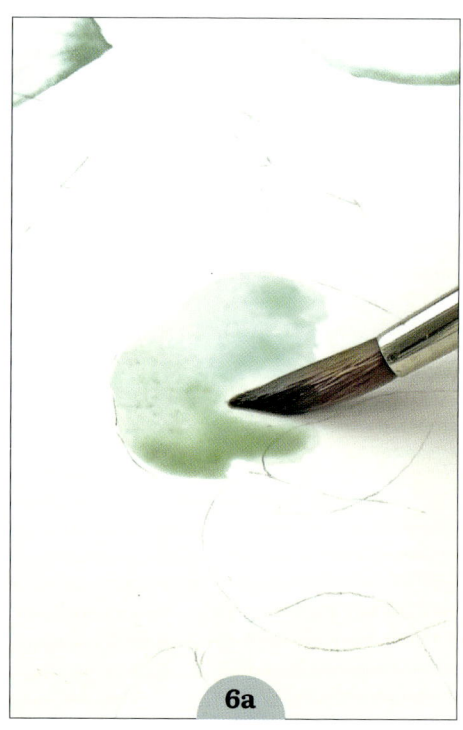

6a

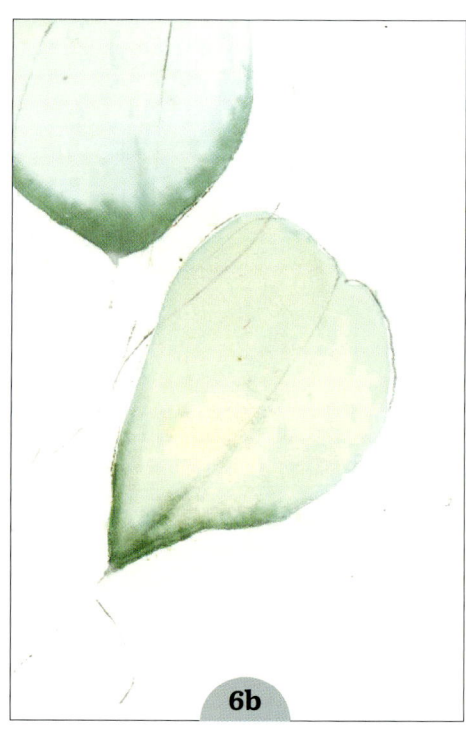

6b

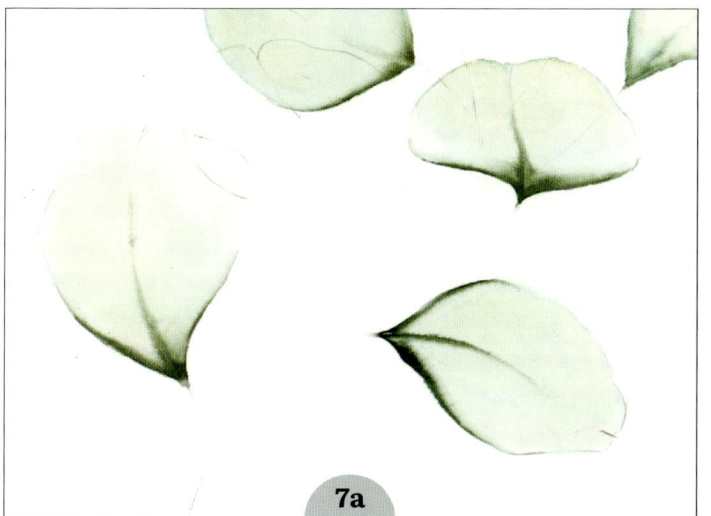

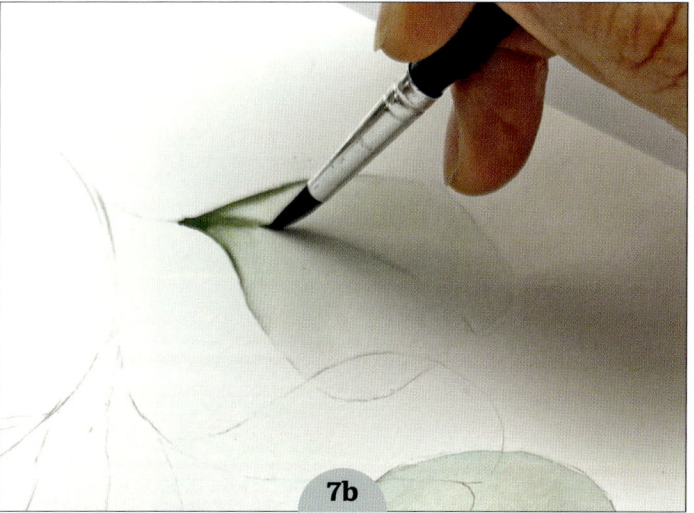

First layer of leaves: bottom section. With the no. 6 brush, wet the leaves with clean water then glaze the bottom three leaves (that aren't overlapping) with the light warm green mix. Add a drop of the dark warm green mix to the bottom of each leaf and distribute the darker colour up and along the edges. With the tip of the no. 4 brush, drag out the dark colour along the middle vein (**7a**). Sometimes it might be handy to rotate the paper so you can distribute colours more easily by moving your brush from top to bottom (**7b**).

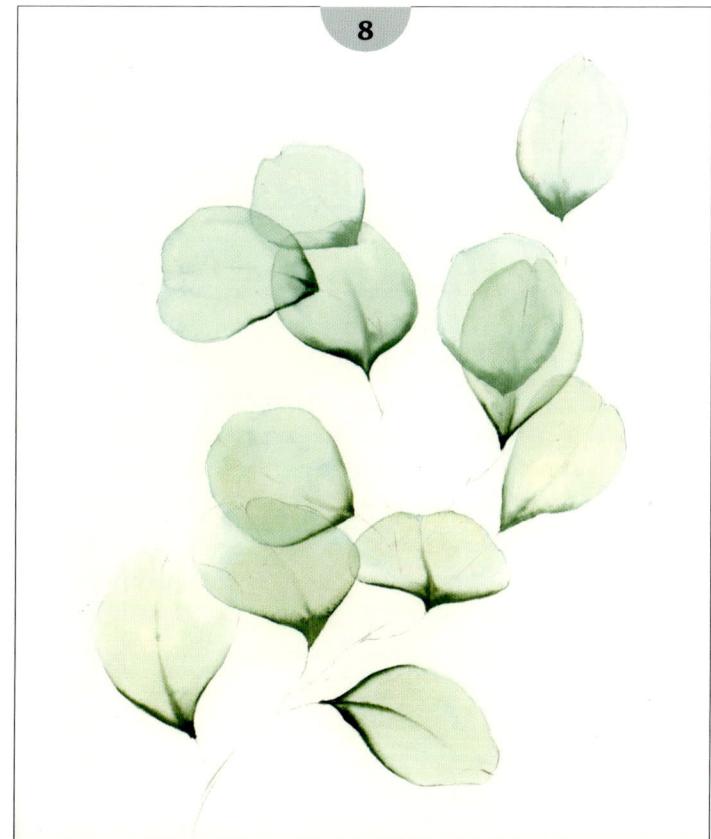

First layer of overlapping leaves. Make sure that all the painted leaves are dry. Then, paint in the leaves that overlap the painted leaves in same way as before, using the lighter green mixes. Remember to use only the cool light green for the top leaves, a mix of cool and warm light green for the middle leaves, and only the warm light green for the bottom leaves.

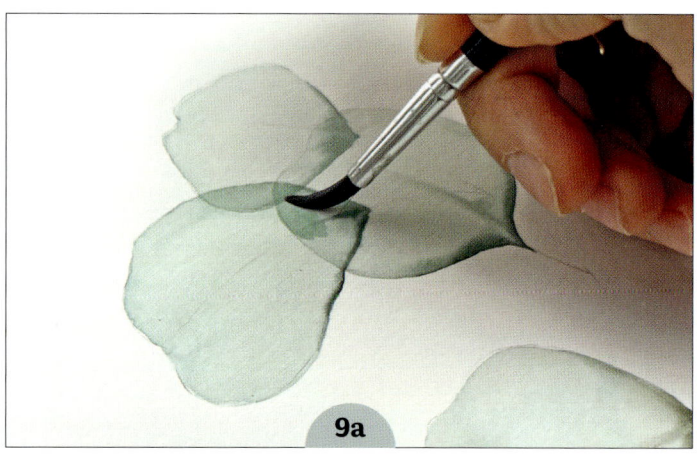

9a

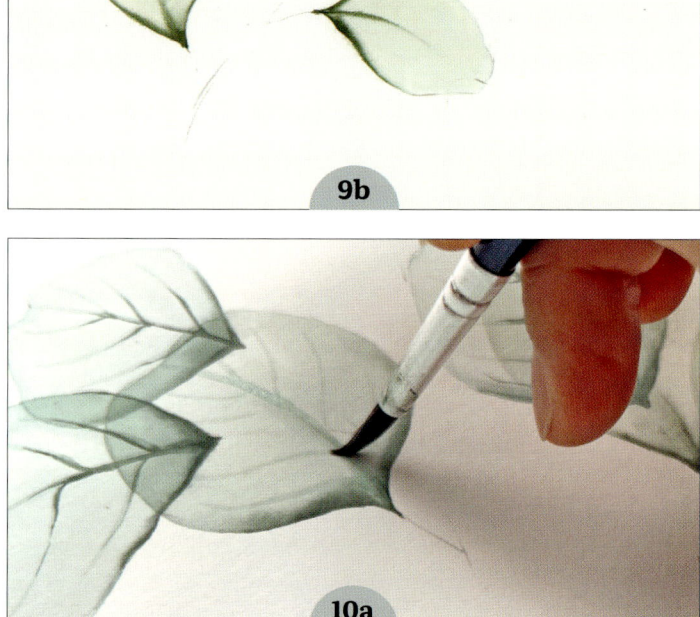

9b

9 Emphasizing the overlapping areas. Now glaze all the overlapping areas with the appropriate light green mix and the no 4. brush: if the leaf was painted with a cold green mix, glaze the intersection with the light cold green mix; if it was painted with a warm green mix, glaze the overlap with a light warm green mix; or if it was painted with both warm and cold greens, glaze the intersection with a combination of light cold and warm greens. When there are many overlaps, as shown in **9a**, it's best to paint one part at a time and allow each layer to dry completely before painting the next. The image in **9b** is after all the intersections have been painted.

10 Painting veins. For painting veins, use either a cold or a warm mix, or a combination of both, depending on the leaf you're working on. We are not going to paint all of the veins on each leaf – only a central one and a few on either side.

With the tip of the no. 4 brush and using the appropriate light green mix, paint a central vein, applying a little bit of pressure as you hit the very bottom of the leaf. In the same way, map out the side veins, keeping the strength of colour in the bottom half of the leaf. Repeat to strengthen the colour (**10a**).

While the vein areas are still wet, use the no. 4 brush to touch in a drop of the appropriate dark green mix at the bottom of the central vein, and allow the colour to spread through the veins – the diluted mix will serve as a capillary for the bolder colour. Use a clean, damp brush to soften the mix as needed (**10b**).

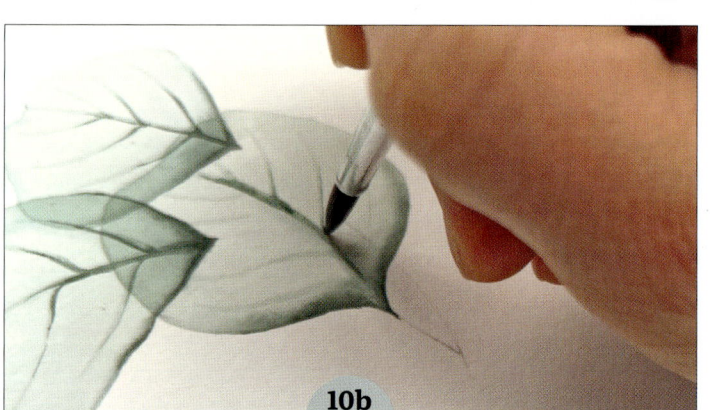

10a

10b

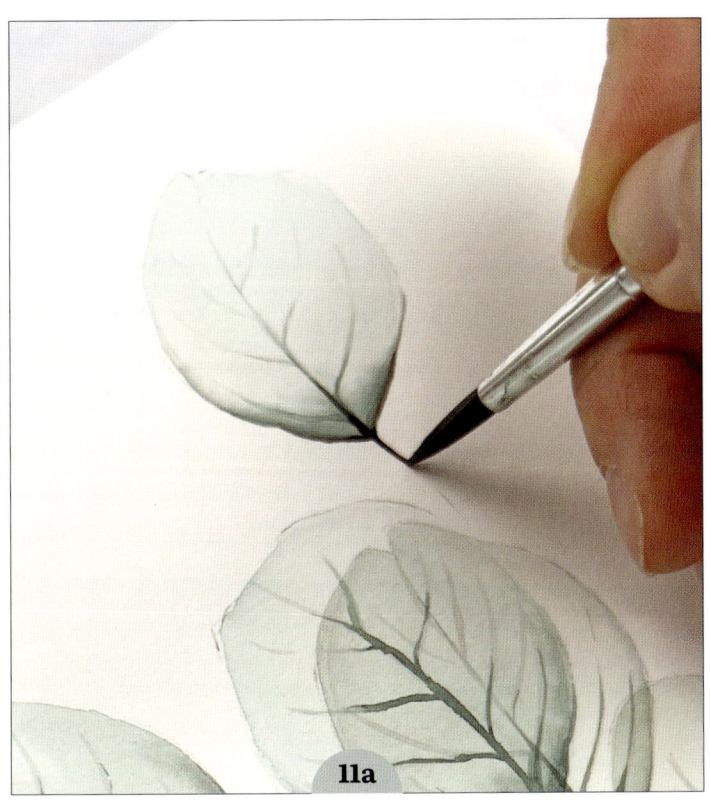

11 Painting stems and branches. Make up the brown mix, referring to the details on page 48. Using this mix, and with the tip of the no. 4 brush, paint in the stem. Starting from the bottom area of the leaf, slightly inside the leaf, will create a smooth transition from leaf to stem or branch (**11a**). When painting the stems and branches, vary the pressure on the brush to create natural curves and textures (**11b**).

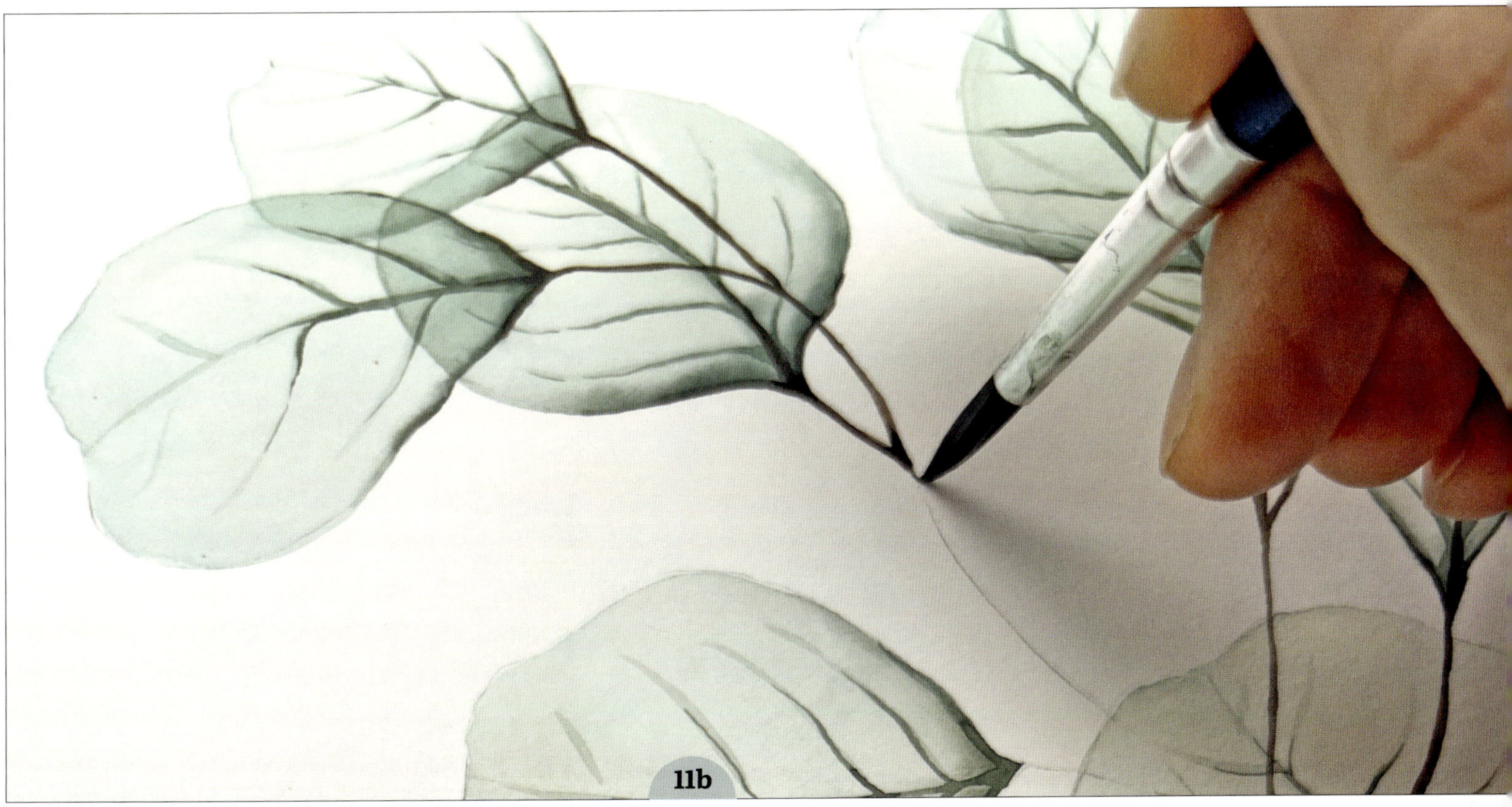

11a

11b

Eucalyptus-inspired
Gallery

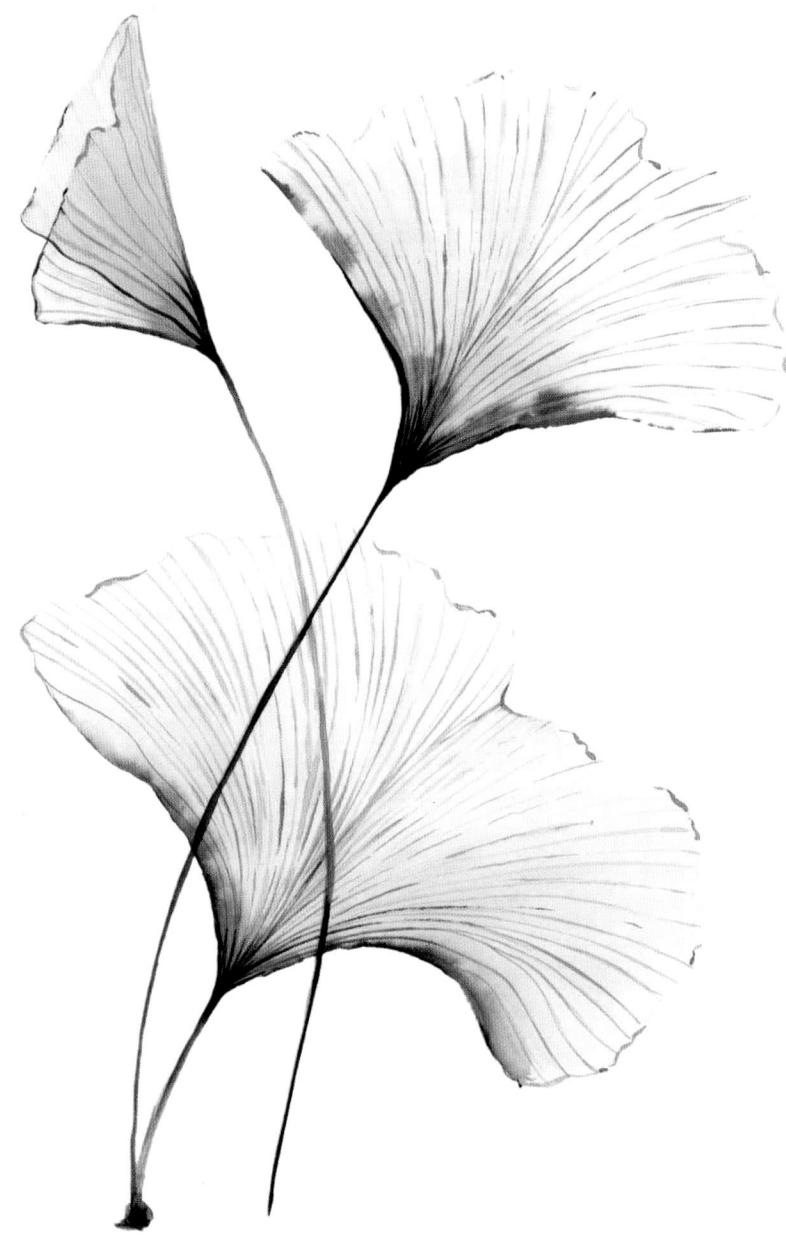

Right

'Ginkgo Biloba Leaves'

18 x 26cm (7 x 10¼in)

Paint: *Perylene Green.*

Painted using the same basic process as for the eucalyptus.

Opposite

'Trailing Willow Leaves'

25 x 36cm (10 x 14¼in)

Paint: *Phthalo Green, Ultramarine Blue, Cadmium Yellow, Burnt Sienna.*

Similar technique as for the eucalyptus, but including more leaf intersections and fewer vein details.

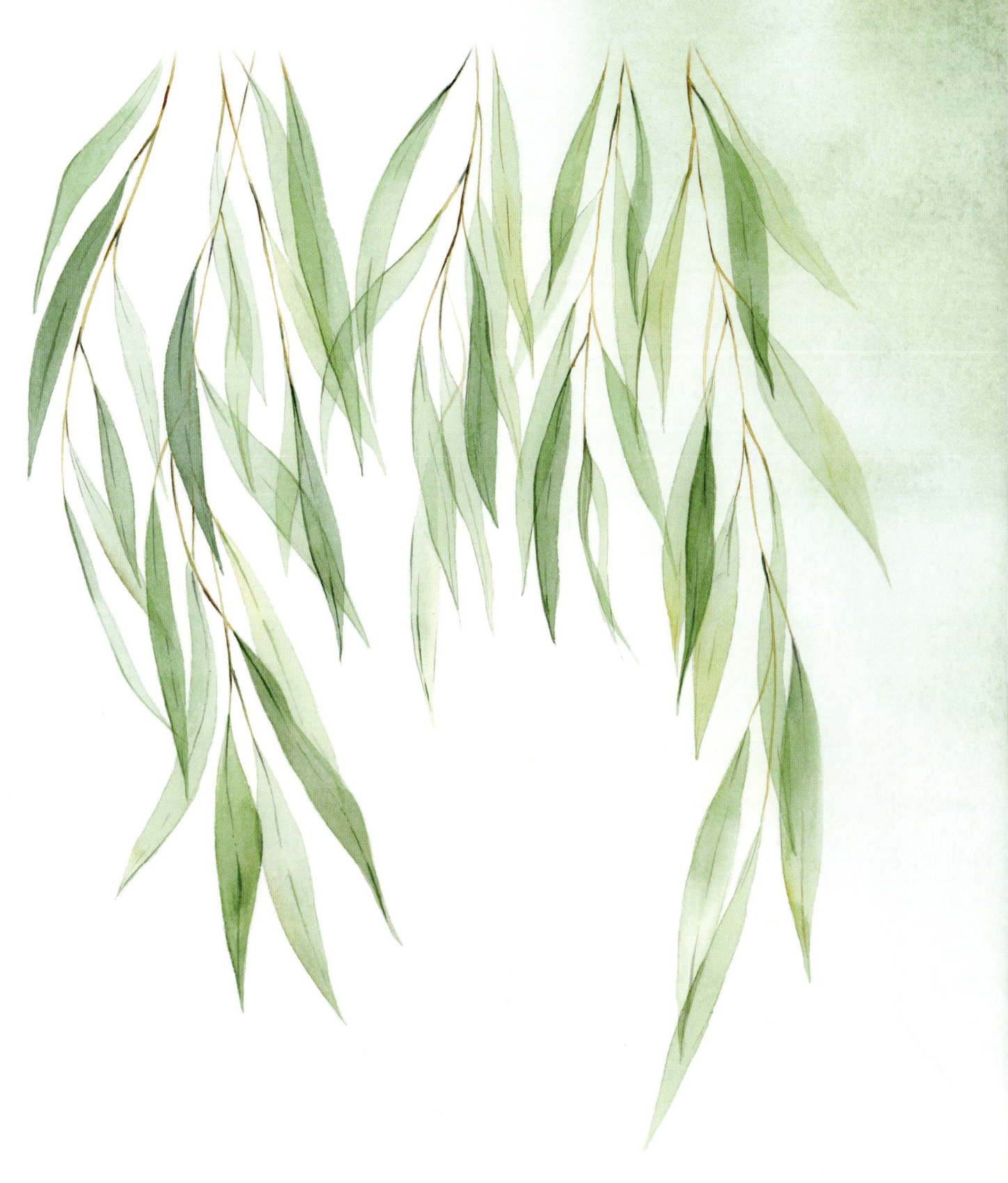

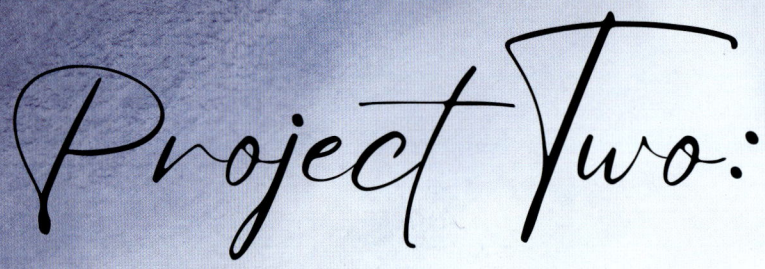

Project Two:

Bellflowers

Bellflowers are one of my favourite species because of their simplicity,
for their lovely variety of blue and purple shades, and for their wonderful,
fairy-tale look.

In this project, I will show you how to make different hues with the same set of
basic colours, and how to vary their transparency to suggest whether certain
areas of the flowerhead are facing towards you or away from you. One unique
quality of the bellflower to bear in mind is that it does not have separate petals,
so we have to be clever about how we create the transparent effect. Although
the painting technique is the same for both flowers in this piece, the sequence
of steps are different, bringing more depth to our composition.

You will need

WATERCOLOUR PAINTS:
Ultramarine Blue, Quinacridone Rose, Phthalo Green,
Burnt Sienna

MATERIALS AND TOOLS:
22 x 30cm (8½ x 12in) sheet of hot-pressed paper;
sharp (or mechanical) HB pencil; putty eraser and
soft white eraser; kitchen paper or cloth; no. 4 and no. 6
round synthetic brushes with very fine tips

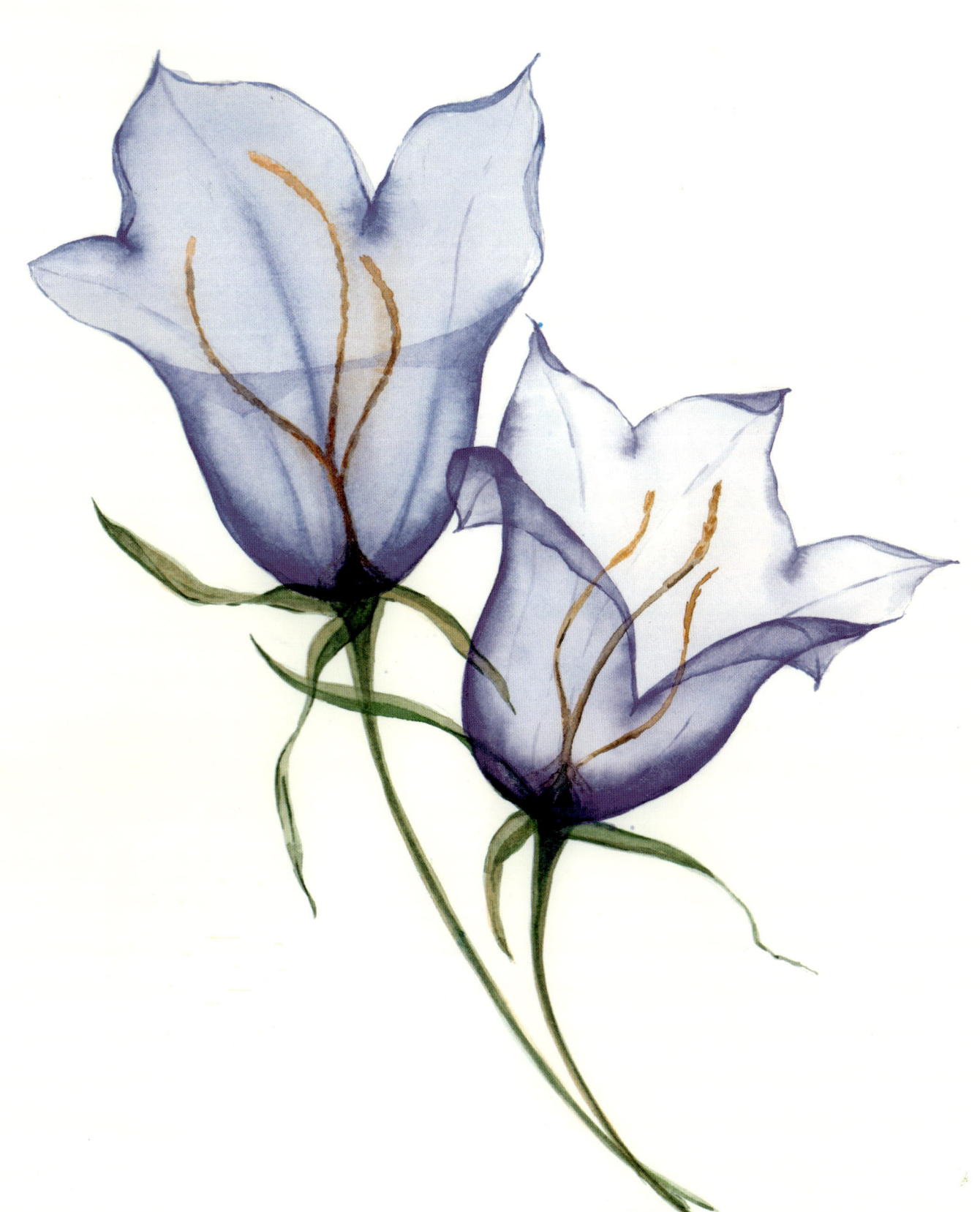

Basic mixes

 **DARK BLUE**
Ultramarine Blue

 **DARK PURPLE**
Ultramarine Blue and
Quinacridone Rose with
Burnt Sienna

 **DARK GREEN**
Phthalo Green
with a hint of
Quinacridone Rose

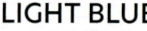 **LIGHT BLUE**
As detailed above,
but very diluted

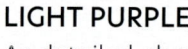 **LIGHT PURPLE**
As detailed above,
but very diluted

 **LIGHT GREEN**
As detailed above,
but very diluted

 **BURNT SIENNA**
Pure pigment, slightly
diluted with water

Tip

Ultramarine Blue is a granulating colour (as it has larger
particles of pigment than other paints), so always stir your
mix with a brush before painting with it.

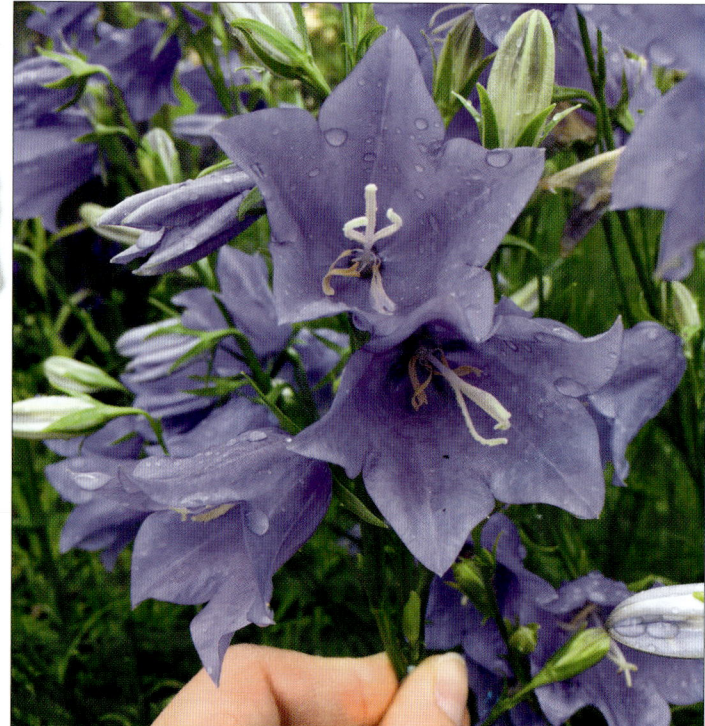

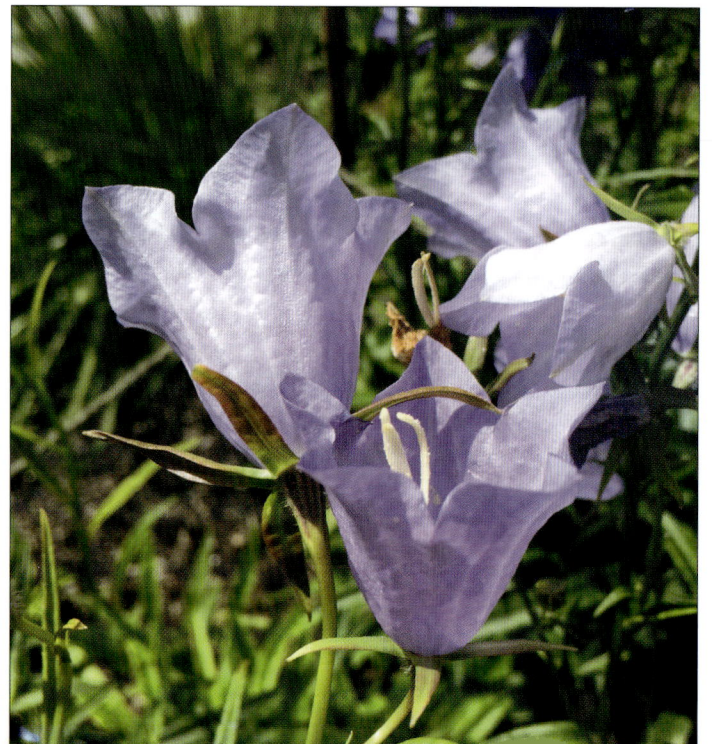

Reference photographs

*It was quite a challenge to take a picture of just a few
bellflowers, instead of a big cluster, so I had to add more
detail to the composition later on to emphasize the lines
and beauty of the individual flowers.*

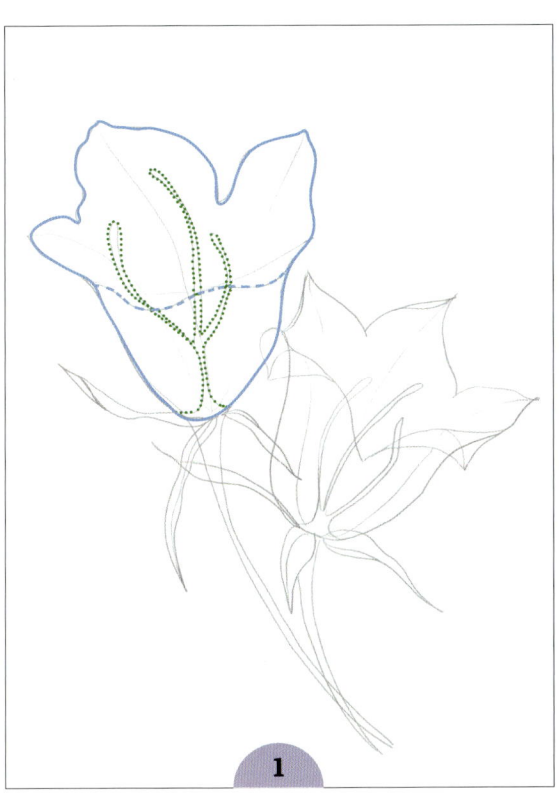

1 Drawing the flowers: left flower. Using the outline on page 123 or the far-left larger reference photograph opposite, draw what would be the visible parts of the left-hand bellflower. This includes the stem, the leaf-like shapes (sepals) and main flower shape (refer to the solid blue outline). Then draw in the outlines of the petals facing away from you (refer to the blue dashed horizontal line), making sure the shape suggests the petals are folded away from you. To finish the flower, outline the 'hidden' style and three stigmas (refer to the green dashed lines).

2 Drawing the flowers: right flower. Similarly, draw in the visible parts of the right-hand bellflower (refer to the solid purple outline). Note the folded edges of the front petals. Then draw in the 'hidden' sections of the flower (refer to to dashed purple lines), tucked behind the folds of the front petals. Make sure they follow the shape of the overall flower. To finish the flower, outline the style and add three stigmas: the bottom of the stigmas and style are hidden inside the flower (refer to the red dashed outlines) and the tops of the stigmas will be visible (refer to the solid red outlines).

3 Softening lines. Once you are happy with your drawing, rub back the lines with a putty eraser, leaving a faint outline.

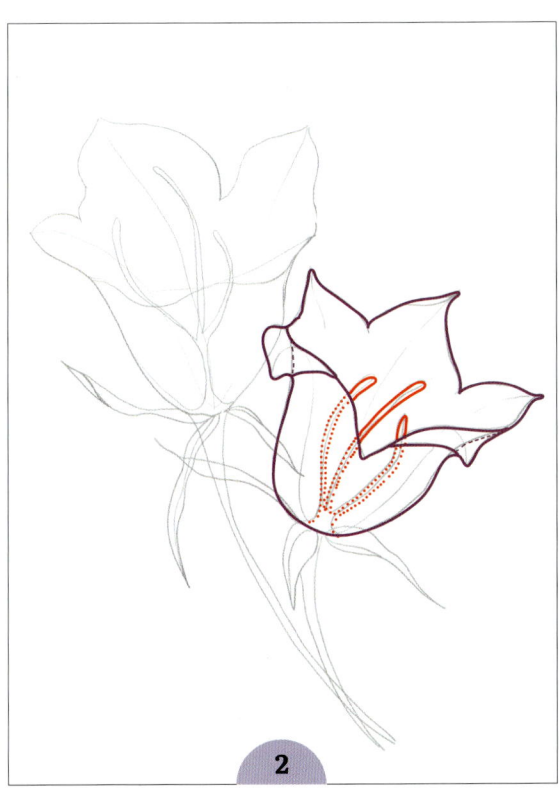

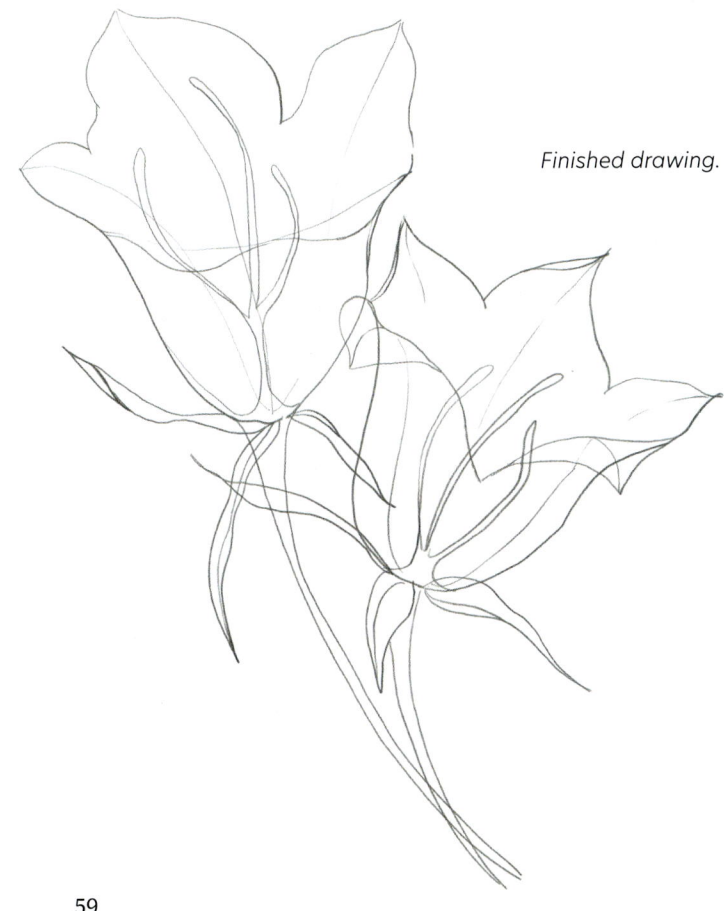

Finished drawing.

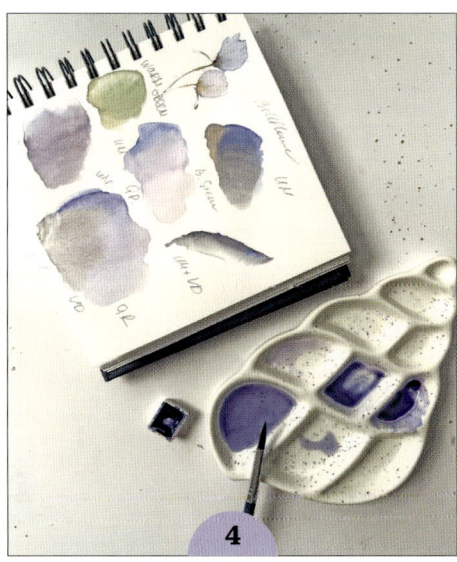

4

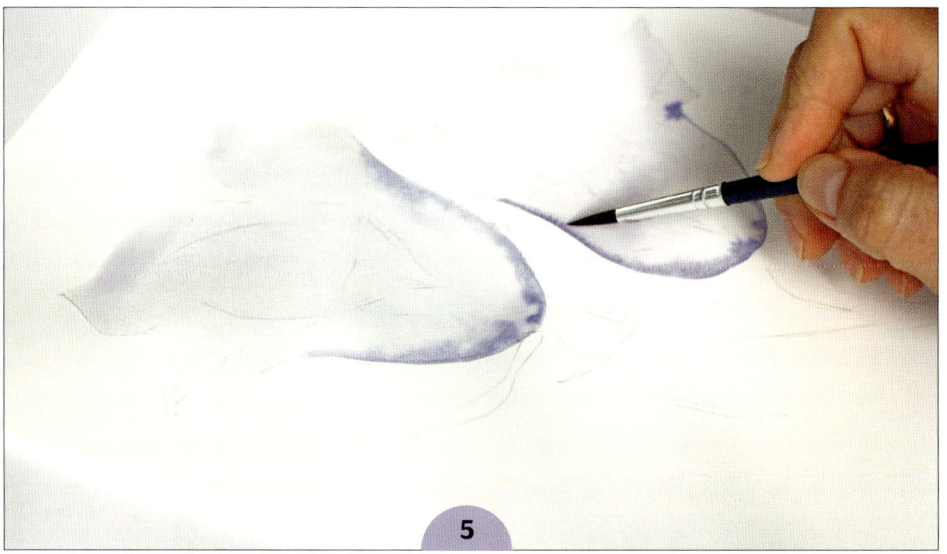

5

Mixing the paints. Make up the two blue and two purple mixes, referring to the swatches and their details on page 58. Start with the two darker mixes then, once you are happy with the colours, take a drop of each mixture, place in separate wells in the palette and dilute each with a large amount of water to create the lighter blue and purple mixes.

First layer. Glaze both bellflowers with clean water using brush no. 6. Make sure the water is applied evenly on the paper and there are no puddles. Start with the left bellflower. Drop in the light blue mix and gently distribute it inside the whole flower, following the shape of the petals. While the paint is still wet, use the tip of a clean, damp no. 4 brush to pick up the dark blue mix and run this along the bottom and side edges. Soften the dark colour with a clean, damp brush. Repeat the process with the right bellflower, but this time with the purple mixes.

Tip

If you are left-handed, I'd recommend starting with the right bellflower to avoid smudging the paint. This will mean using the purple mixes first, rather than the blue mixes.

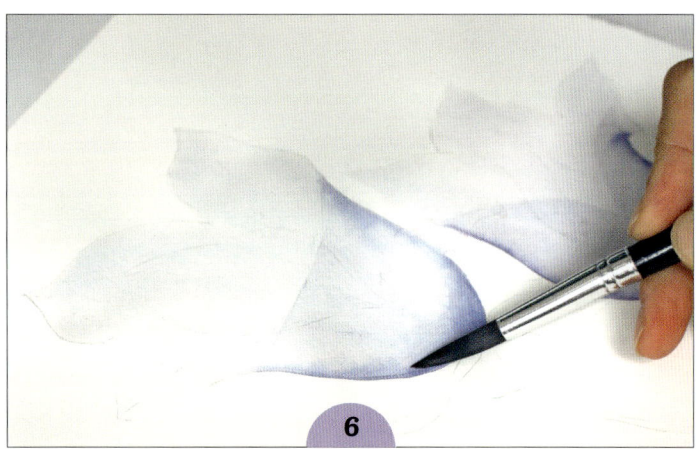

6

Second layer. As the 'opening' of the left-hand bellflower is facing away from us, we should paint it with softer colours to accurately capture the perspective. Using a damp no. 6 brush, glaze the bottom area of the bell with the light blue mix up to the border where the petals bend. Then, with a damp no. 4 brush, run the dark blue mix along the edges of the area, gradually increasing the intensity of colour towards the centre of the flower. Repeat the process for the right-hand bellflower bloom, using the purple mixes. Leave the whole painting to dry completely. Note that where the petals bend for the right-hand flower, there is a V-shaped indent; make sure to follow this shape for its next washes (see steps 10-12) later on.

7 Left bellflower: bent petals. The petals facing away from you are slightly folded over, so we need to suggest this with the transparency effect. Wet this area with a clean, damp no. 4 brush then, using the same brush, glaze it with the light blue mix. While the paint is still wet, paint a shadow by running the dark blue mix along the top folded edge with the no. 4 brush. Distribute this colour from the fold to the edges of the petal, as shown. Leave the painting to dry completely.

8 Left bellflower: emphasizing transparency. Gently glaze the whole area of the bellflower bloom with water, including the recently painted area. Run the dark blue mix along the top edges of the flower with the no. 4 brush, then soften the colour with a clean, damp no. 6 brush, in towards the centre of the flower. As the petals have a wavy shape with some folds and indents, touch in and distribute drops of the dark blue mix into some areas. Leave the painting to dry completely.

9 Left bellflower: adding depth and contrast. Glaze the whole flower again with clean water. Add a drop of Burnt Sienna to the dark blue mix to darken it further. Paint along the bottom part of the bell with this mix, adding more tone in the centre of the flower. Soften the edges with a clean, damp brush. Leave to dry.

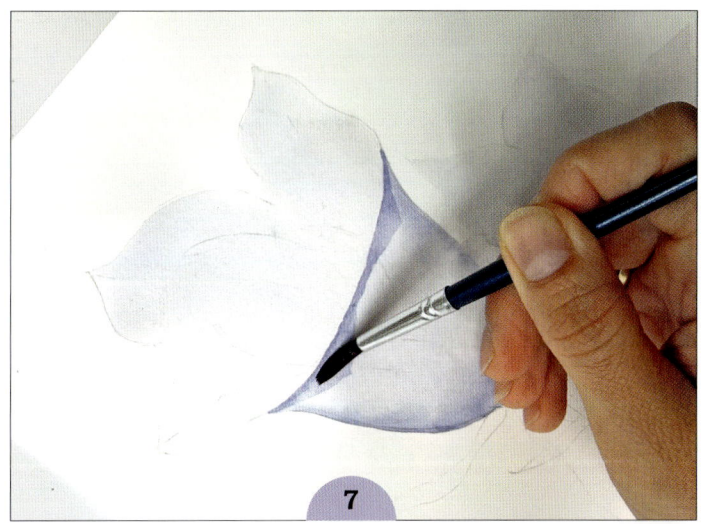

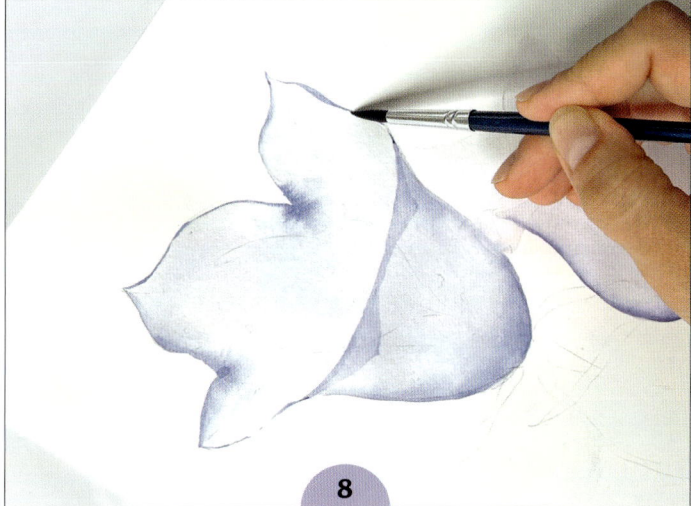

Tips

- You will notice that, with every glaze, the border of overlapping areas gets softer and loses contrast.

- If you find the level of depth isn't quite enough, glaze the paper with clean water once again and paint another layer to emphasize the contrast.

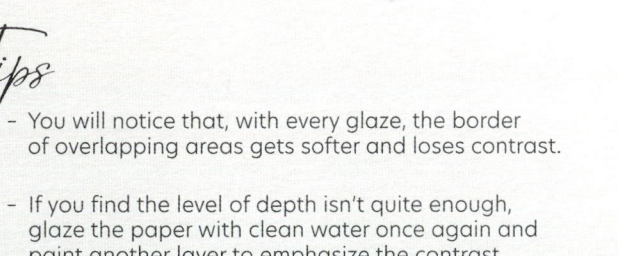

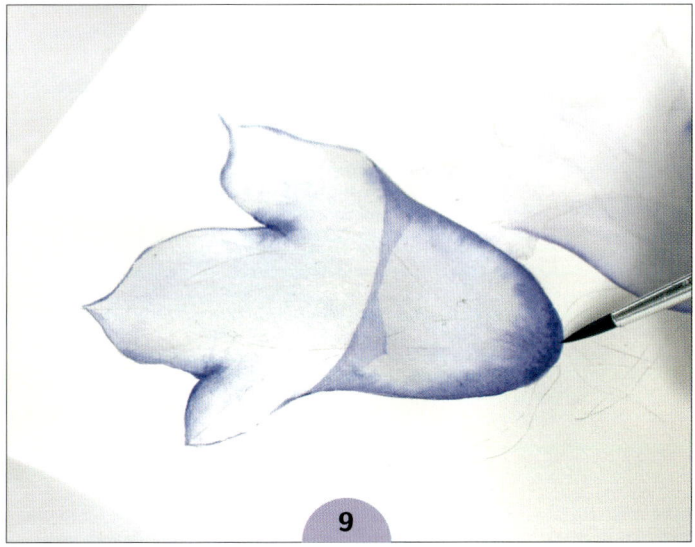

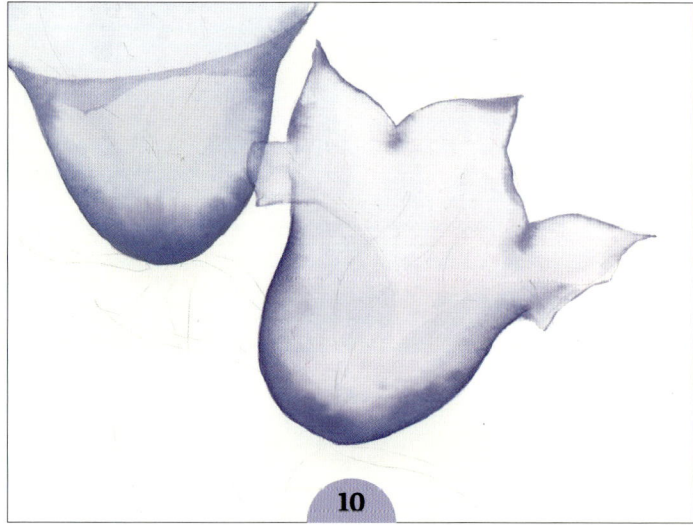

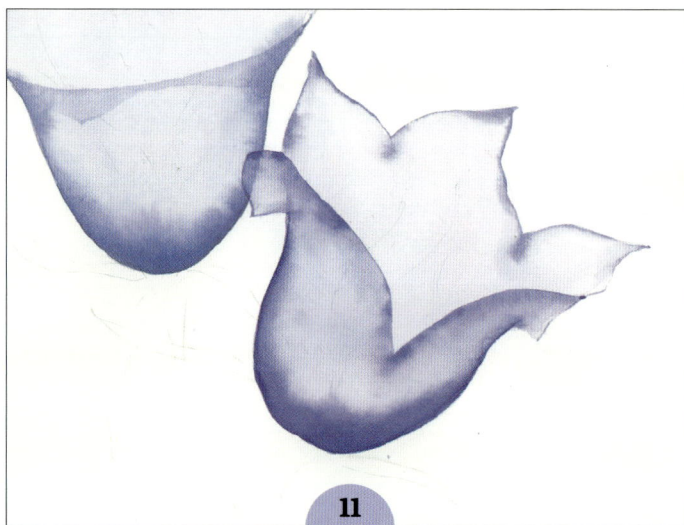

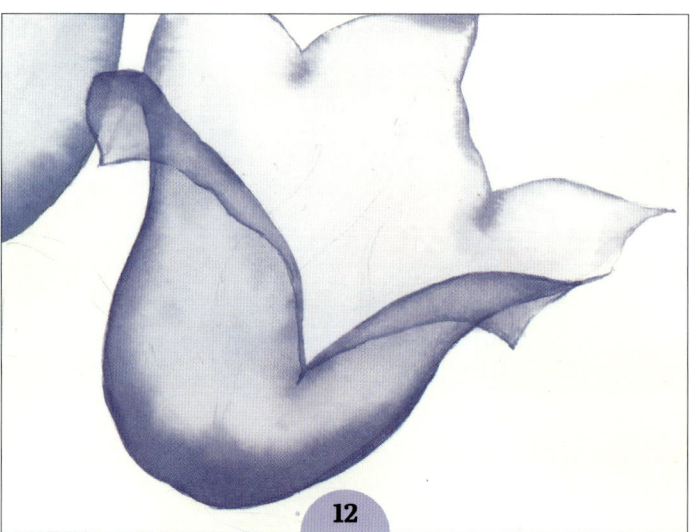

10 Right bellflower: emphasizing outline. As the right flower is facing us, we can see the front petals. To highlight this in the painting, you will need to add more contrast. Using the no. 6 brush, wet the whole bloom with clean water then glaze it with the light purple mix. Next, run the dark purple mix along the edges of the bellflower with the no. 4 brush: there should be almost no pigment around the edges of the top petals, and a very thin line around the front-facing petals. Gradually increase the intensity of colour towards the base of the flower. Leave the painting to dry completely, as before.

11 Right bellflower: front petals. Using the no. 6 brush, wet the front area only with clean water. Glaze this same area with the light purple mix. With the no. 4 brush, run the dark purple mix all around the edge of the front petal section, then soften and distribute the colour inwards with the same brush. 'Dot' then gently distribute the dark purple mix below the folded-over front-left petal, to suggest a shadow. Again, leave the whole painting to dry completely.

12 Right bellflower: front petals continued. Paint the outer edges of the folded-over front petals with the dark purple mix, using the no. 4 brush. Along the top edge of the fold, pull the line of dark purple gently downwards to distribute the colour.

13 Painting veins. Bellflowers have thin veins, one along the middle of each petal. With the tip of the no. 4 brush, paint the veins with the diluted purple mix. Try to vary pressure on the brush, and leave some gaps, to make the veins look more delicate and soft. Do not try to paint a long fine line in one go, as there is a high risk of it going wrong. Rather, paint small 'dashes' to have more control.

14 Adding details. Run the dark purple mix along the edges of the top petals with the no. 4 brush to emphasize how these edges are slightly turned over.

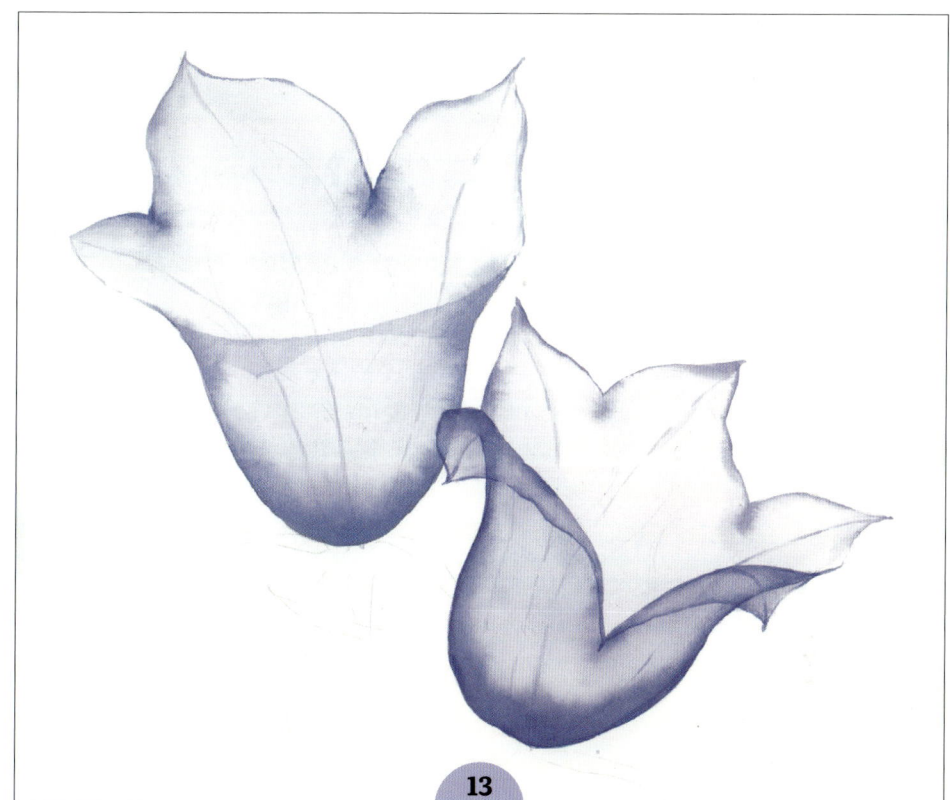

13

Details

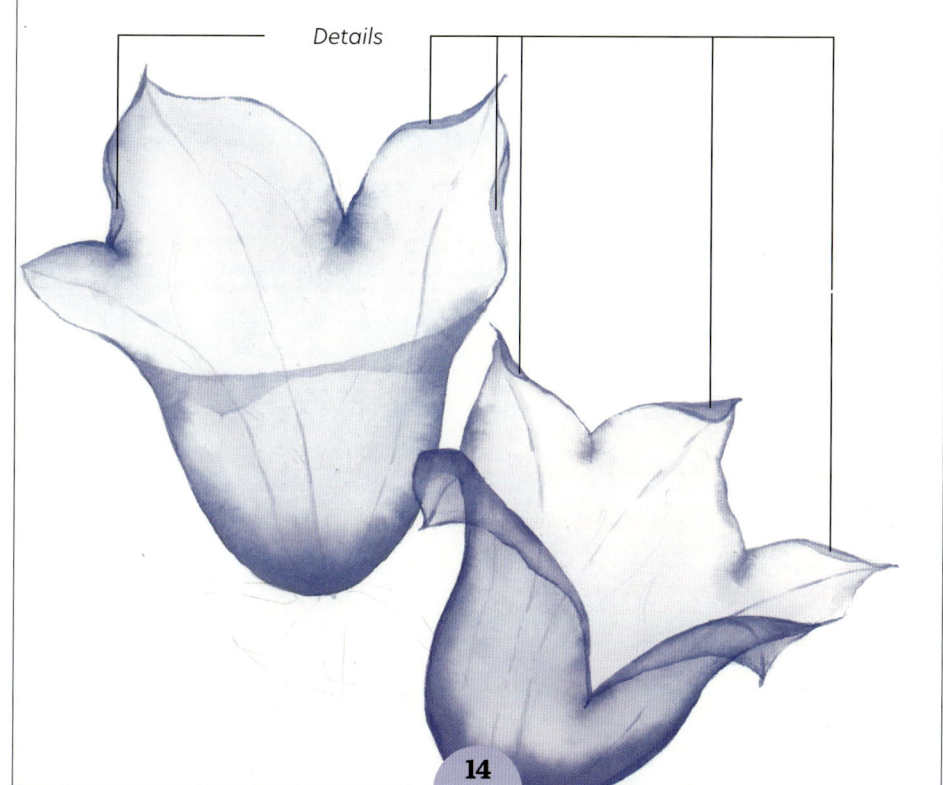

14

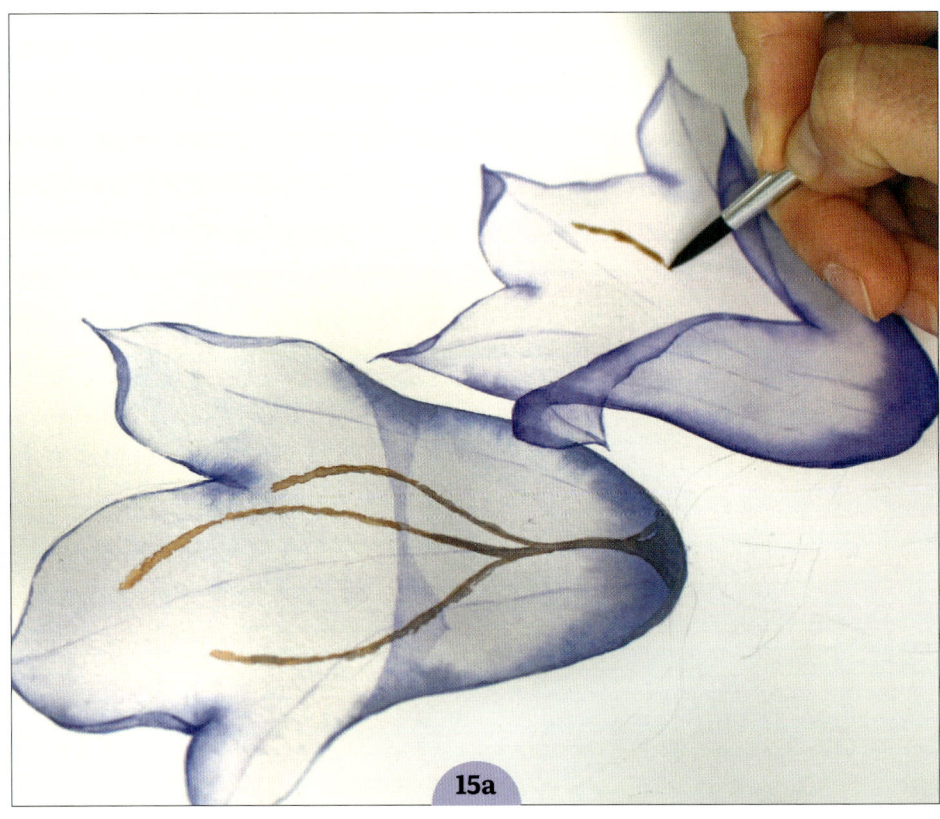

15a

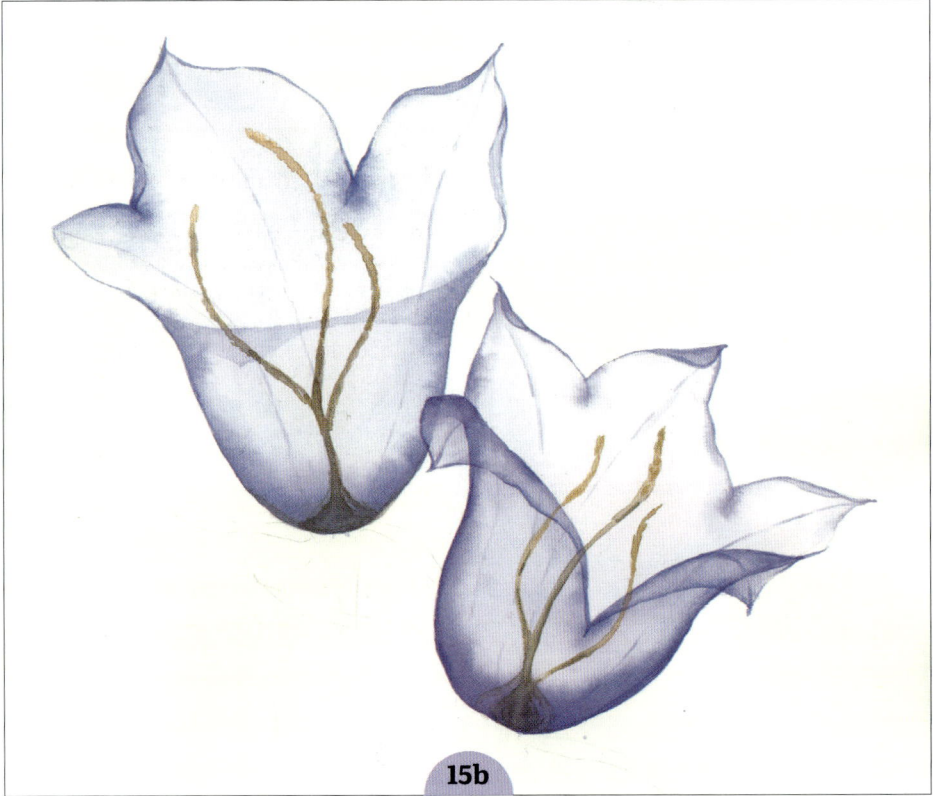

15b

15 Style and stigmas. With the no. 4 brush, run three curving lines of a diluted mix of Burnt Sienna along the pencilled-in stigmas, working from the top downwards. Gently wiggle your brush as you stipple to create the fluffy texture of the stigmas. Add a drop of pure Burnt Sienna to the diluted mix when moving towards the base of the flower, and paint in the ovary (at the bottom of the style).

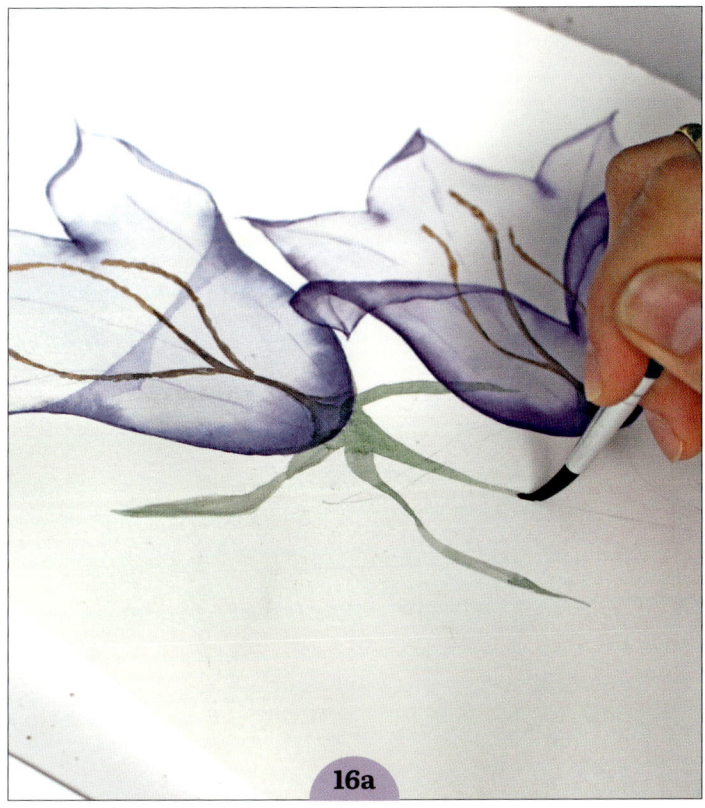

16a

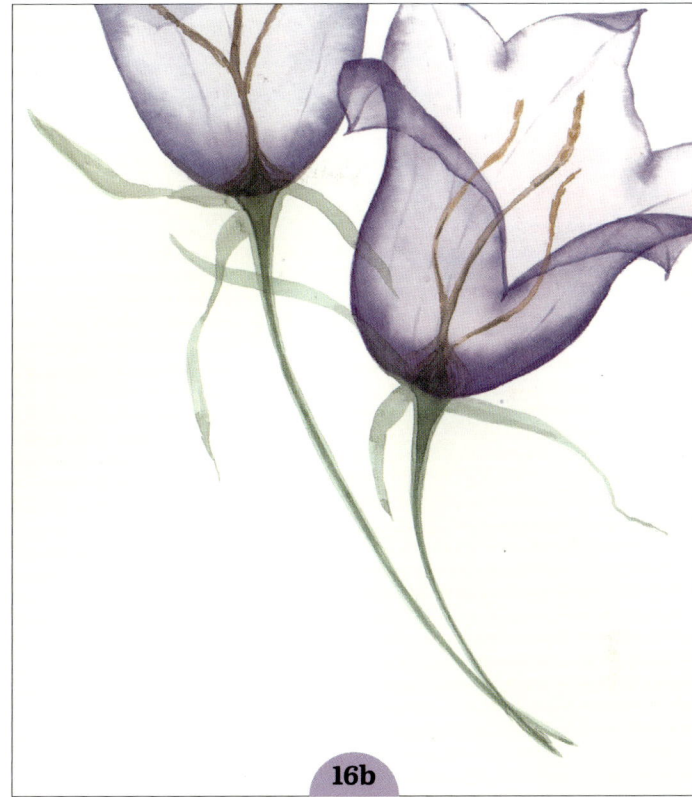

16b

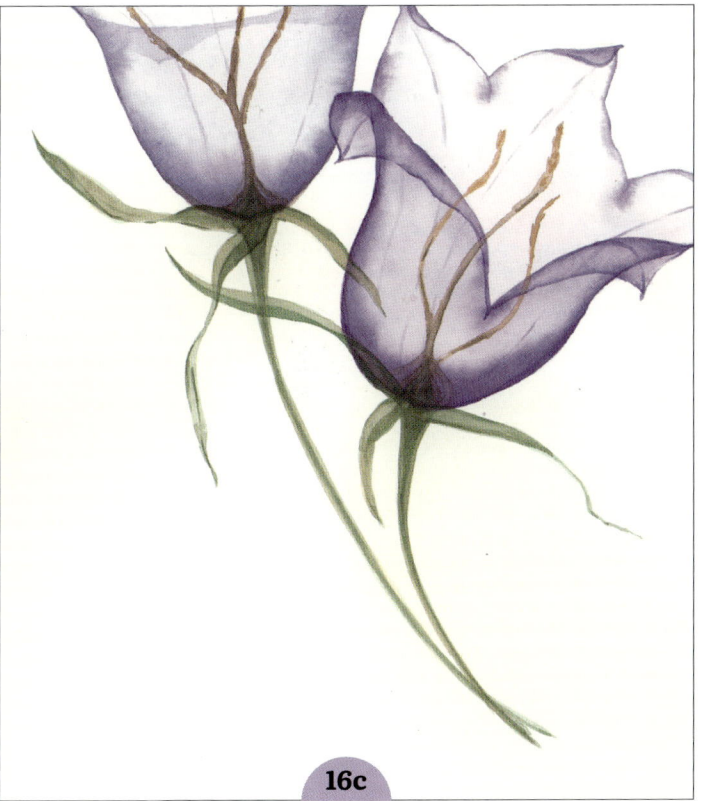

16c

16 Leaf-like shapes (sepals) and stems. Make up the two green mixes, referring to the swatches and details on page 58. As with the blue mixes, start with the darker mix then, once you are happy with the hue, take a drop of the mixture, place it in a separate well in the palette and dilute it with a large amount of water to create a lighter mix.

Begin by painting in the basic sepal and stem shapes for the left bellflower, using the light green mix and the no. 6 brush. Work from the top then distribute the colour towards the bottom. Repeat with the right bellflower (**16a**). While the paint is still wet, and starting from the top of the stem and working downwards, run the dark green mix down the centre of the stems, leaving a light green 'border' on each side (**16b**). Finish by defining the curves and shadows of the sepals with a second layer of the light green mix (**16c**) – this is simply running lines along only a few sections of the sepals here and there, but being mindful of perspective and light direction.

Bellflower-inspired *Gallery*

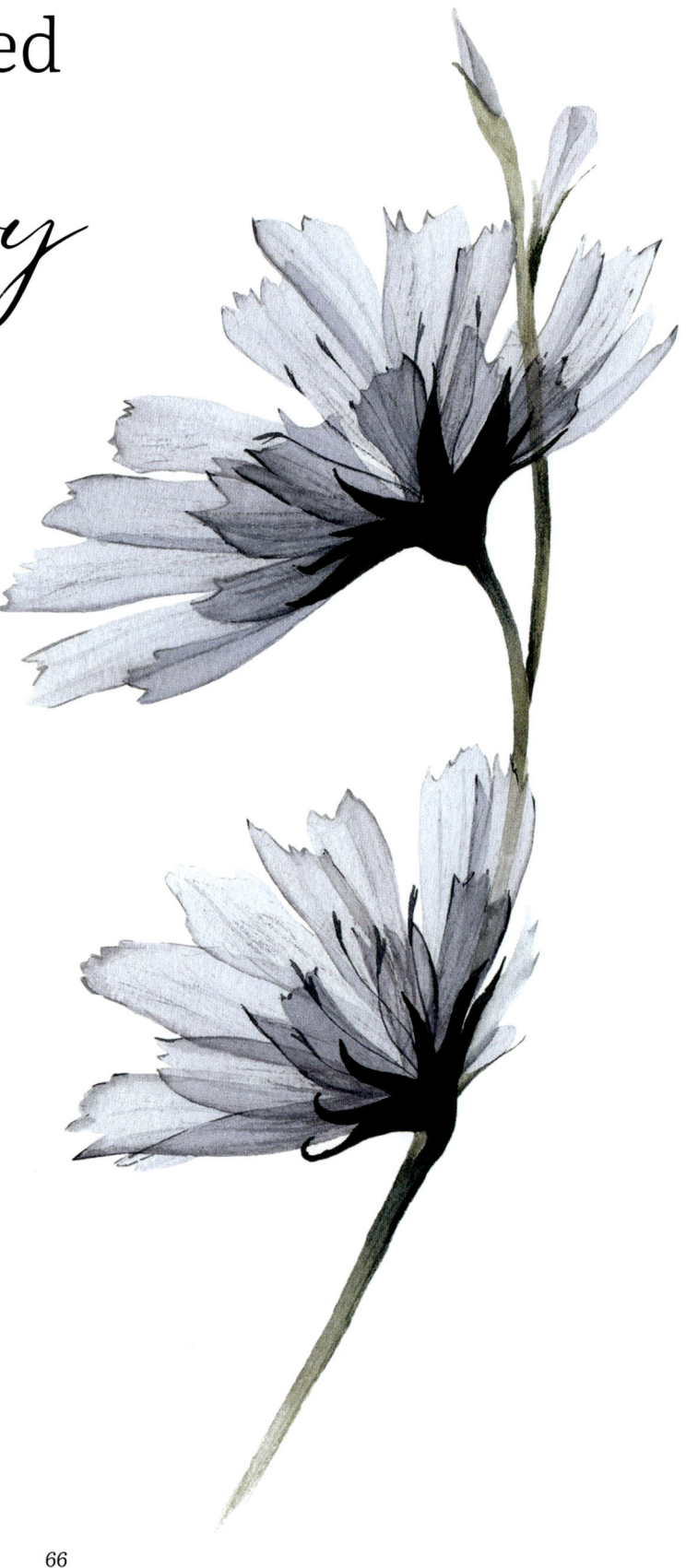

Right

'Chicory Flowers'

18 x 26cm (7 x 10¼in)

Paint: *Indigo Blue, Phthalo Green, Sepia.*

Painted using a similar technique as for the bellflowers, except that each petal was painted separately.

Opposite

'Bohemian Calla Lilies'

25 x 36cm (10 x 14¼in)

Paint: *Madder Lake Deep, Burnt Sienna, Phthalo Green.*

A calla lily's structure is a similar to a bellflower's in that it has a spathe that looks like one large petal. In this case, I needed to emphasize the edges of the spathes to help suggest their shape.

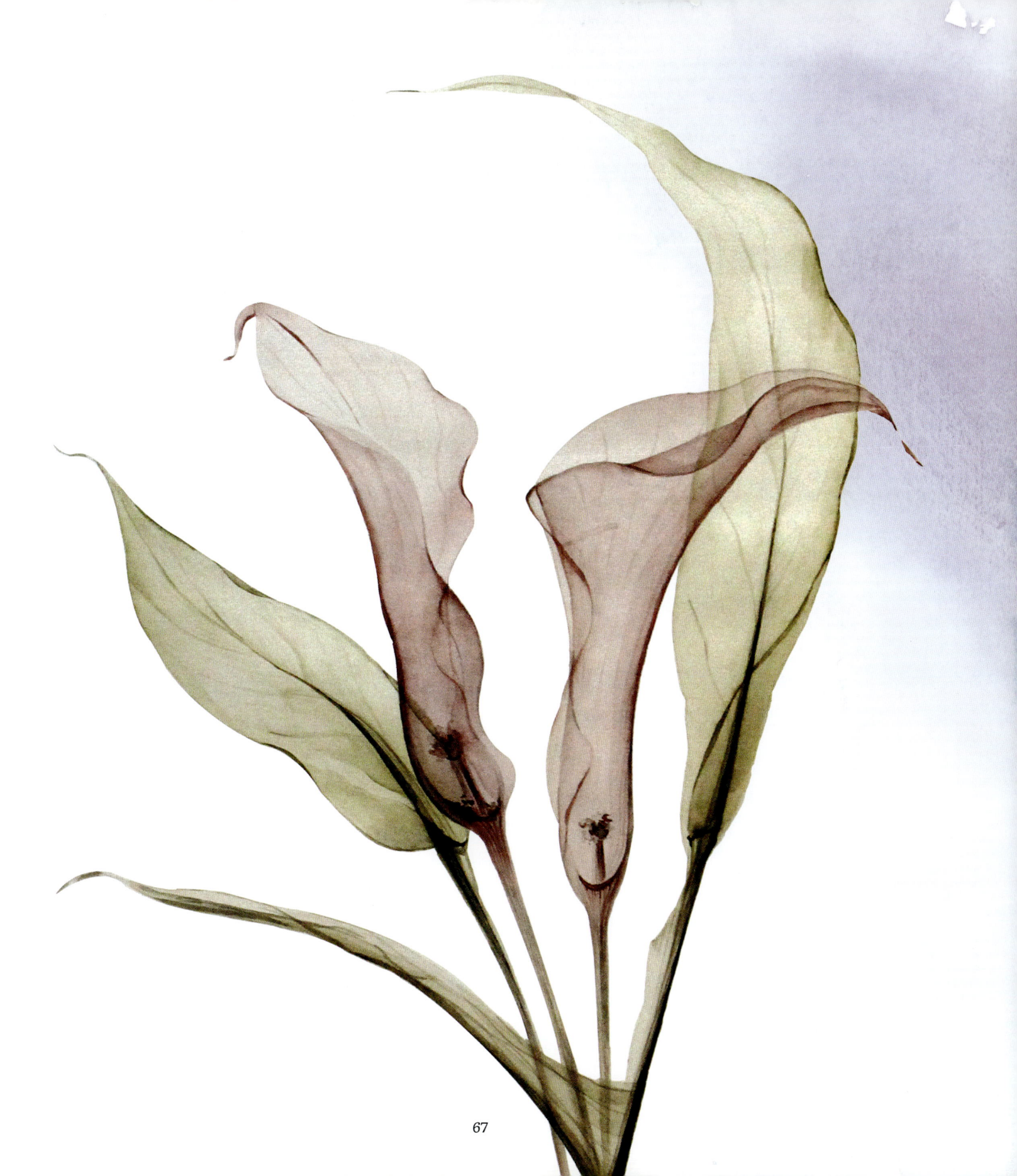

Project Three:

Magnolia

For this project, we'll be looking at painting petals and leaves that overlap each other and the stem. This looks complicated, but is easier to achieve than you might think. As long as you take your time, and work stage by stage, you can create a stunning magnolia of your own.

I took a picture of the magnolia that inspired this painting in one of the botanical gardens in Bergen, Norway, on a beautiful late-spring day. Although the flower was mainly white, I decided to turn it into a transparent pink flower for the painting, and play around with alternative colours and shades.

You will need

WATERCOLOUR PAINTS:
Quinacridone Rose, Burnt Sienna, Phthalo Green, Sepia

MATERIALS AND TOOLS:
22 x 30cm (8½ x 12in) sheet of hot-pressed paper;
sharp (or mechanical) HB pencil; putty eraser and
soft white eraser; kitchen paper or cloth; no. 10 sable brush
with a pointed tip; no. 4 and no. 6 round synthetic brushes
with very fine tips

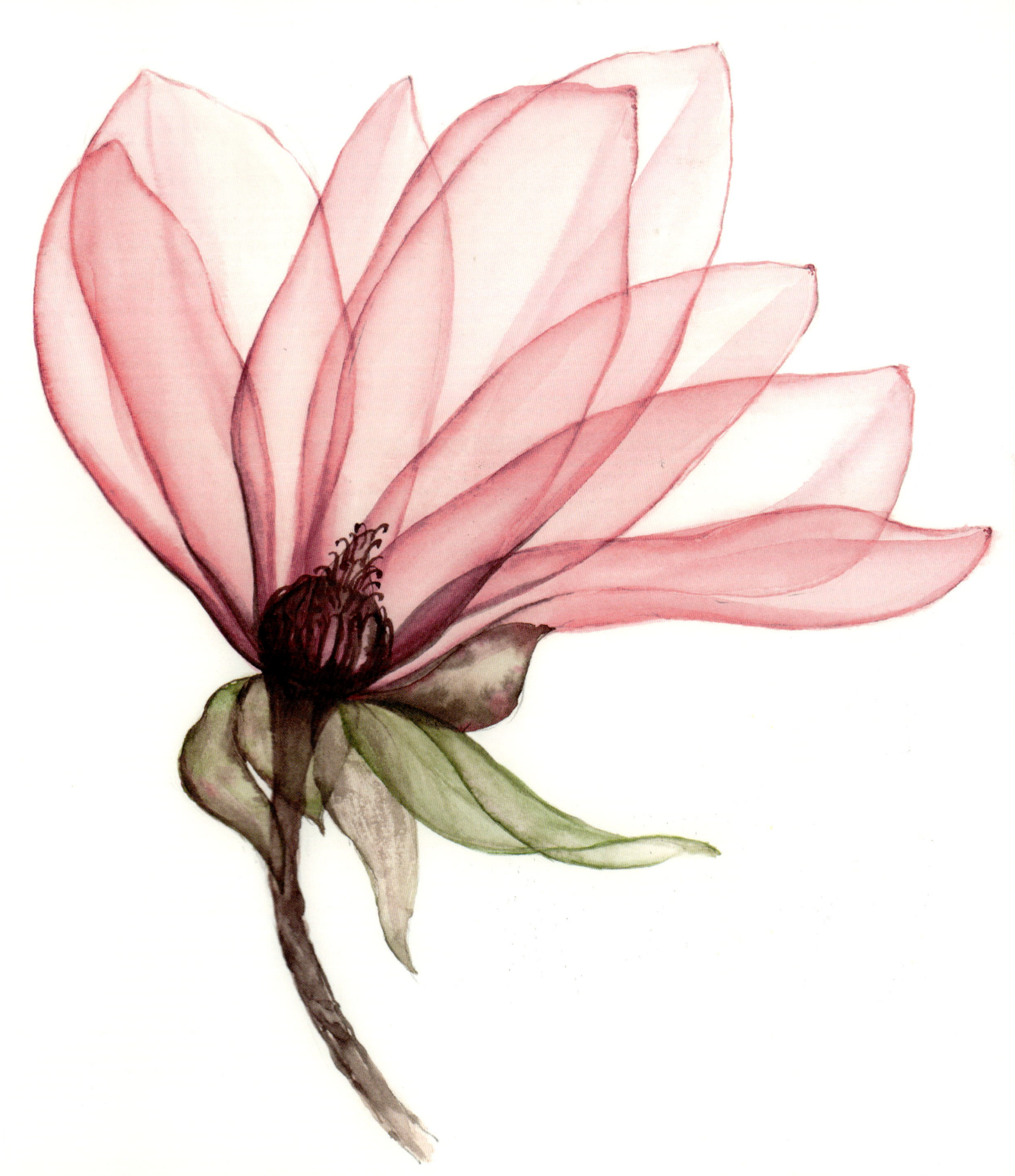

Basic mixes

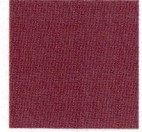

DARK PINK
Quinacridone Rose with
a hint of Burnt Sienna

DARK BROWN
Sepia with a hint of
Quinacridone Rose

SAGE GREEN
Phthalo Green with Burnt
Sienna and a hint of
Quinacridone Rose

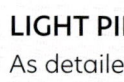

LIGHT PINK
As detailed above,
but very diluted

LIGHT BROWN
As detailed above,
but very diluted

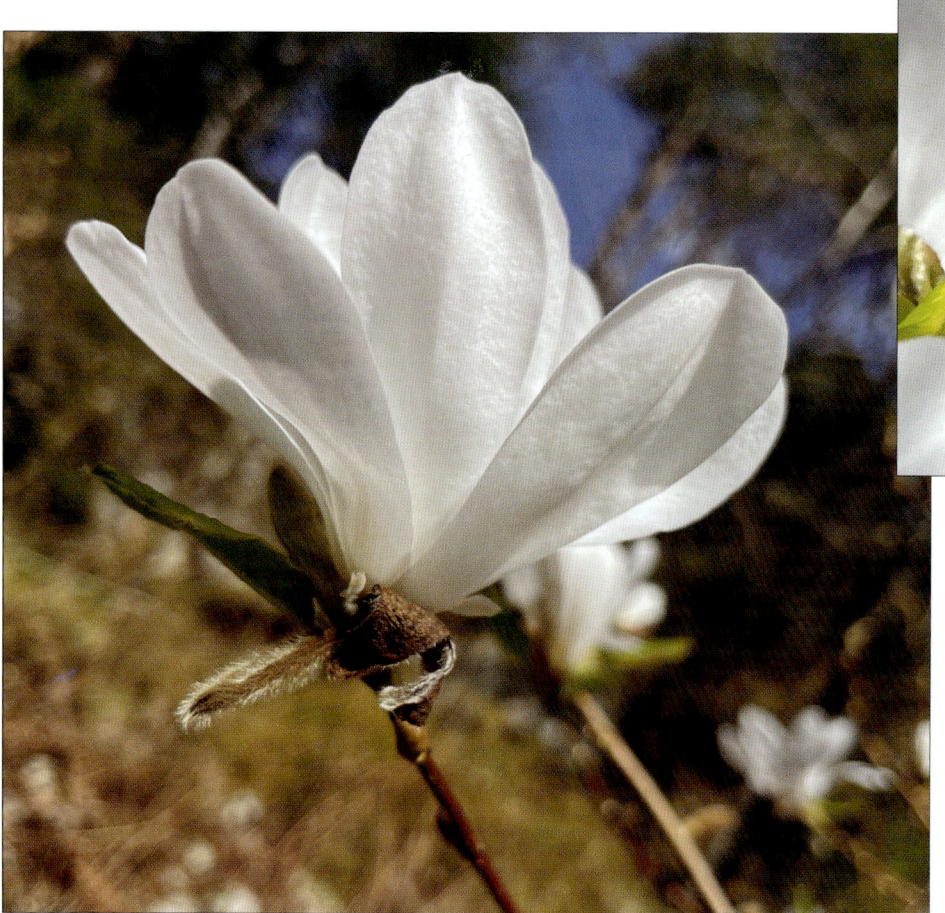

Reference photographs

*The original flower was white in colour
(see left image). Knowing that I was going
to paint the flower with the transparent
technique, I also took a close-up of the
flower centre, with its spiral of stigmas
surrounded by stamens (see top image).*

*When hunting for flower references, take
as many pictures as possible, and from
different angles (and from inside!) – it will
help you to understand the flower structure,
so you can draw it more accurately later.*

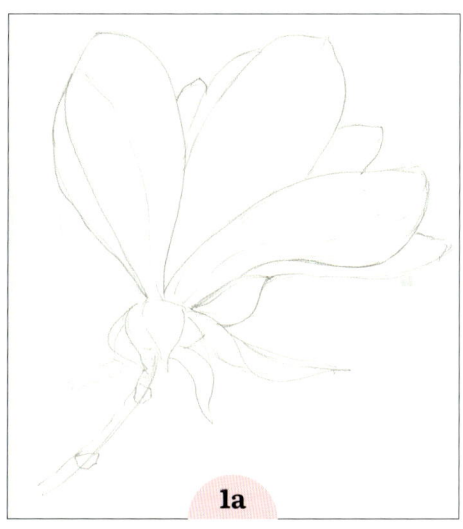

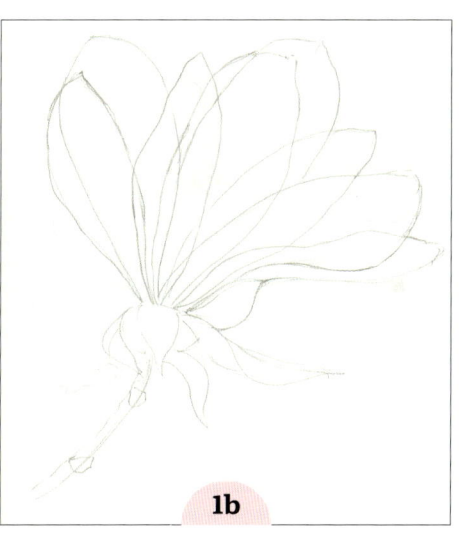

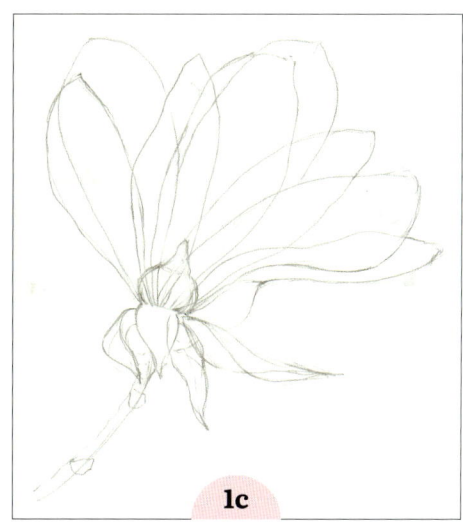

Drawing the flower. Using the outline on page 124 or the reference opposite, draw the visible part of a magnolia flower. Extend the petal outlines to the base of the flower centre.

Add a few 'invisible' petals at the back, emulating the shape of the front ones.

Outline the mass of stigmas and stamens in the flower centre but do not go into detail at this stage. We will circle back to this later.

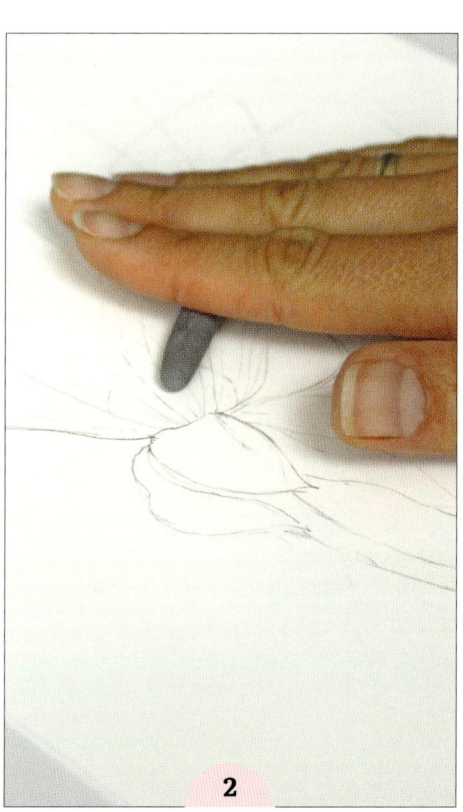

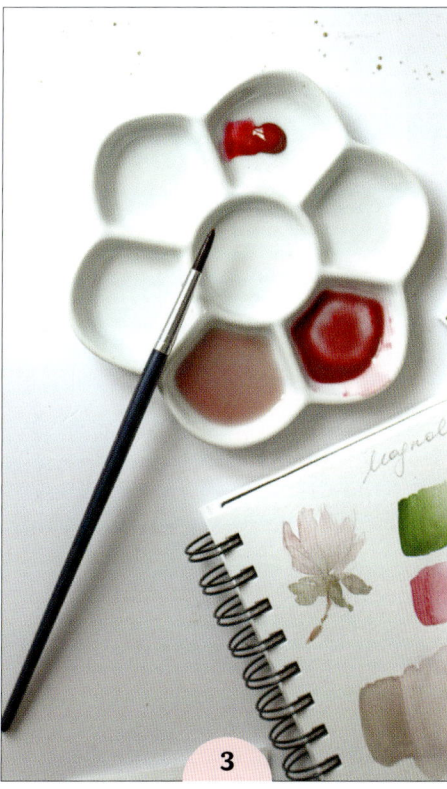

2 Softening lines. Once you are happy with your drawing, rub back the lines with a putty eraser, leaving a faint outline.

3 Mixing the paints. Make up the dark pink and light pink mixes, referring to the swatches and their details opposite. Start with the darker mix then, once you are happy with the colour, take a drop of the mixture, place it into another well in the palette and dilute it with a large amount of water to create the lighter mix.

Tip
You will need quite a lot of the light mix, so prepare plenty in advance.

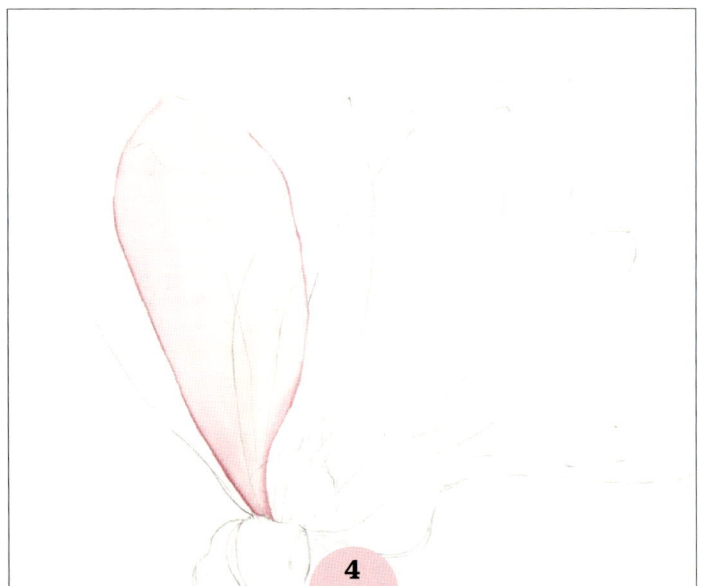

4

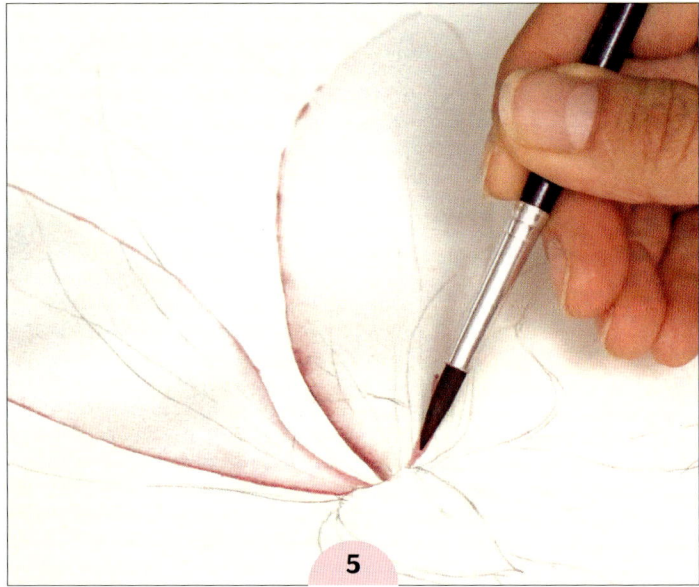

5

First petal. Start with one of the large front petals. Glaze the petal with water using the no. 10 sable brush. Make sure the water is applied evenly on the paper with no puddles. Now paint in the light pink mix, gently distributing it with the brush from bottom to top and following the shape of the petal. While the paint is still wet, and with the tip of a damp no. 4 brush, add the dark pink mix around the edge of the petal. Soften the dark colour with a clean, damp brush.

Second petal. Choose a petal that does not overlap the first one – we do not want to touch the first petal while it is still wet. Repeat the painting process as for the first petal. Add the dark pink mix along the edges of the petal with almost no pigment around the top edge, then gradually increasing the intensity of colour towards the flower centre.

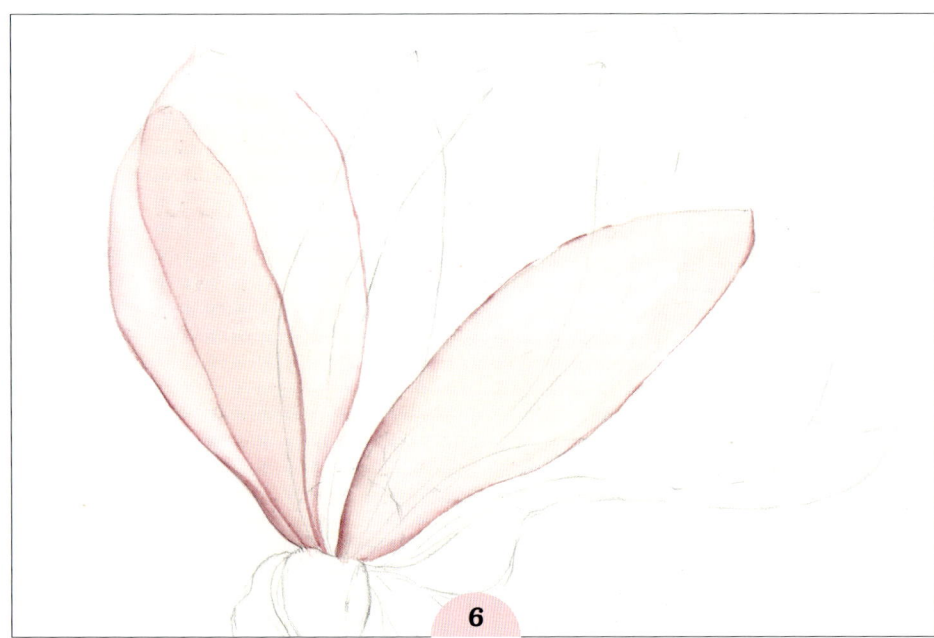

6

Overlapping petals: middle. Check the first petal to see if it is thoroughly dry. If it is, gently wet the whole of the petal 'lying' on top of it with clean water using the no. 10 sable brush. Using the same brush, add the light pink mix to the petal, working from the top and then distributing the colour downwards. Using a damp no. 4 brush, add the dark pink mix along the edges in the same way as you did before. Leave the petal to dry completely.

7 Overlapping petals: middle continued. Paint a few more petals in the same way. Always make sure that the previous petals are completely dry (see the tip below).

8 Folded petal. When a petal is folded in places, it has more weight and density in the folded areas. This needs to be reflected in the painting. Wet the petal with clean water using the no. 10 sable brush and add the light pink mix. While the paper is still wet, paint a line of dark pink mix along the top edge of the petal with a damp no. 4 brush then distribute it gently from the top edge (the 'fold') downwards. While the glaze is still wet, run the dark pink mix around the edges with the no. 4 brush then soften the colour with a clean, damp brush. Leave the petal to dry completely, then finish it by subtly mapping the outline of the 'invisible', folded-over side of the petal with the light pink mix and no. 4 brush.

9 Final petals. Paint the remaining petals one by one using the same techniques and brushes. Remember to strengthen the edges of the petals that are closer to the centre of the magnolia, using the dark pink mix.

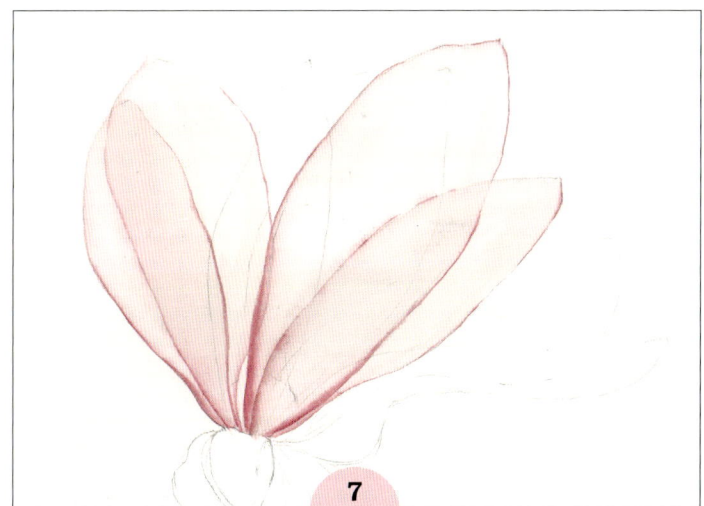

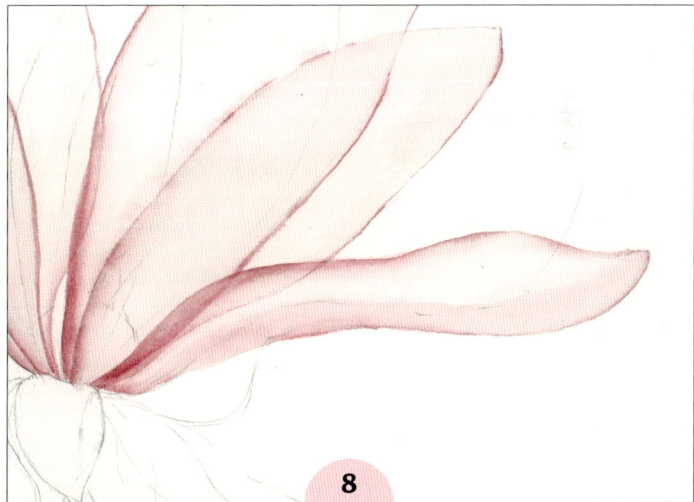

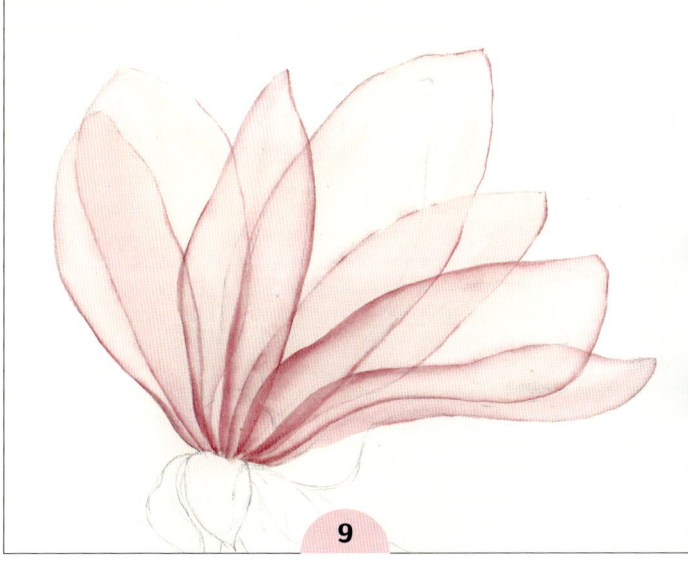

Tip

Always let the glaze of a petal dry completely before painting a new one over the top. If necessary, use a hairdryer to speed up the process.

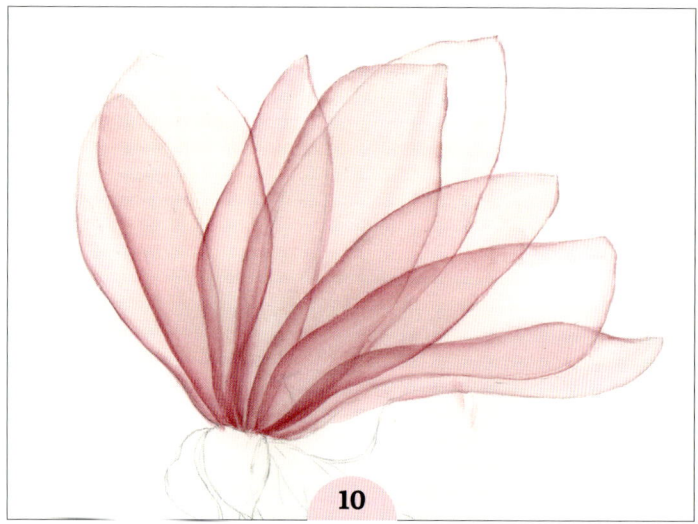

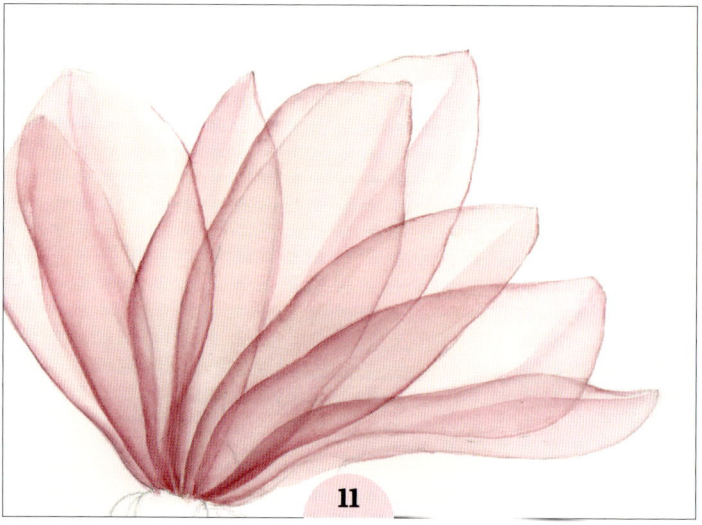

Overlapping petals: back. Once the painting is dry, add an extra back layer of petals - overlapping the previously painted petals using the same process described before. This strengthens the pink colour in the front and middle layer petals, and increases the contrast between all the layers too.

Painting veins. A magnolia petal has one main central vein (it looks like a thicker area) that we are going to map. Gently wet the petal area with clean water and a clean no. 10 sable brush then add a dark line along the centre of one large petal, using the light pink mix. Immediately soften the line with a clean, damp brush, sweeping towards one side of the petal. Repeat for all of the petals.

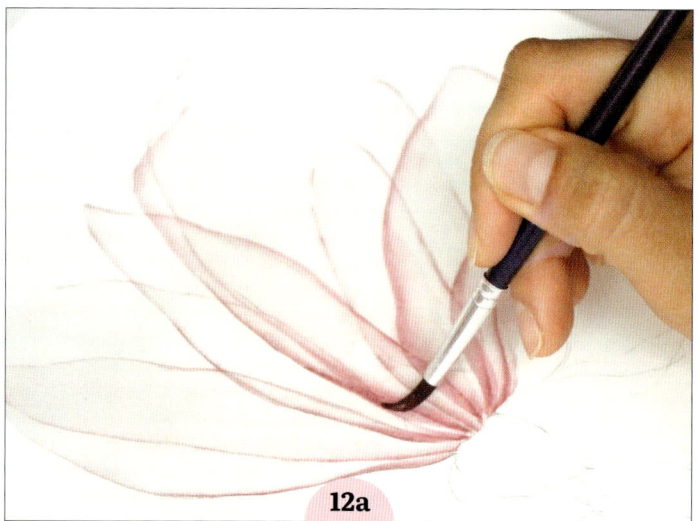

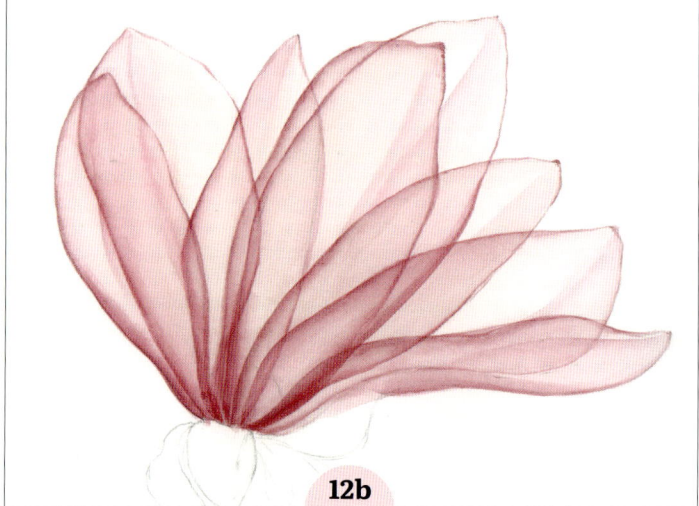

Adding contrasting outlines. Darken and warm the dark pink mix with a drop of Sepia. Paint along the edges of the petals with this mix, adding more of the mix to the edges of the petals nearest the centre of the flower. Soften the edges with a clean, damp brush as you finish each petal. Always follow the shape of the petal edge by rotating your hand as you paint.

Painting a stem. Make up the two brown mixes, referring to the swatches and details on page 70. As with the pink mixes, mix up the darker colour first then use this to create a lighter mix, in another palette well. Using the no. 6 brush, apply the light brown mix to the stem, from the top and distributing the colour towards the bottom. While the paint is still wet, run the dark brown mix around the edges of the stem with a damp no. 4 brush, starting from the top and tapering off towards the bottom. Soften the edges immediately with a clean, damp brush. Leave the painting to dry completely.

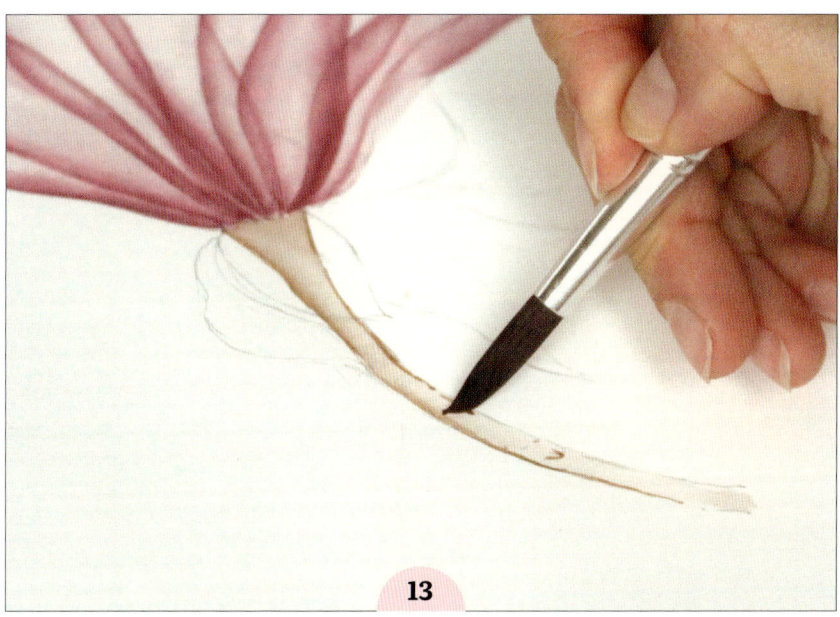

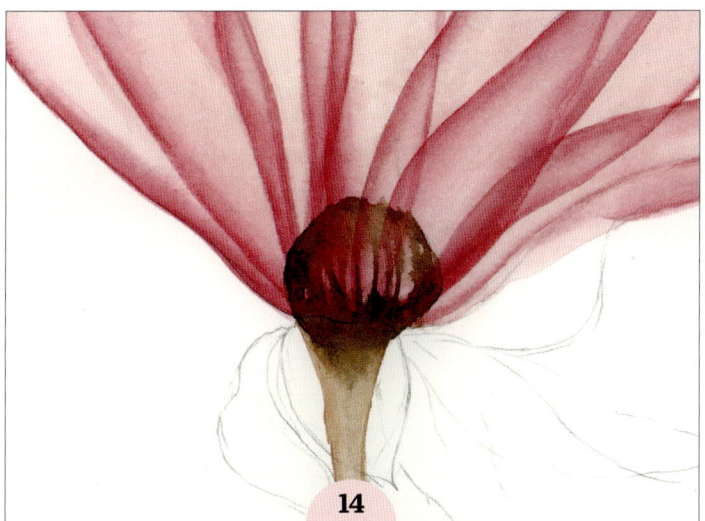

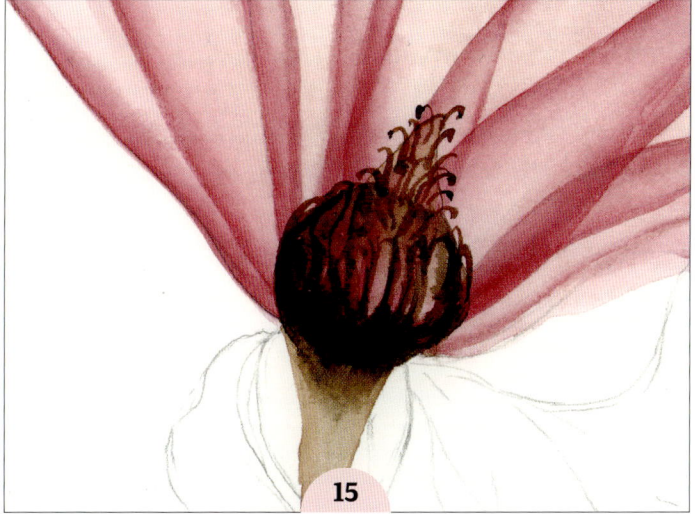

Painting the flower centre. When the flower is dry, wet the top of the stem and the sketched-in, ball-like shape of the flower centre with clean water using the no. 6 brush. Glaze a circular shape with the dark brown mix, using the same brush. While the paint is still wet and with the tip of the damp no. 4 brush, run the dark brown mix around the edges of the shape. With the same mix and brush, suggest stamens around the form with C-shaped strokes, working from the bottom up.

Painting a cluster of carpels. Using the stronger dark brown mix and the tip of the no. 4 brush once again, paint in tall carpels around the top of the ball-like shape, adding curvy tips to each to hint at textures. Darken the bottom of the rounded shape with a very strong dark brown mix, using the no. 6 brush.

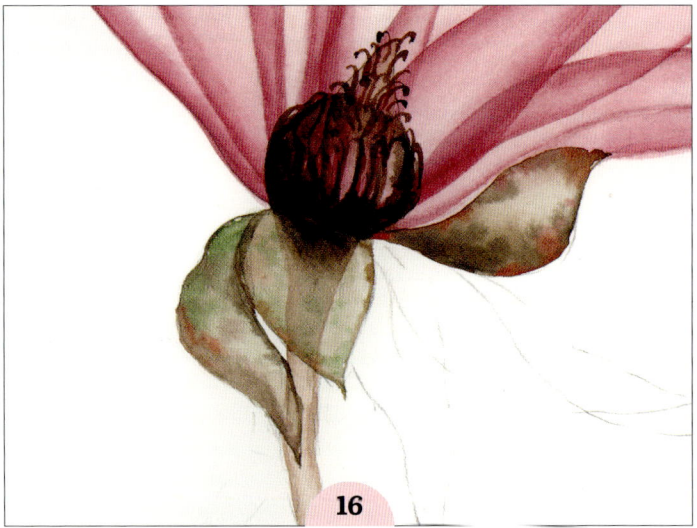

16 Painting separate leaf-like petals (bracts). Mix the sage green mix, referring to the swatch and details on page 70. Wet the bracts that don't overlap one another with the no. 6 brush and clean water, then glaze in the light brown mix, working from the section of the bracts closest to the flower centre outwards. While the paper is still wet, run the dark brown mix around the edges of the bracts with a damp no. 4 brush, again working from the carpel outwards. Here and there, 'dot' the sage green, light brown, dark brown and pure Burnt Sienna inside the bracts with the tip of a brush to create a dappled texture. Alternate between brushes as you do this, and emphasize the placement of the bracts by using the dark brown mix and Burnt Sienna for the back sections, and the sage green and light brown for parts of the bracts that sit closer to the foreground.

17 Painting overlapping bracts. Add a hint of pure Sepia to the sage green mix. Paint in the remaining bracts, wetting them with clean water first with the no. 6 brush then glazing in this new sage green mix (**17a**). Leave the paint to dry for a minutes then, using the tip of the no. 4 brush, define the edges of these bracts with the new sage green mix (**17b**).

18 Defining the stem. With the tip of the no. 4 brush and dark brown mix, outline the edges of the stem. Start from the flower centre, then work downwards.

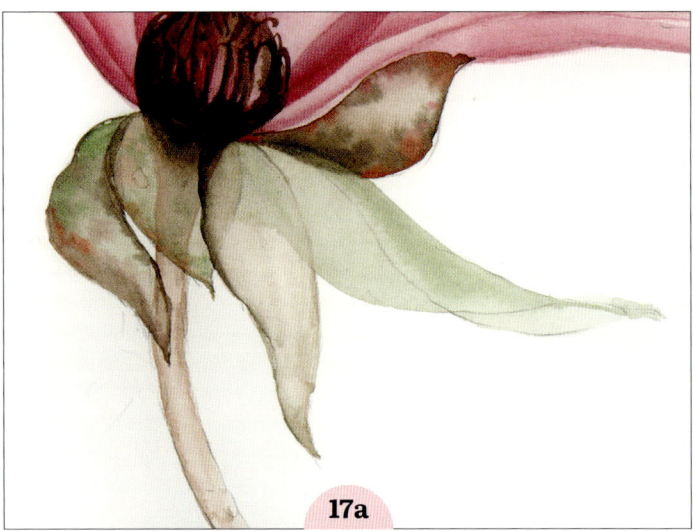

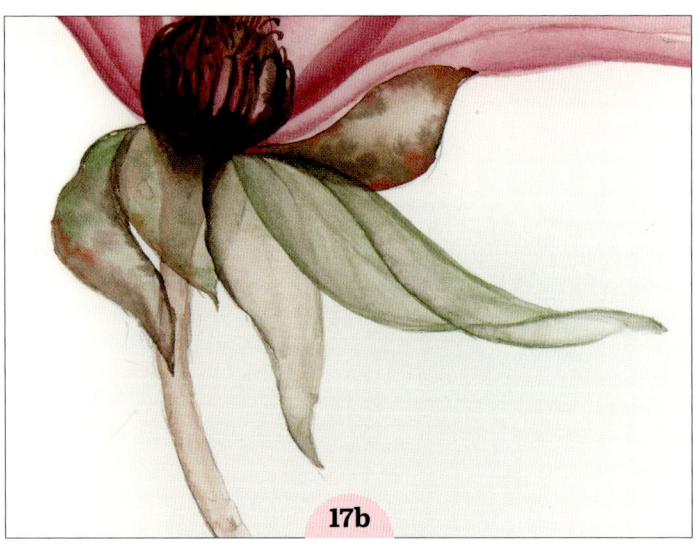

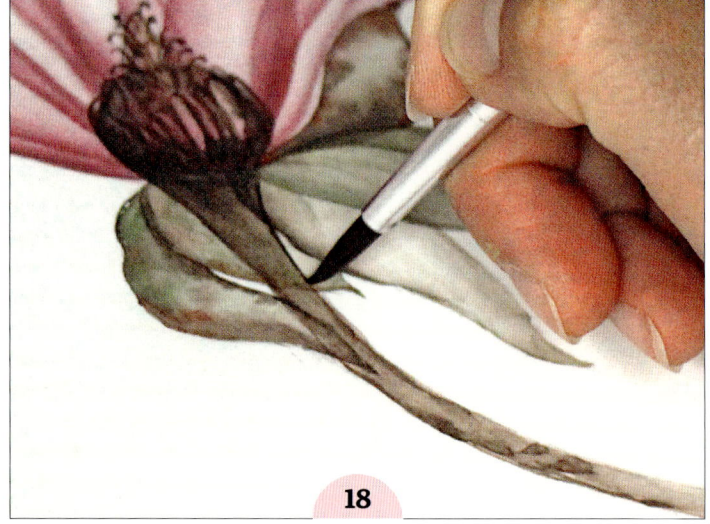

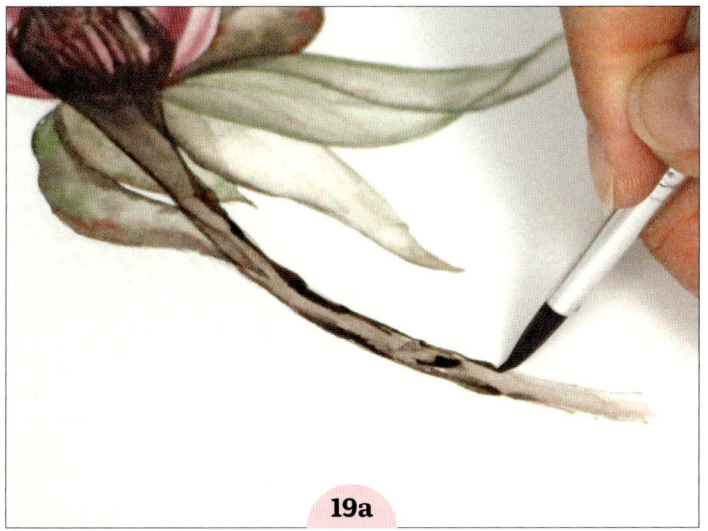

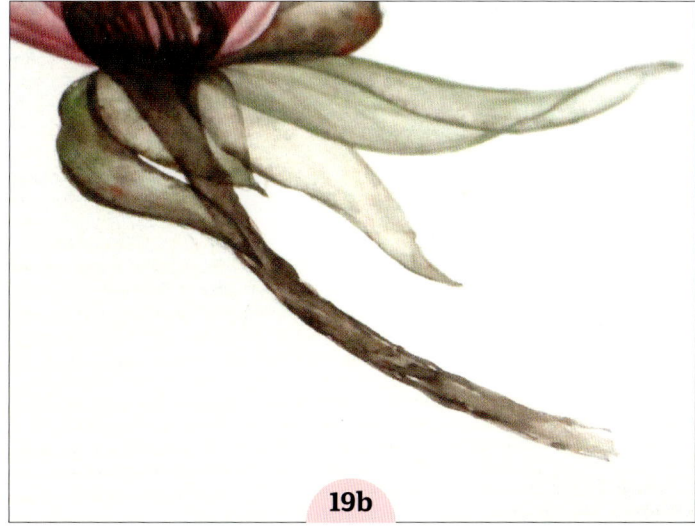

Adding texture to the stem. With a dry no. 6 brush, 'dash' in the dark brown mix along the stem, from top to bottom. Gently shake and wiggle your brush as you work, to emulate the knotted texture of a magnolia stem.

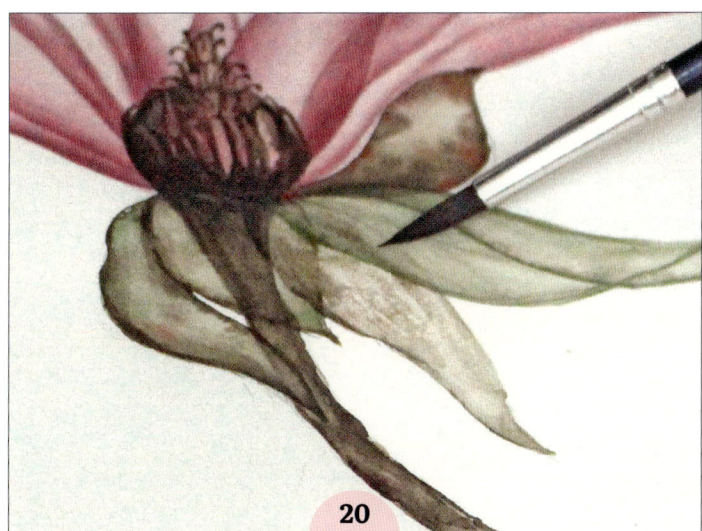

Adding texture to the bracts. Load the brush with a strong dark brown mix then remove any excess paint on the bristles by dabbing the brush on kitchen paper. Flatten the tip of the brush and paint over the bracts with the mix, using fast but gentle strokes, following their shape.

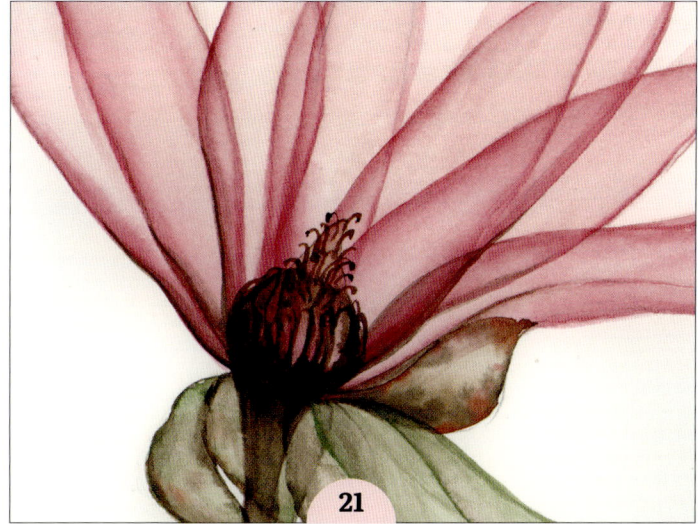

Final details. Using the tip of the no. 4 brush and the stong dark brown mix, outline the bottom edges of some of the petals and the bracts, to define their outlines and add shadows.

Magnolia-inspired
Gallery

Below

'Delicate Magnolia'

30 x 20cm (12 x 8in)

Paint: *Ultramarine Blue, Quinacridone Rose, Sepia.*

Painting this magnolia was much simpler than painting our magnolia project, as it had fewer petals and I didn't have any greenery.

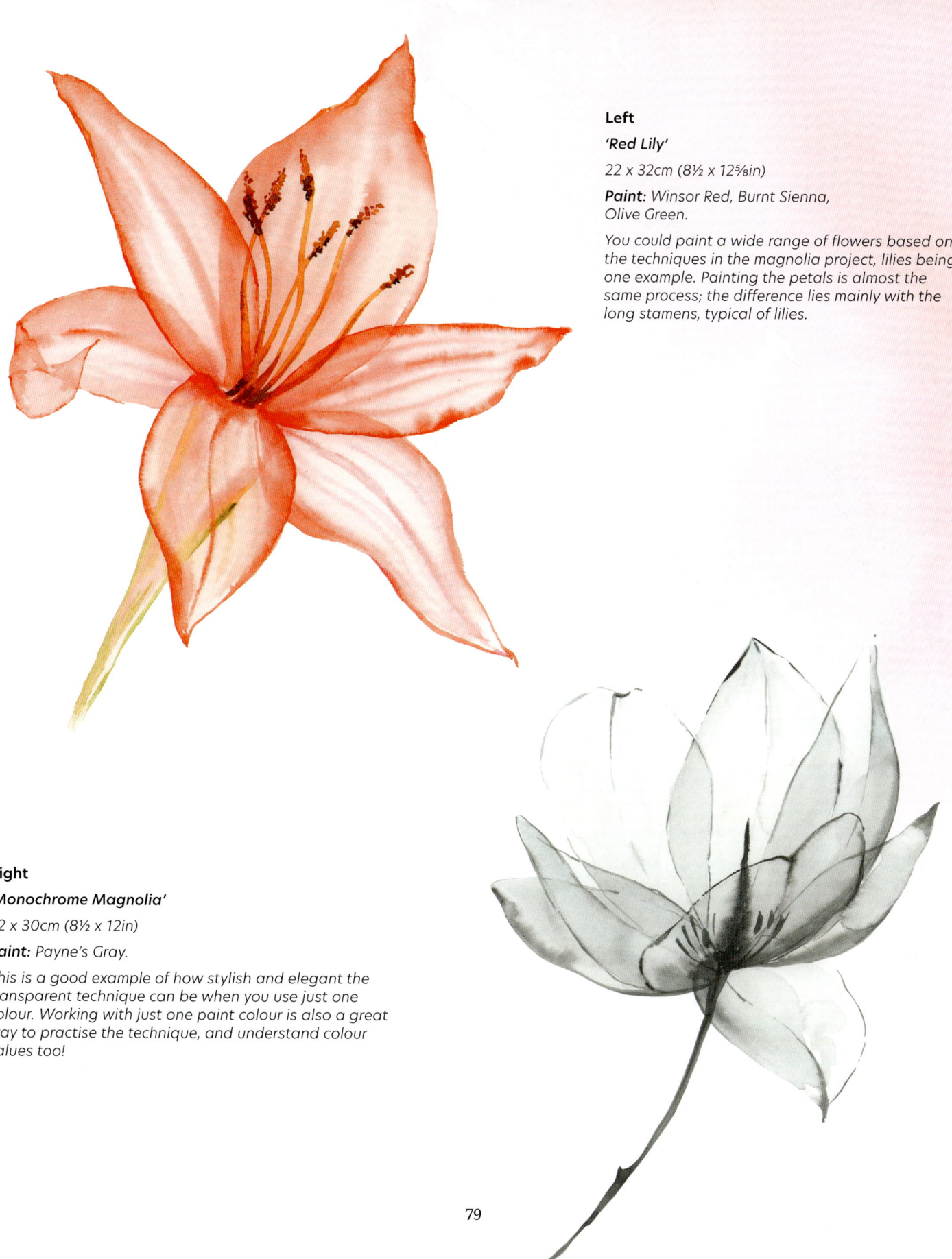

Left

'Red Lily'

22 x 32cm (8½ x 12⅝in)

Paint: *Winsor Red, Burnt Sienna, Olive Green.*

You could paint a wide range of flowers based on the techniques in the magnolia project, lilies being one example. Painting the petals is almost the same process; the difference lies mainly with the long stamens, typical of lilies.

Right

'Monochrome Magnolia'

22 x 30cm (8½ x 12in)

Paint: *Payne's Gray.*

This is a good example of how stylish and elegant the transparent technique can be when you use just one colour. Working with just one paint colour is also a great way to practise the technique, and understand colour values too!

Project Four:

Iris

I love irises for their special shape – to me, their petals look like
butterfly wings. Although irises come in a wide range of colours,
my favourites are the traditional deep blue bearded ones.

Because irises have a complex structure of petals, I recommend painting
the petals in separate layers, one after another. In the steps on the
following pages, you'll see I work from the back petals towards the front
ones; this approach adds a more organic look to your iris.

You will need

WATERCOLOUR PAINTS:
Ultramarine Blue, Sepia, Phthalo Green

MATERIALS AND TOOLS:
22 x 30cm (8½ x 12in) sheet of hot-pressed paper;
sharp (or mechanical) HB pencil; putty eraser and soft
white eraser; kitchen paper or cloth; no. 4 and no. 6 round
synthetic brushes with very fine tips; no. 10 sable brush

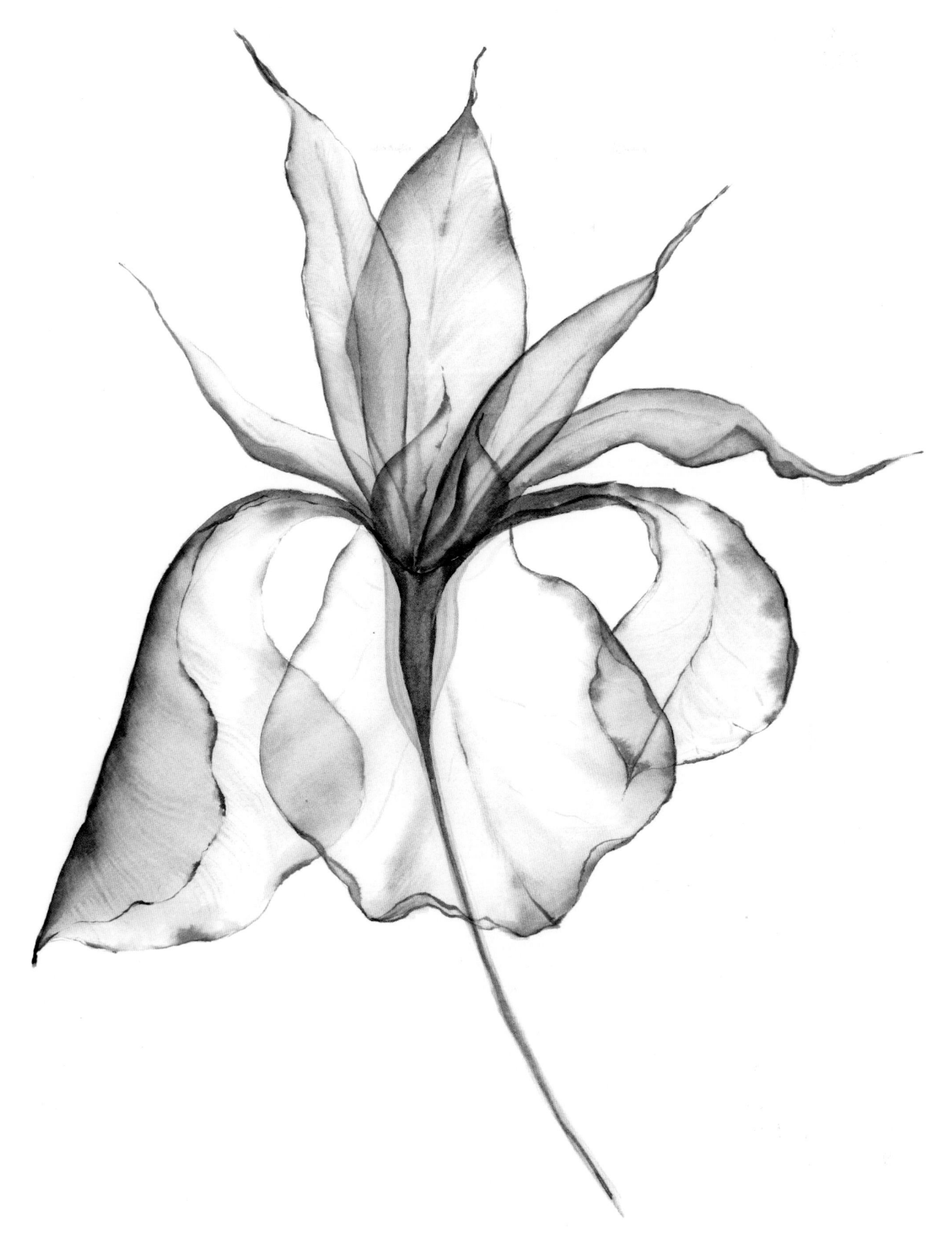

Basic mixes

DARK BLUE
Ultramarine Blue
with a hint of Sepia

DARK GREEN
Phthalo Green
with a hint of Sepia

LIGHT BLUE
As detailed above,
but very diluted

LIGHT GREEN
As detailed above,
but very diluted

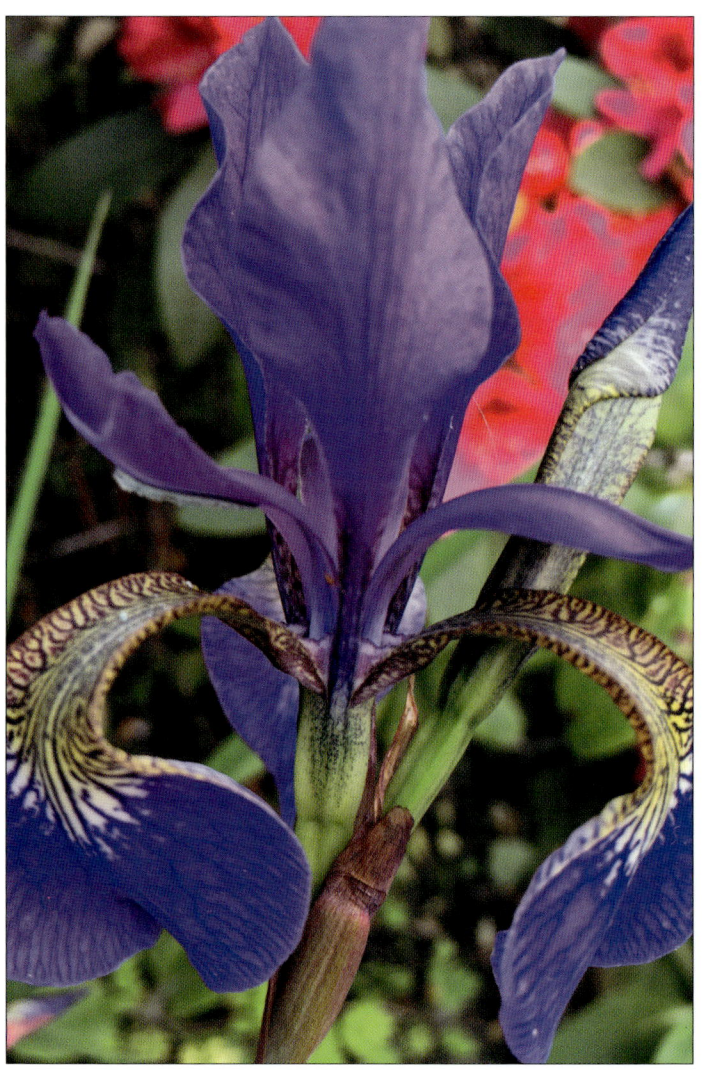

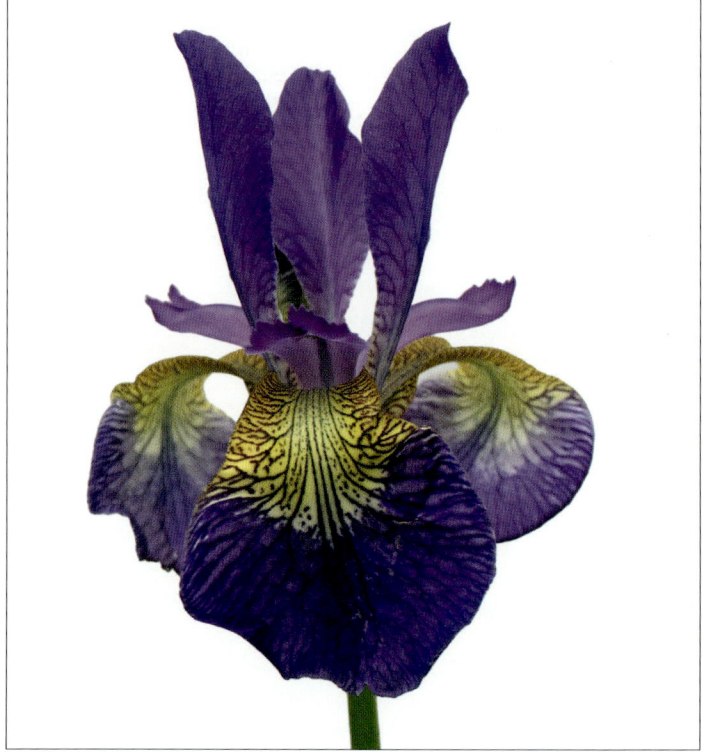

Reference photographs

A single iris can look quite different in appearance, depending on whether you view it from the front or from the back. That is why I usually take pictures from both sides of the flower, to make a more precise drawing.

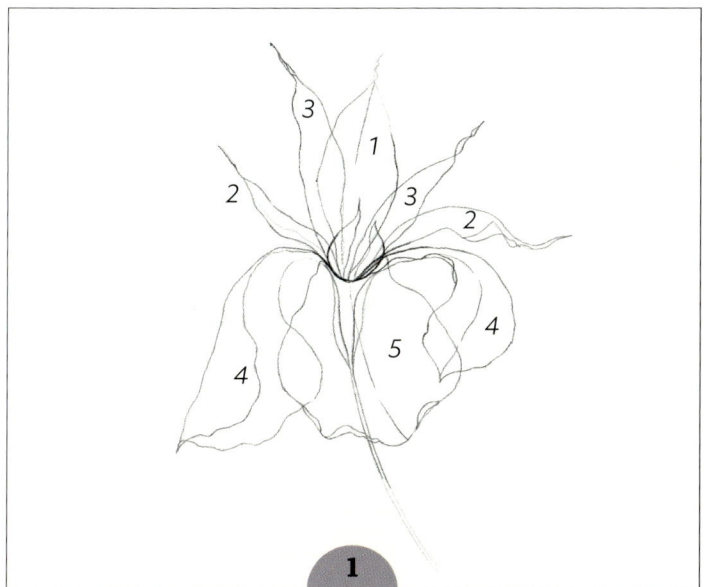

Drawing the flower. Using the outline on page 125 or the references opposite, draw the iris. Although the iris stem is quite straight and thick, I prefer to add some curves and make it thinner for artistic purposes. To help paint the flower's petals in an order that will achieve the best transparent effect, lightly pencil numbers over the petals in a sequence that means you work from the back of the flower towards the front.

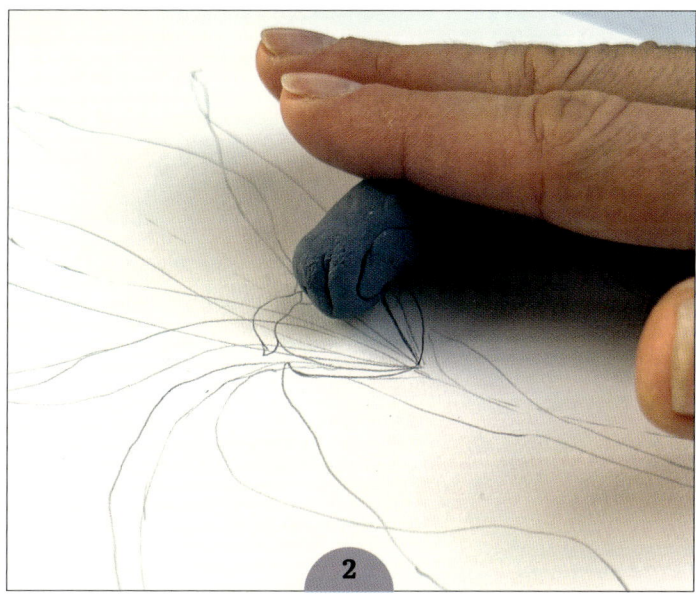

Softening the outline. Once you are happy with the drawing, rub back the lines with a putty eraser, leaving a faint outline.

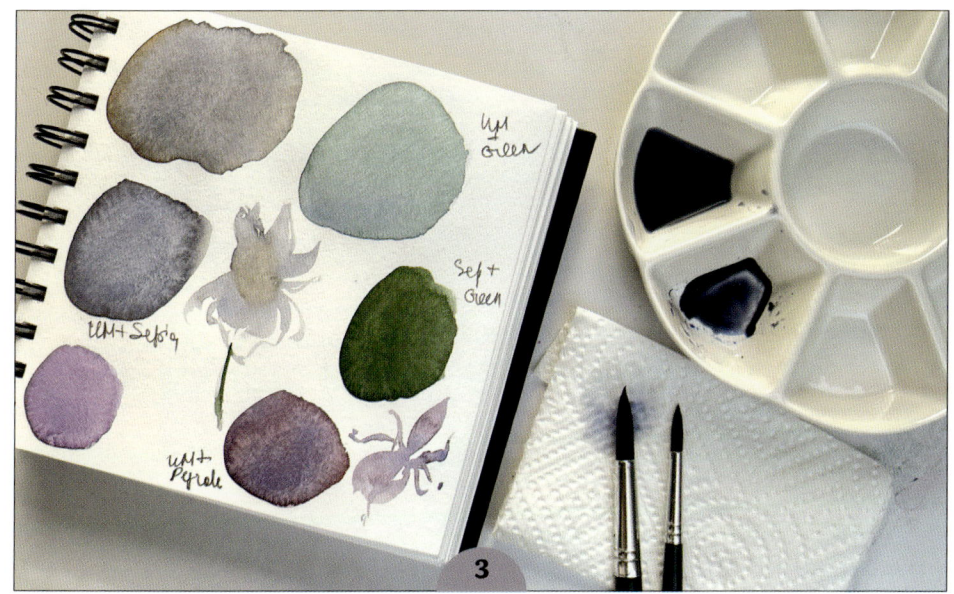

Mixing the paints. Make up the blue mixes, referring to the swatches and their details opposite. Start with the darker mix then, once you are happy with the colour, take a drop of it, place it in a separate well in the palette and dilute it with a large amount of water to create the lighter mix.

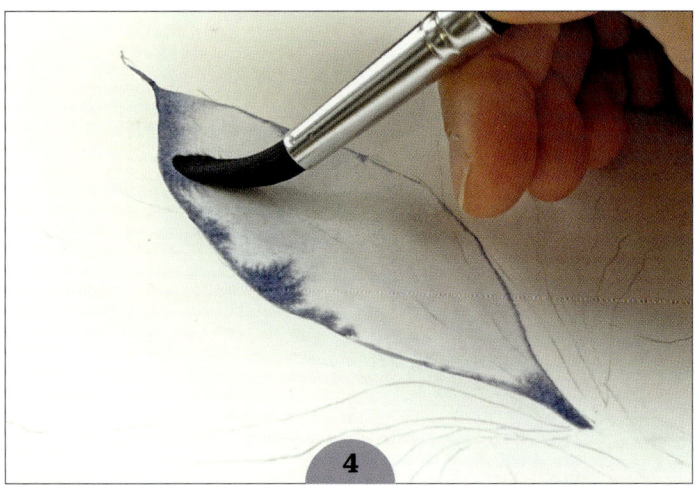

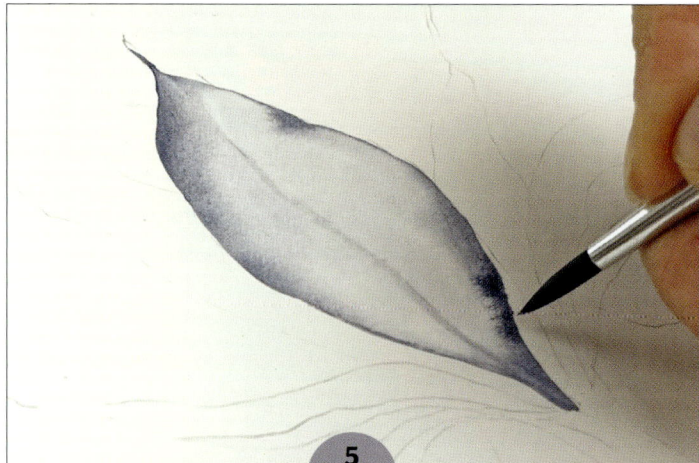

4 Top petal. Wet the inside of the petal with clean water using the no. 6 round brush. Make sure that the water is applied evenly on the paper with no puddles. Drop in the light blue mix at the top of the petal then gently distribute it downwards and throughout the petal. While the glaze is still wet, switch to the no. 4 brush then, using only the tip, sweep in the darker blue mix along the edges of the petal. Soften the darker colour with a clean, damp no. 6 round brush.

5 Adding detail. With the tip of the no. 4 brush and using the light blue mix, paint in the central vein.

6 Adding detail continued. Flatten the no. 4 brush and, while the paint for the vein is still wet and with a gentle movement, move your brush from the central vein towards the outer edges of the petal. Repeat along the length of the vein, working from top to bottom and following the shape of the petal to produce slightly curvy lines. This creates the impression and texture of side veins.

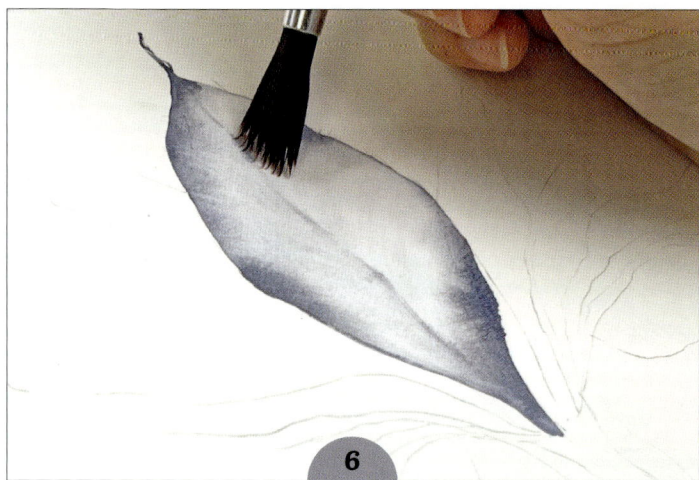

7 Second row of petals: left-hand petal. Wet the whole petal with clean water using the no. 6 round brush, then glaze in the light blue mix with the same brush. With the no. 4 brush, run the dark blue mix along the bottom edge of the area, from left to right, gradually increasing the intensity of colour towards the flower centre. Then, with the tip of the no. 4 brush and the light blue mix, and working from the centre of the flower to the end of the petal, run a thin, delicate line along the top of the petal. While the paper is still wet, add more intensity to the bottom area of the petal, as shown.

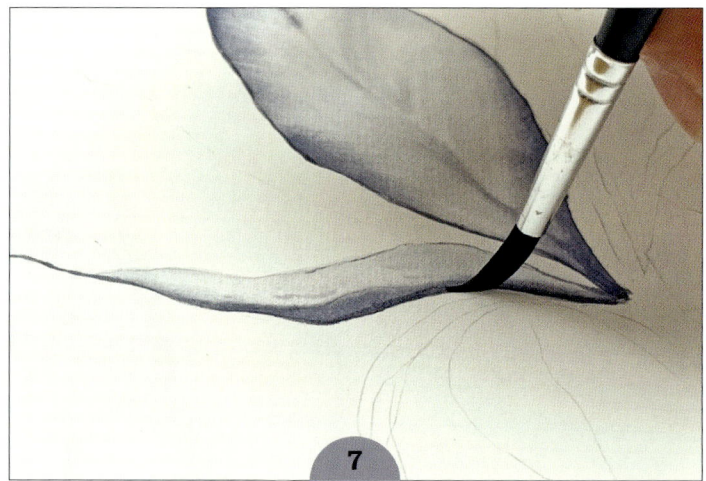

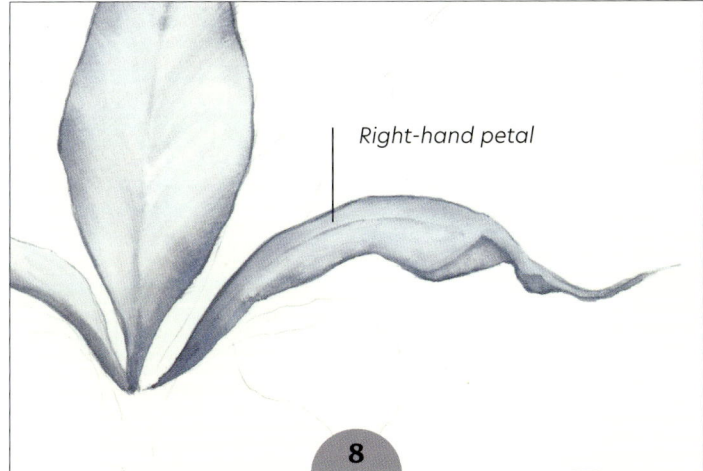

Right-hand petal

8 **Second row of petals: right-hand petal.** Using the no. 6 round brush, wet the petal then glaze it with the light blue mix as before. Then, with the tip of the no. 4 brush and the dark blue mix, paint in the central and side veins as described in steps 5 and 6. Try to vary the pressure on the brush as you paint in the veins, to add realism. Soften any hard edges where the dark blue meets the light blue with a clean, damp brush. To paint the small folded areas, run the dark blue mix along the bottom edges with the no. 4 brush then blot out the colour that has bled upwards with a clean, dry brush.

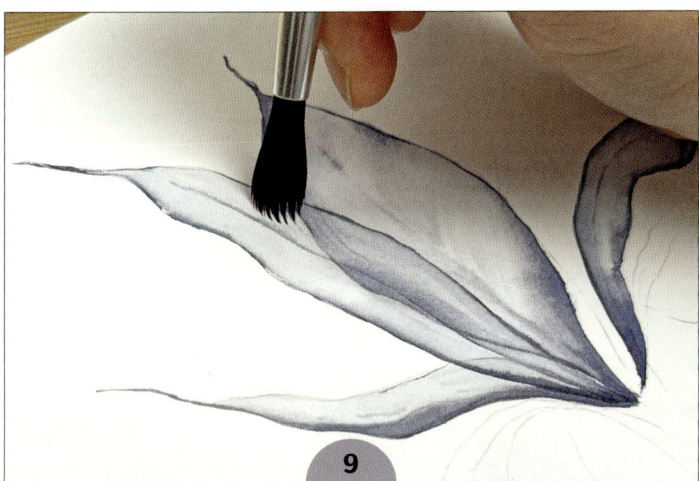

9 **Third row of petals: left-hand petal.** Paint the petal in the same way as described in steps 4–6, opposite. Make sure to wet and glaze the area of the petal where it overlaps the top petal. Note that, while the paper and colours are still wet, there is no need to pick up extra paint from the palette. By 'dragging' the colours already present in the painting, the lines are softer, and appear more delicate and organic.

10 **Third row of petals: right-hand petal.** Paint the right-hand petal in the same way described in steps 4–6, again making sure to wet and glaze in the areas that overlap the top petal and the right-hand petal from the second row. Outline the small top area with the dark blue mix and the no. 4 brush to suggest the way the petal is folded.

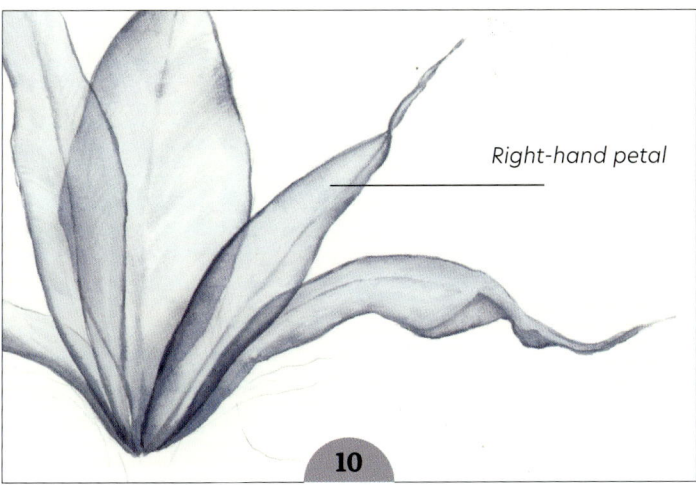

Right-hand petal

11 Fourth row of petals: left-hand petal. As this petal is bent and one side is folded over, the left edge of the petal needs to have a denser, more intense application of colour to suggest the fold. Using the no. 6 round brush, wet the whole petal area with water then glaze in the light blue mix, working from left to right.

12 Fourth row of petals: left-hand petal continued. While the glaze is still wet, glaze in another layer of the light blue mix on the left-hand side of the petal only, within the sketched folded edge. With the tip of a damp no. 4 brush, run the dark blue mix along the left edge of the petal. Soften the dark colour with a clean, damp brush, as before.

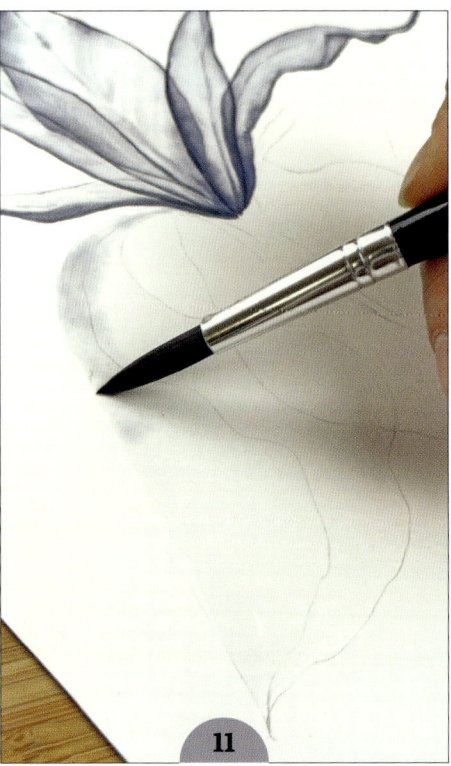

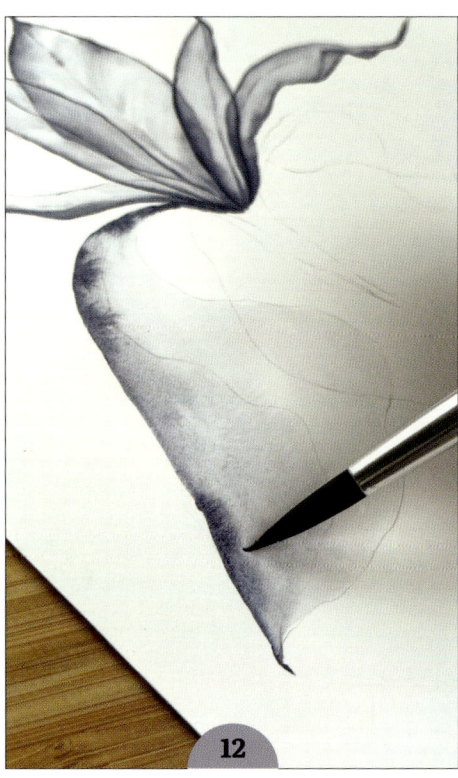

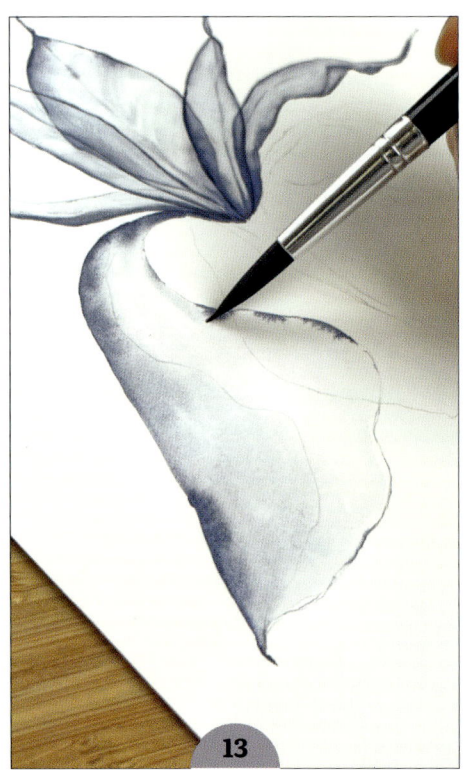

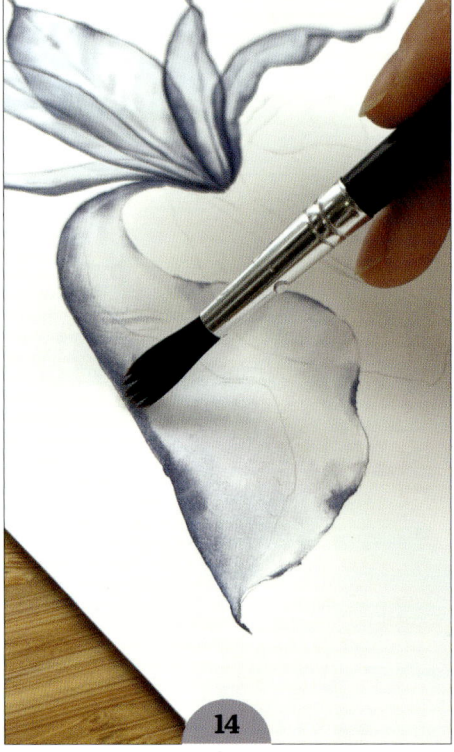

13 Fourth row of petals: left-hand petal continued. While the paint is still wet, add random spots of the dark blue mix along the right-hand edge of the petal with the tip of the no. 4 brush, to suggest wavy, folded areas.

14 Fourth row of petals: left-hand petal continued. With the tip of the no. 4 brush and using the dark blue mix, run a thin, delicate line along the left edge of the petal. Vary the pressure on the brush for realism, and occasionally 'wobble' the brush towards the inside of the petal to allow the mix to bleed here and there. Flatten the no. 4 brush and pull a few strokes from the dark paint on the left-hand side towards the right-hand edge.

15 Fourth row of petals: right-hand petal. Using the no. 6 round brush, wet the petal with clean water then glaze it with the light blue mix. With the tip of the brush, 'dot' the dark blue mix along the edges of the petal, working from top to bottom. Vary the amount of colour applied along the edges to emulate the wavy structure of the petal. Soften the dark colour with a clean, damp brush, as shown.

Tip

When softening the outline around the petals, you may find it easier to rotate the paper as you go.

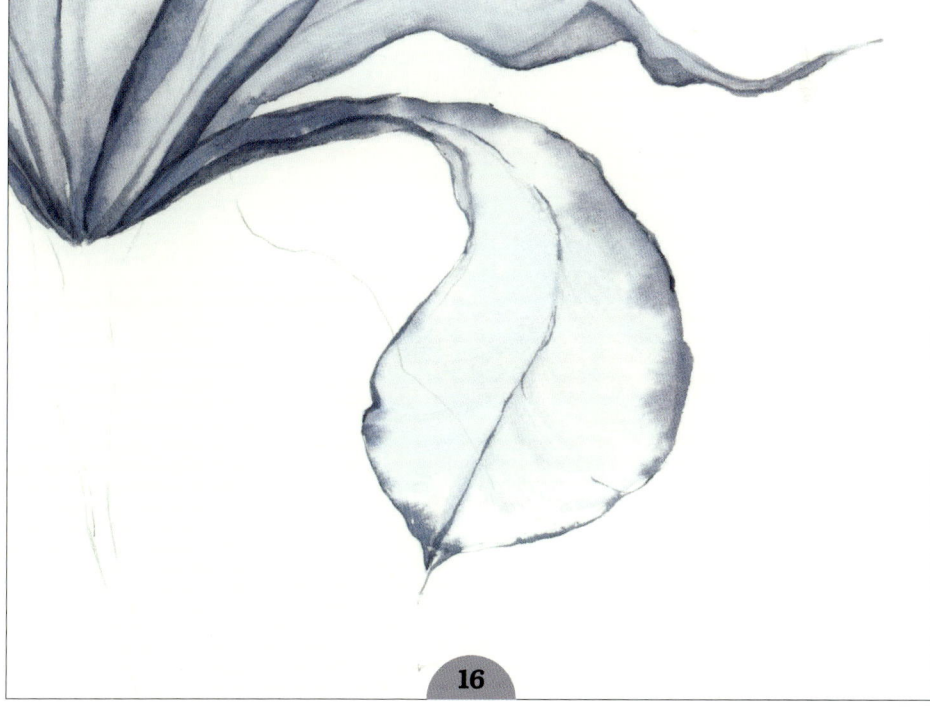

16 Fourth row of petals: right-hand petal continued. Using the tip of the no. 4 brush and with the dark blue mix, paint in the central vein, soften it with a clean, damp brush, then suggest little veins either side of it in the same way described in step 6 (see page 84). Finish the petal by running in a thin, delicate line of the light blue mix along the left- and right-hand edges of the petal using the no. 4 brush.

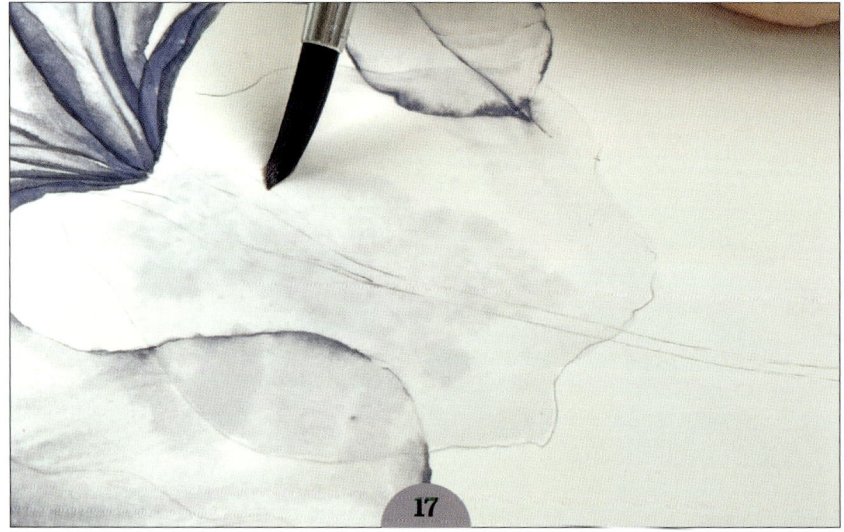

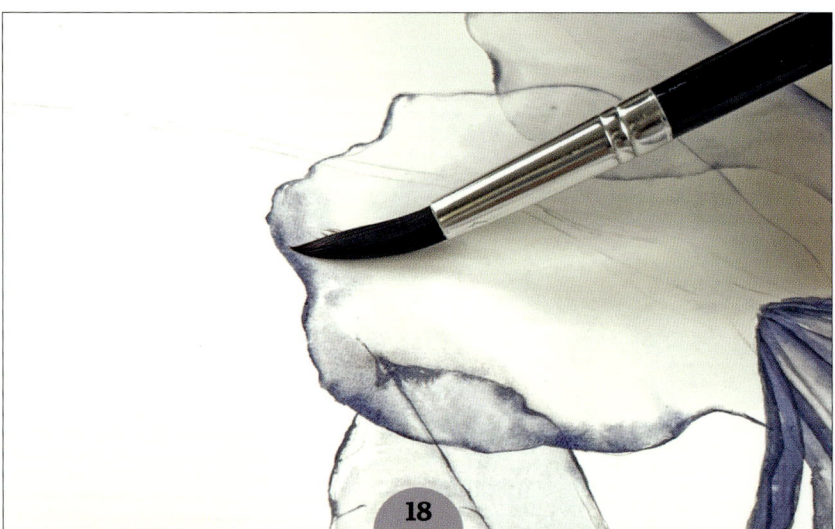

17 Bottom petal. This petal has a very large surface area. First wet it with water using a no. 6 round brush or no. 10 sable brush (including the areas where it overlaps the fourth row of petals), then glaze in the light blue mix, working from the centre of the petal outwards.

18 Bottom petal continued. With the tip of the no. 4 brush, run the dark blue mix around the edge of the petal, then soften the colour with a clean, damp brush. Note that I've rotated the painting to make it easier to paint all around the edge (see also the tip box on page 87).

19 Bottom petal continued. 'Dot' in some dark blue mix to the edges here and there with the no. 4 brush, forming small 'triangles'; these imitate the folds of the petal. Soften these shapes with a clean, damp brush.

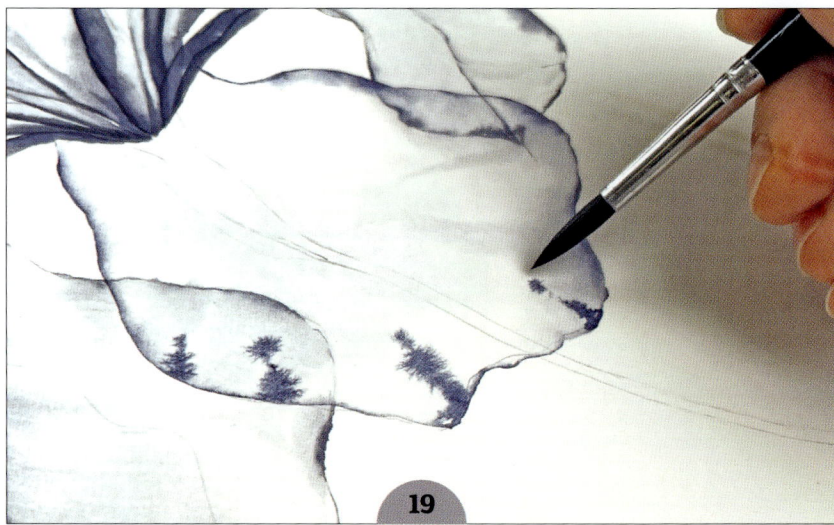

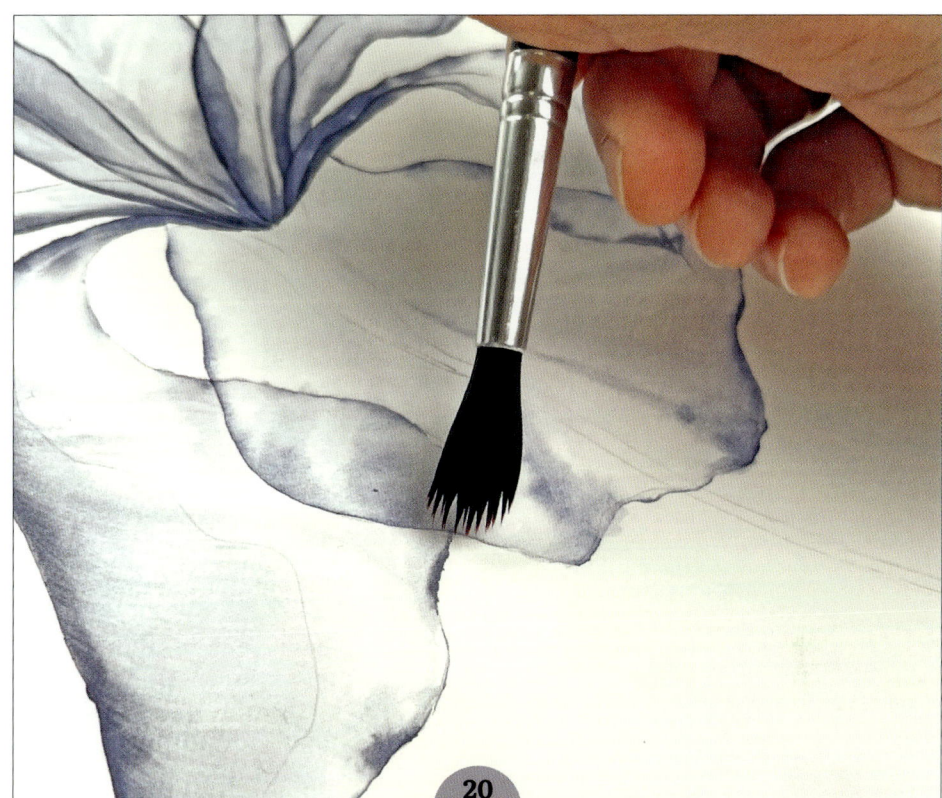

20 **Bottom petal continued.** With the light blue mix and using only the tip of the no. 4 brush, paint the central vein, starting from the bottom of petal and stopping just before you reach the centre of the flower. To add further texture to the petal, flatten the no. 4 brush then pull some of the colour from the small 'triangles' on the outside edges inwards. Leave the painting to dry completely.

21 **Bottom petal continued.** With the tip of the no. 4 brush and using the dark blue mix, brush paint in the curling edges along the bottom and right-hand sides.

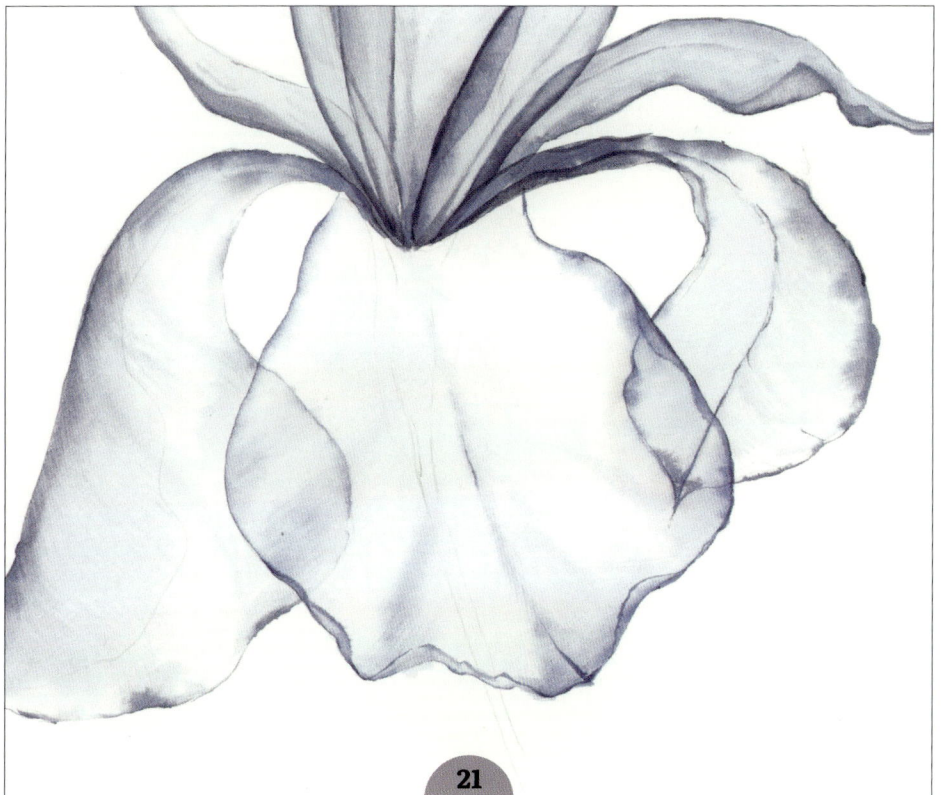

22 Fourth row of petals: folded area of the left-hand petal. Working within the darker folded-over area only, glaze the area with the light blue mix using the no. 6 round brush. Run the dark blue mix along the left-hand edge of the petal only, then with a clean, damp brush soften the colour, as shown.

23 Fourth row of petals: folded area of the left-hand petal continued. While the paint is still wet, flatten the no. 4 brush and drag out the darker colour from the left- to the right-hand edge of the folded area. With the tip of the no. 4 brush, 'dash' in the dark blue mix along the right-hand edge of the folded area.

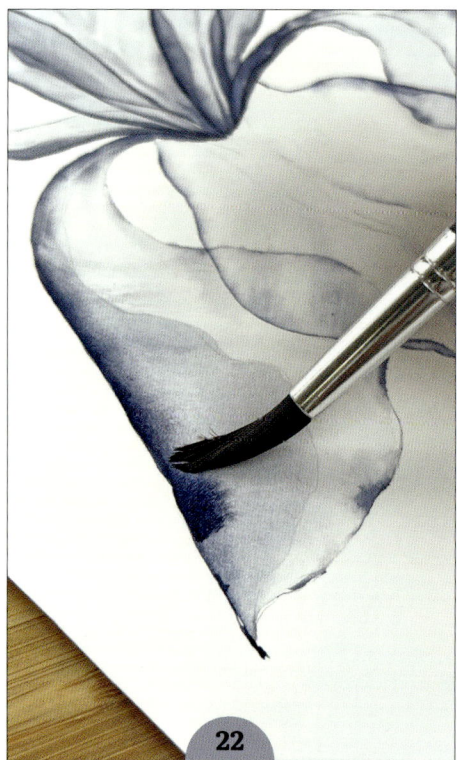

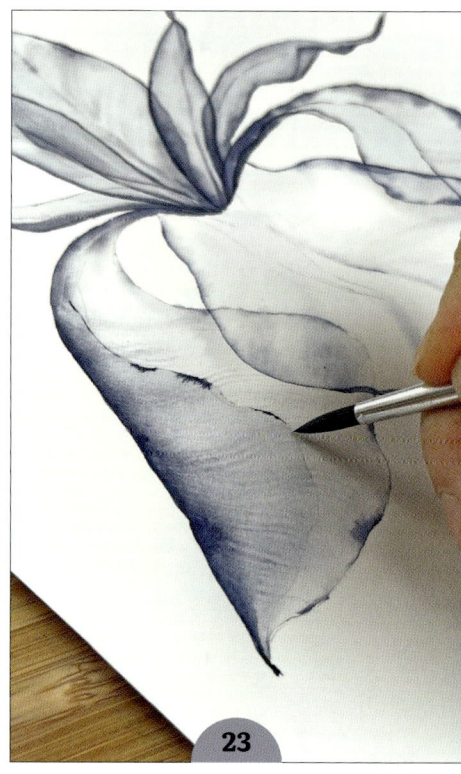

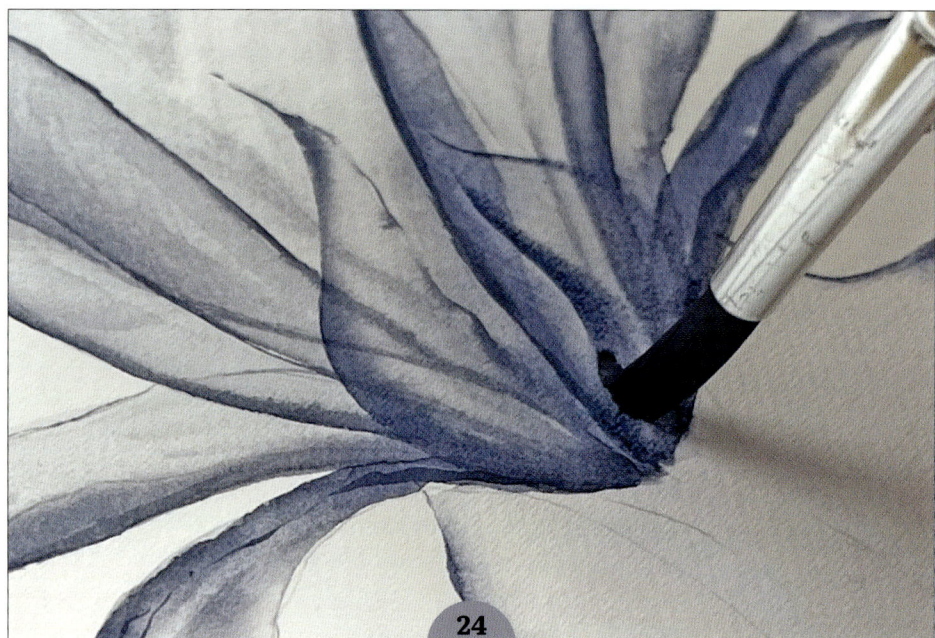

24 Two central petals. With the no. 6 round brush and light blue mix, glaze in the small left-hand petal. Work from top to bottom, starting with the tip of the brush, adding some pressure around the middle of the shape to widen the brush, then releasing the pressure at the very bottom to taper the brush. With this approach, you can paint a petal in just one brush stroke. Using the tip of the no. 4 brush, run the dark blue mix along some of the edges. Repeat the process with the small right-hand centre petal.

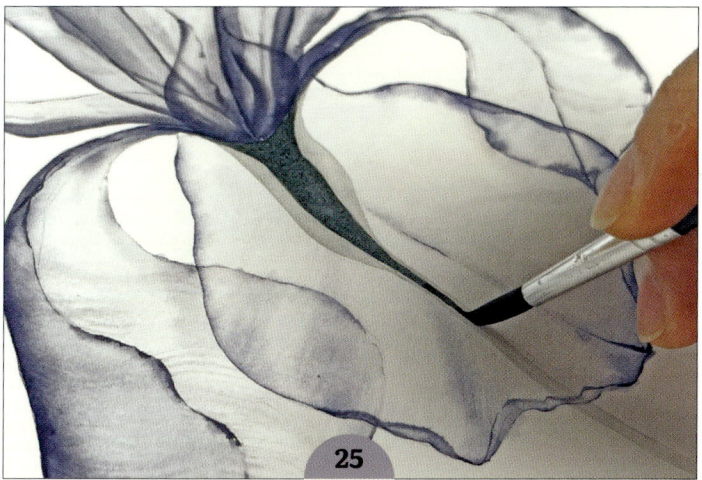

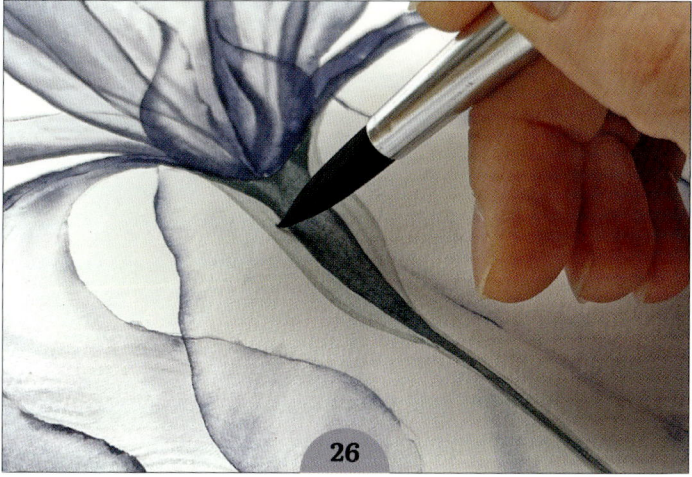

25 The stem. Make up the two green mixes, referring to the swatches and their details on page 82. As with the blue mixes, prepare the dark green mix first then use this to make up the light green mix. With the no. 6 round brush, paint the whole stem with the light green mix, including the receptacle. Wait until the stem is completely dry, then glaze in a narrower shape inside the stem and receptacle using the dark green mix and no. 4 brush.

26 The stem continued. While the dark green area is still wet, clean and dry the brush then use it to blot out some paint from the middle of the receptacle. Using the soaked-up paint on the brush, and with just the tip, run a few delicate vertical strokes inside the light green area of the receptacle to suggest the stem texture.

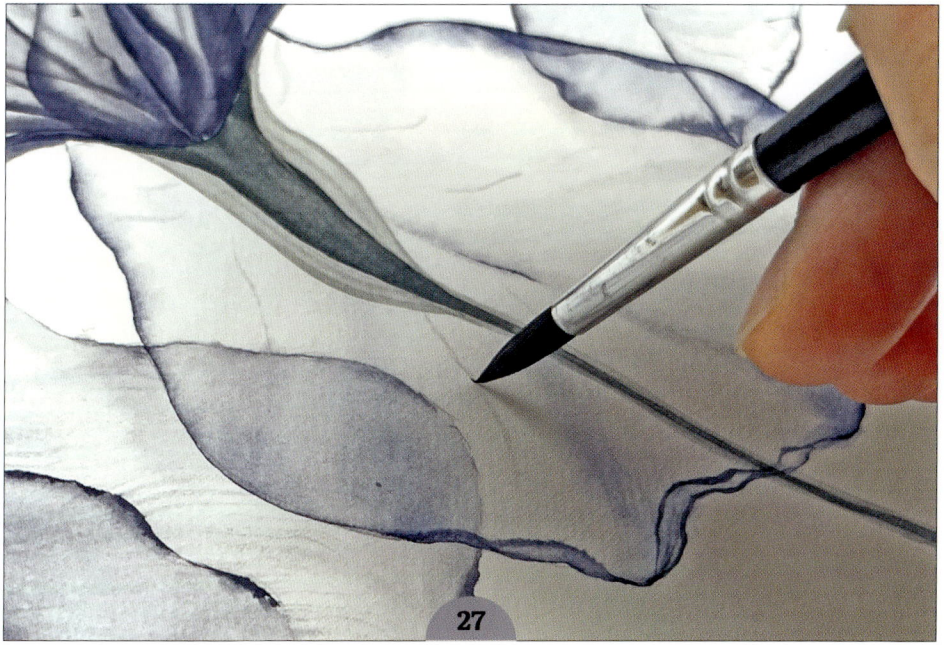

Bottom petal: final details. With the light blue mix and no. 6 round brush, glaze the areas where the bottom petal overlaps the fourth row of petals, to emphasize the intersections of the petals. With the tip of the no. 4 brush and the light blue mix, paint some tiny veins inside the petal, working from the stem outwards. Vary the pressure you apply to the brush as you paint each vein, to add variety and realism.

Iris-inspired *Gallery*

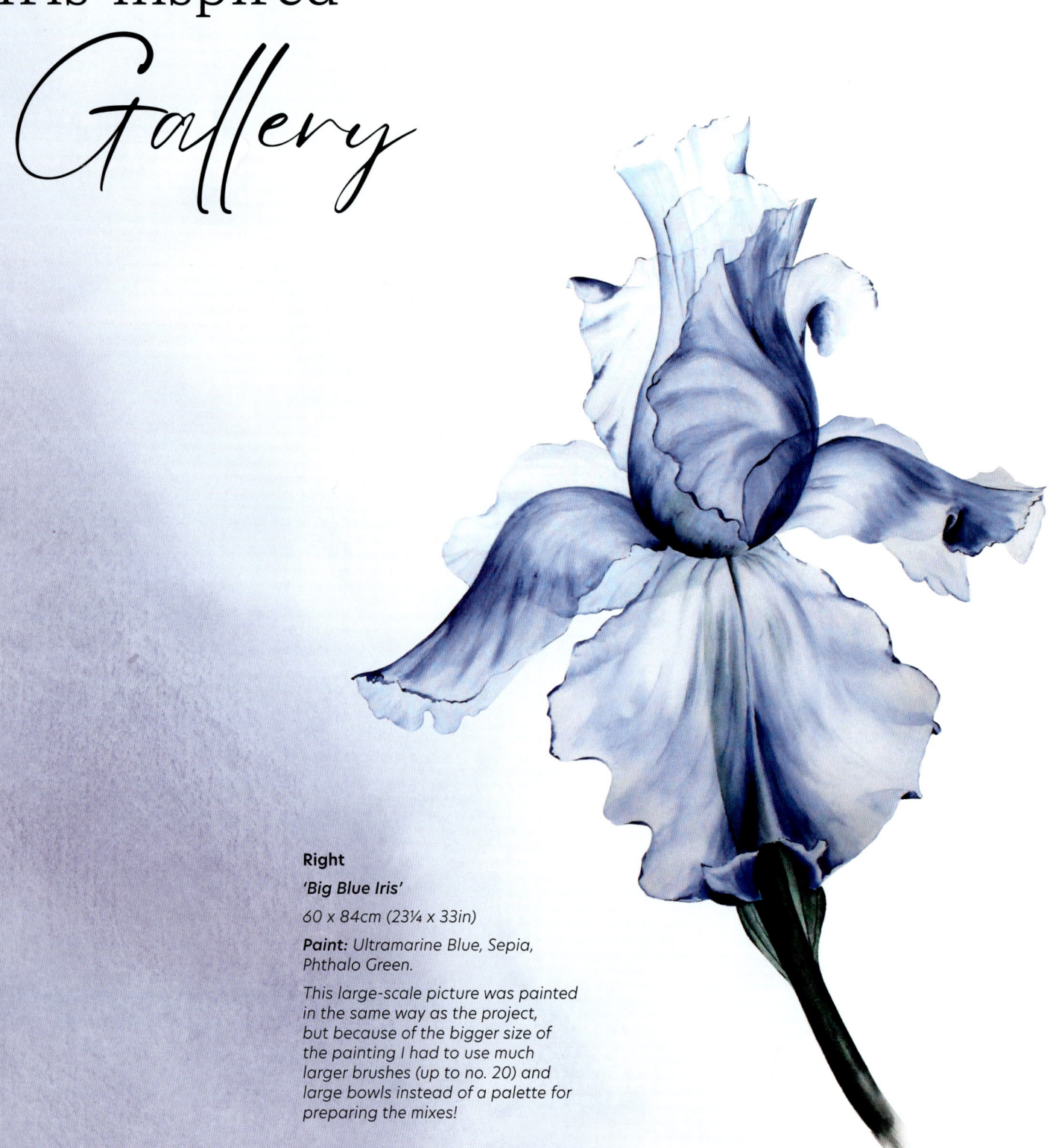

Right

'Big Blue Iris'

60 x 84cm (23¼ x 33in)

Paint: *Ultramarine Blue, Sepia, Phthalo Green.*

This large-scale picture was painted in the same way as the project, but because of the bigger size of the painting I had to use much larger brushes (up to no. 20) and large bowls instead of a palette for preparing the mixes!

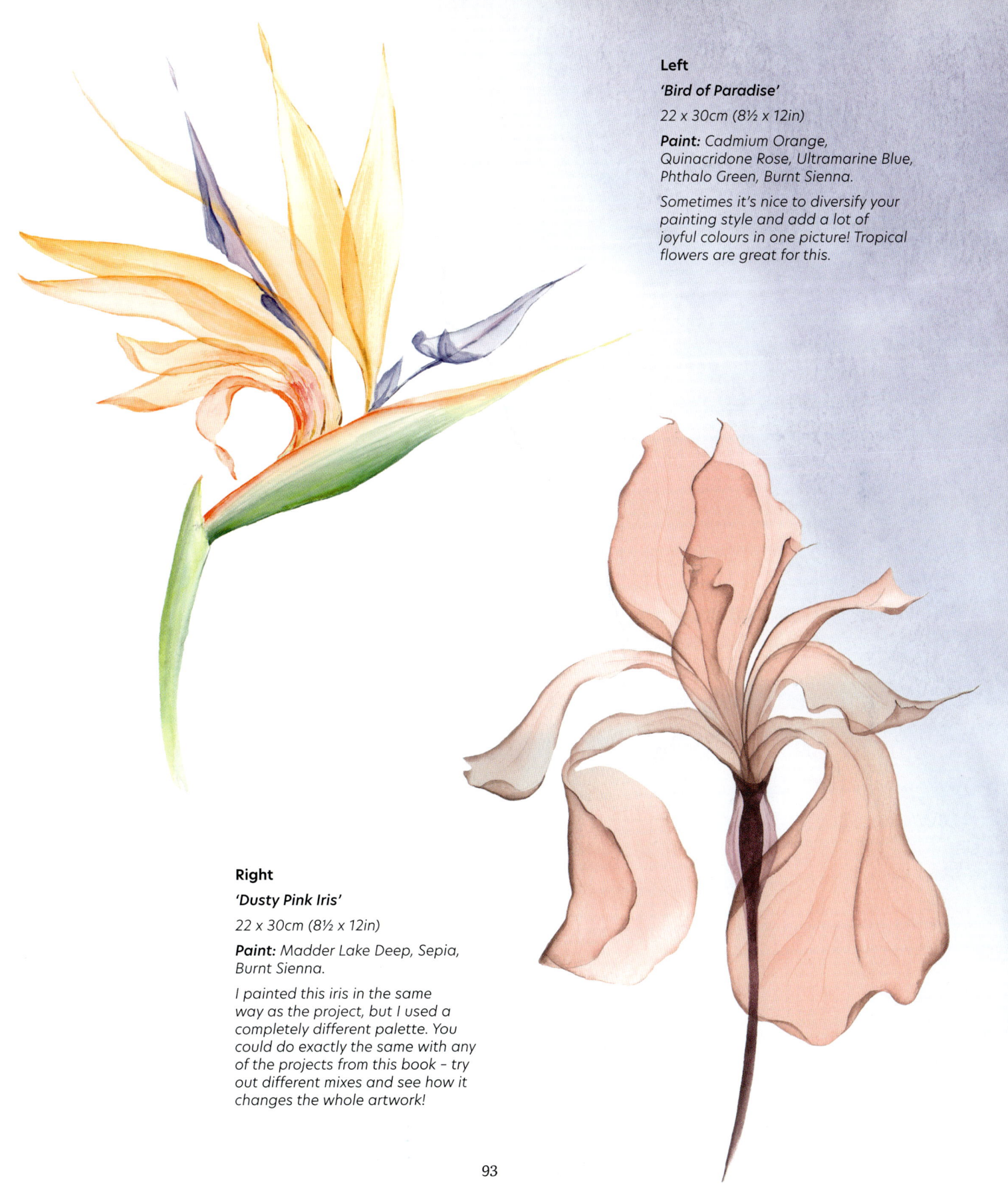

Left

'Bird of Paradise'

22 x 30cm (8½ x 12in)

Paint: *Cadmium Orange, Quinacridone Rose, Ultramarine Blue, Phthalo Green, Burnt Sienna.*

Sometimes it's nice to diversify your painting style and add a lot of joyful colours in one picture! Tropical flowers are great for this.

Right

'Dusty Pink Iris'

22 x 30cm (8½ x 12in)

Paint: *Madder Lake Deep, Sepia, Burnt Sienna.*

I painted this iris in the same way as the project, but I used a completely different palette. You could do exactly the same with any of the projects from this book – try out different mixes and see how it changes the whole artwork!

Project Five:

Peony

Peonies have always been my favourite flowers because they bloom around my birthday, in June. I love having bouquets of these beauties on my desk all month long – their whimsical shapes, countless petals and vibrant colours give so much inspiration!

However, painting peonies in a transparent technique can be a challenge, as their numerous petals can make it easy for the painter to get lost in all the layers. After much experimentation and practice, I have found a methodical approach that suggests the fragility and complexity of a peony that requires less effort than it looks.

Capturing the many layers of a peony in paint requires patience and time but it is very meditative, and allows you to paint at your own pace, step back and appreciate each step of the process.

For this project, you will incorporate everything you have learned in previous lessons, such as layering plenty of petals, emphasizing transparency, and painting greenery.

You will need

WATERCOLOUR PAINTS:

Quinacridone Rose, Cadmium Orange, Burnt Sienna, Phthalo Green, Ultramarine Blue

MATERIALS AND TOOLS:

22 x 30cm (8½ x 12in) sheet of hot-pressed paper; sharp (or mechanical) HB pencil; putty eraser and soft white eraser; kitchen paper or cloth; no. 4 and no. 6 round synthetic brushes with very fine tips

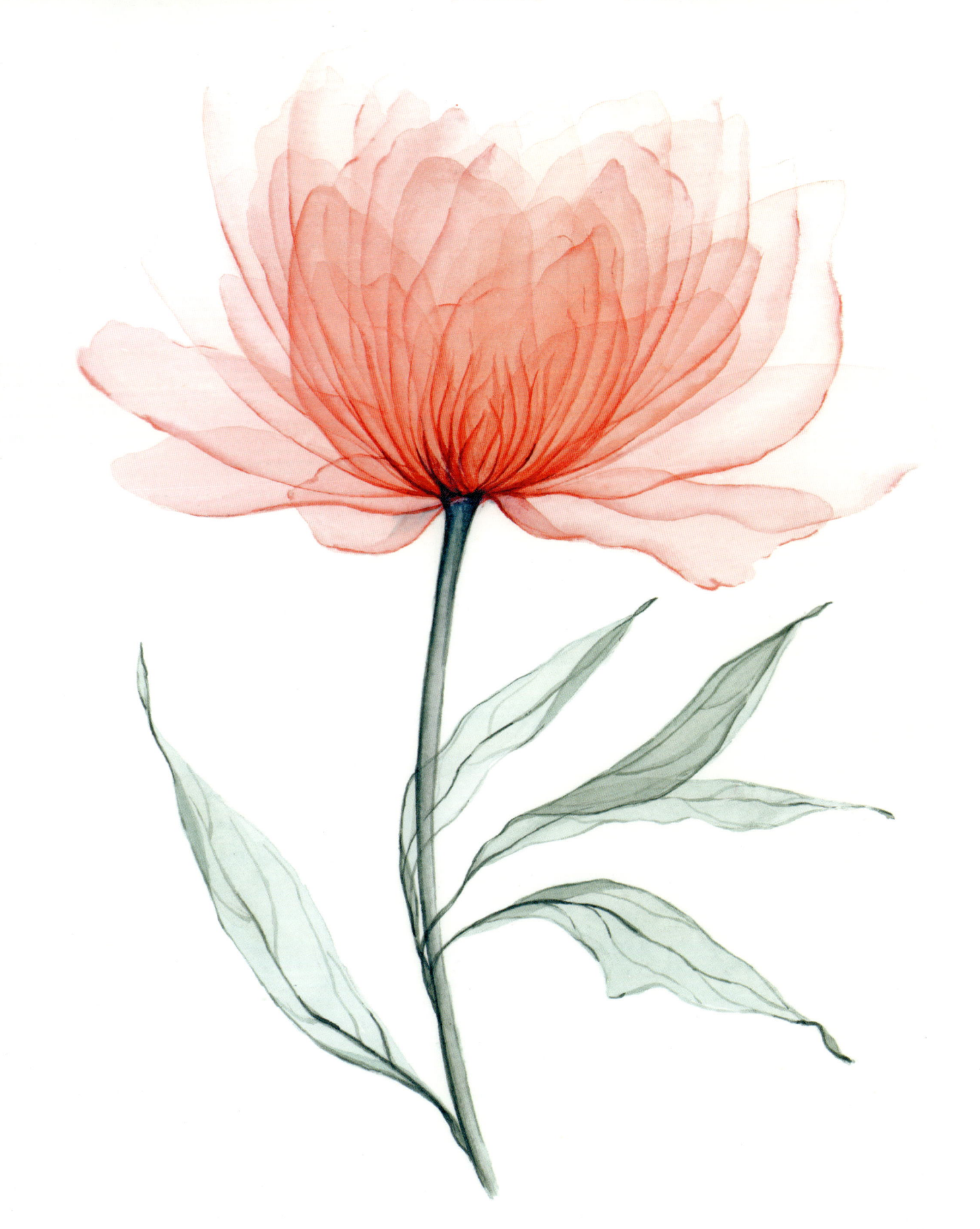

Basic mixes

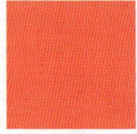

DARK PINK

Quinacridone Rose and Cadmium Orange

MEDIUM YELLOW PINK

As detailed above, but more diluted and with slightly more Cadmium Orange

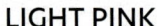

LIGHT PINK

As the Dark Pink mix, but very diluted

DARK GREEN

Phthalo Green, Ultramarine Blue and a hint of Burnt Sienna

LIGHT GREEN

As detailed above, but very diluted

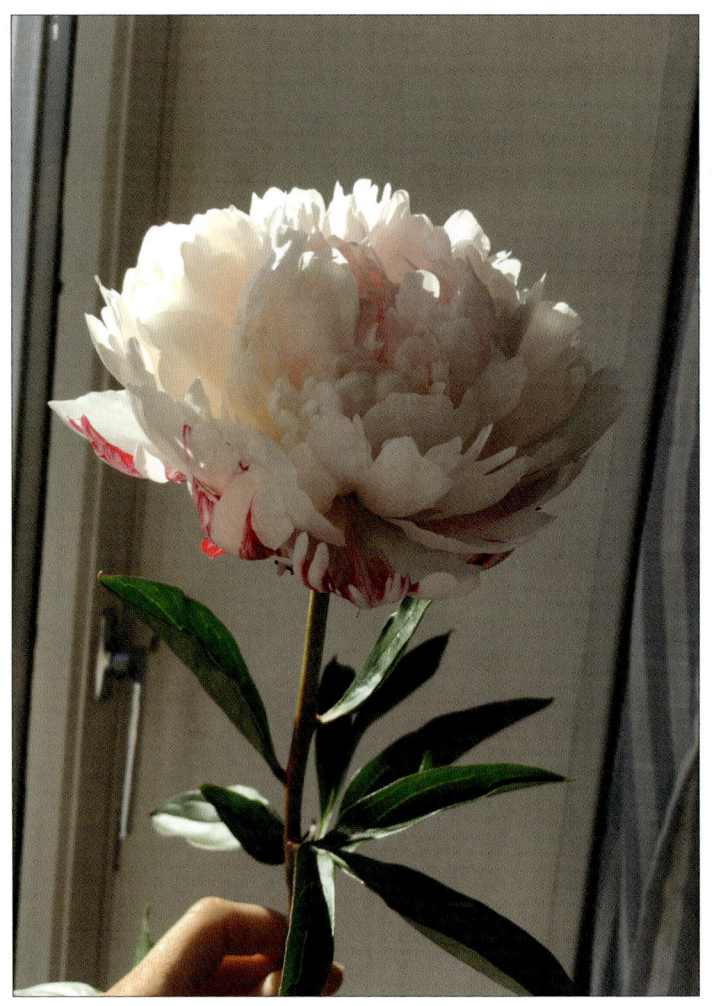

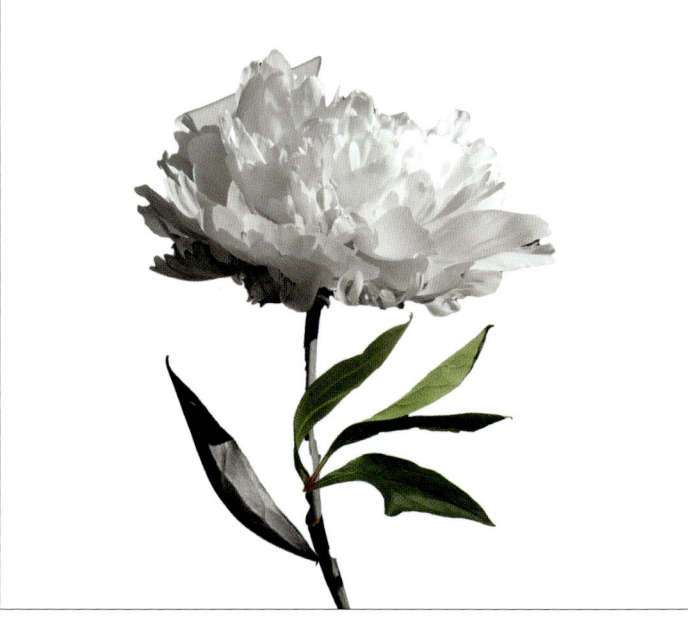

Reference photographs

I took a picture of one peony from my birthday bouquet against a white wall (see left). The bloom, with dozens of petals, looked complex enough, so I removed a number of leaves to make the whole flower's appearance lighter. I added more movement to the petals, stem and the leaves, to suggest a light breeze blowing from the left side. To stay focused on the petals' shapes, I turned my reference black-and-white.

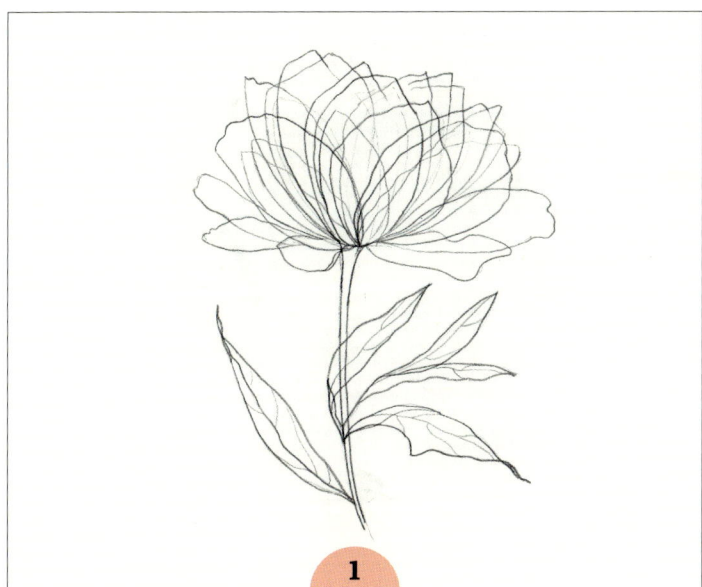

Drawing the flower. Using the outline on page 126 or the references shown opposite, draw the peony. If you are using the photo references, it's better not to draw all the petals; otherwise, the sketch will be too messy and it'll be hard to distinguish the different petals. Focus on the basic flower structure and on the most dominant petals. Remember: you can draw in more petals later. Once you are happy with the drawing, rub back the lines with a putty eraser, leaving a faint outline.

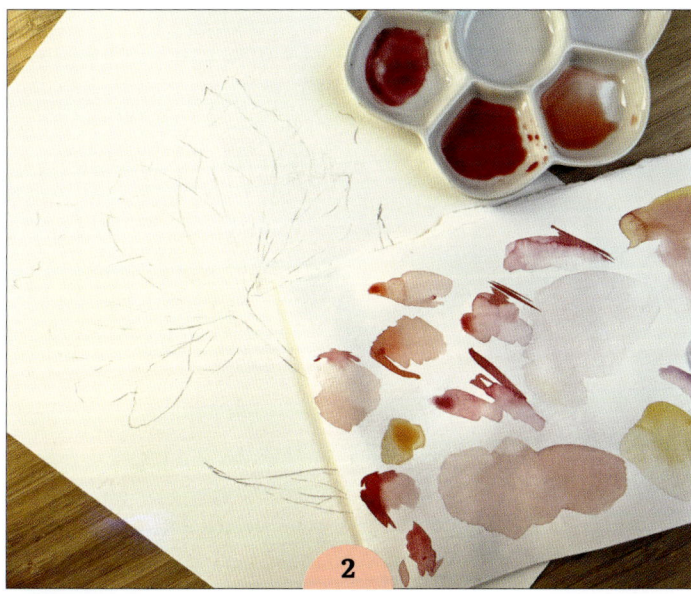

Mixing the paints. Make up the three pink mixes, referring to the swatches and their details opposite. Start with the dark pink mix then, once you are happy with the colour, take a drop of it, place it in a separate well in the palette and dilute it with a large amount of water to create the lighter mix.

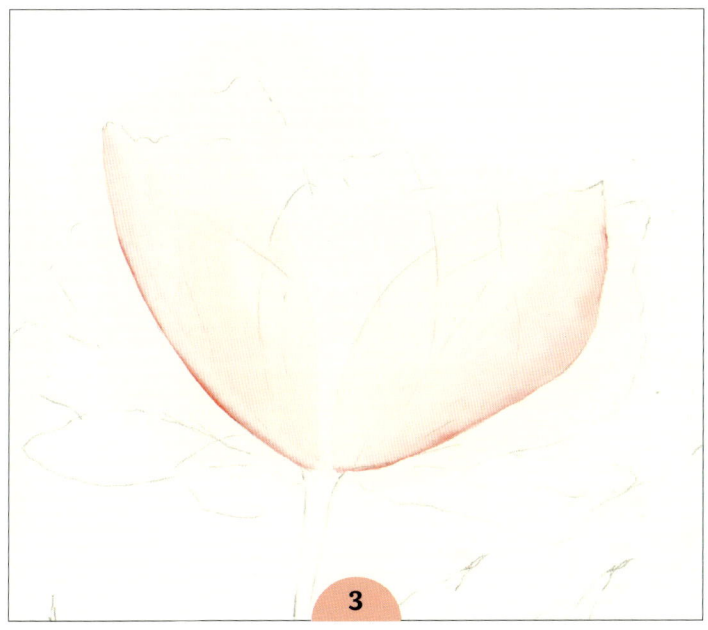

The back petals. These are the outer layer of petals, and the largest ones. With the no. 6 brush, start by wetting the back petals with clean water then glaze in the light pink mix. Distribute the mix evenly on the paper, working from the outer edges inwards, and make sure there are no puddles. Run a little of the medium pink mix along only the outside edges of the petals, using the same brush. While the glaze is still wet, change to the no. 4 brush then, using only the tip of the brush, run the dark pink mix along only the outside edges of the petals. Soften the dark colour with a clean, damp brush. Let these petals dry completely before moving on to the next stage.

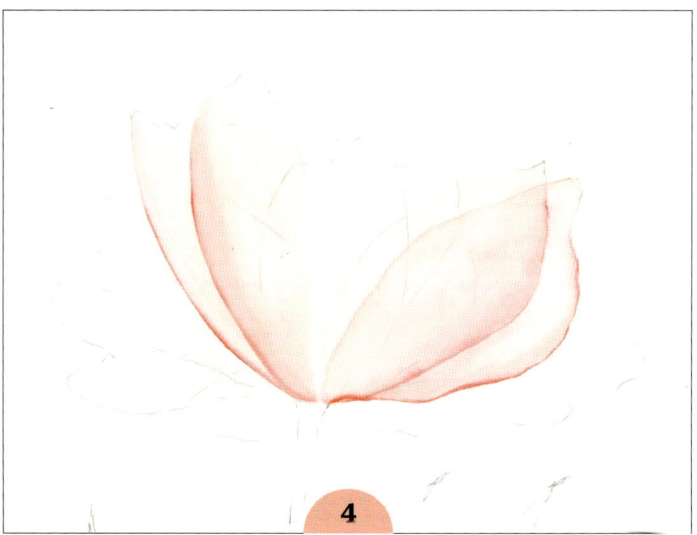

4

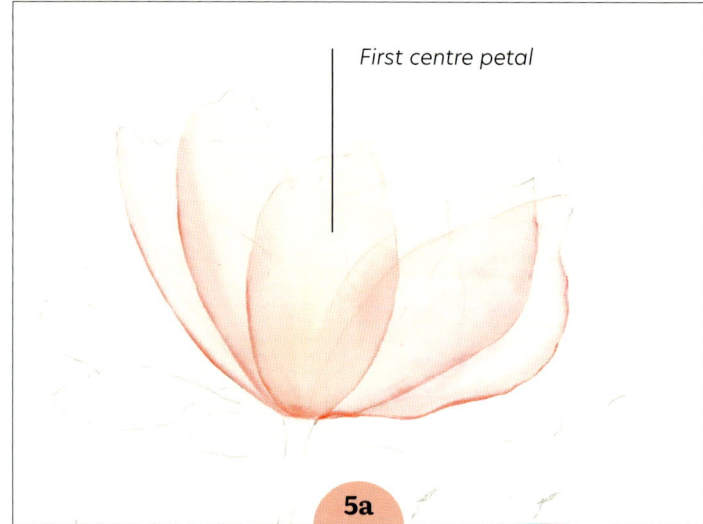

First centre petal

5a

4 The next petals. Paint the next pair of petals in the same way, making sure the inner edges don't overlap in the middle area of the flower. Leave to dry.

5 Adding the centre petals. Paint the sketched central petals in the same way as before, making sure the painting is dry completely before adding the next set of petals. This ensures the different petals don't 'bleed' into each other, and have distinct edges. Remember to add stronger outlines to the edge of the petal that's the farthest away from the centre of flower.

6 Adding more petals. Add another pair of petals either side of the very first set of petals you painted, painting them in exactly the same way as before. To add warmth to the painting, you can create a warm gradient effect by touching in the medium yellow pink mix at the base of a few of the middle petals.

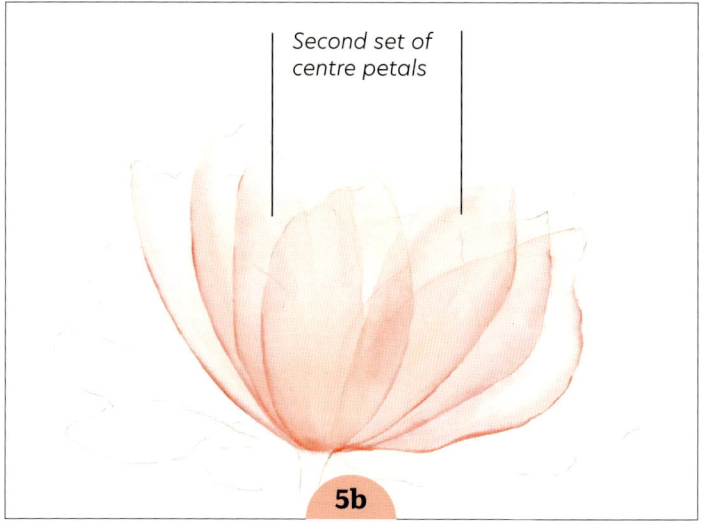

Second set of centre petals

5b

Tip

The reason why we paint only the outer edge of each petal with a darker mix is that this helps suggest the volume delicate quality of petals in a peony, and adds depth and dimension too.

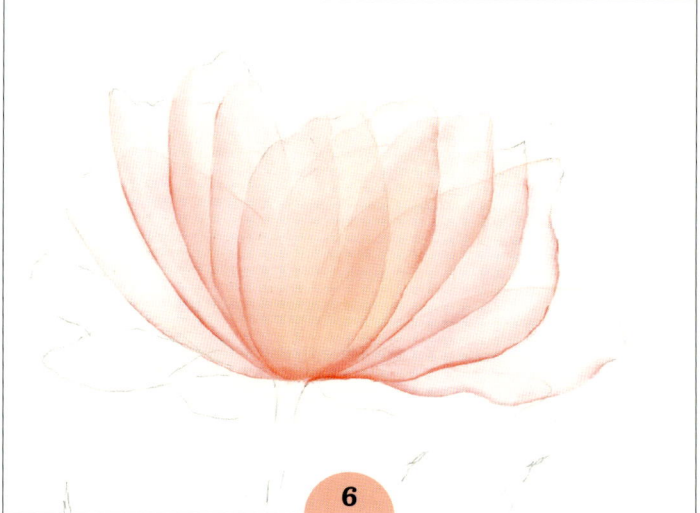

6

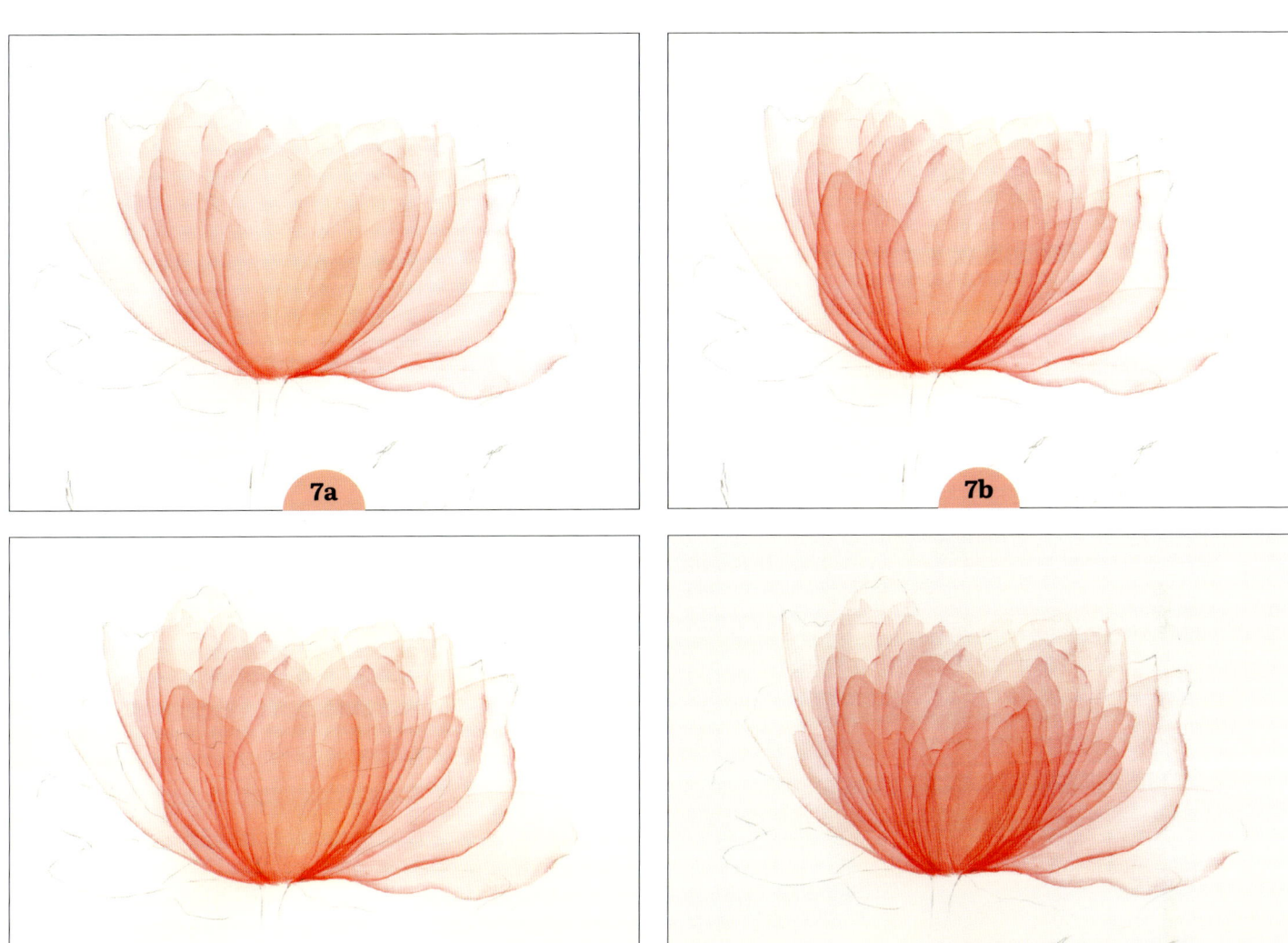

7 Middle layer of petals. Paint the next group of petals located in the middle of the flower in the same way before, painting one petal at a time. Each petal should be slightly shorter than the previous one, as this creates volume. It's crucial to let every petal dry thoroughly before proceeding to the next one, so that each petal has a distinguished outline. To speed up the process, I used a hairdryer. You'll notice in **7c** that I drew in the next group of petals that were then painted in **7d**; I recommend doing this, to help you stay organized and ensure you don't get lost in all the lines.

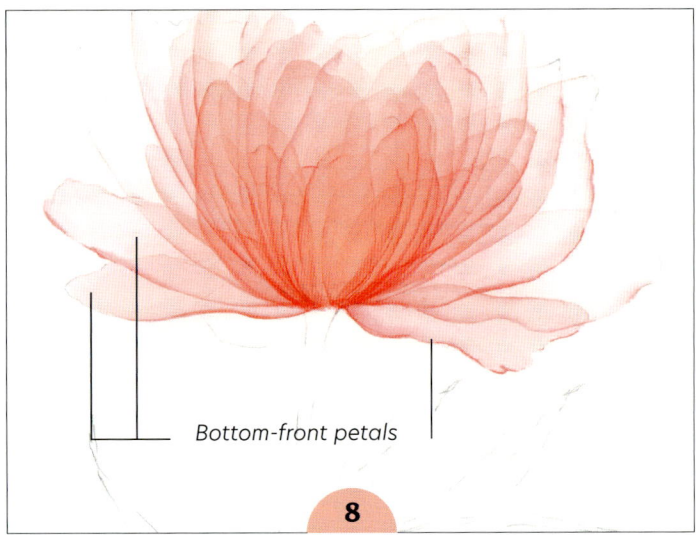

Bottom-front petals

8

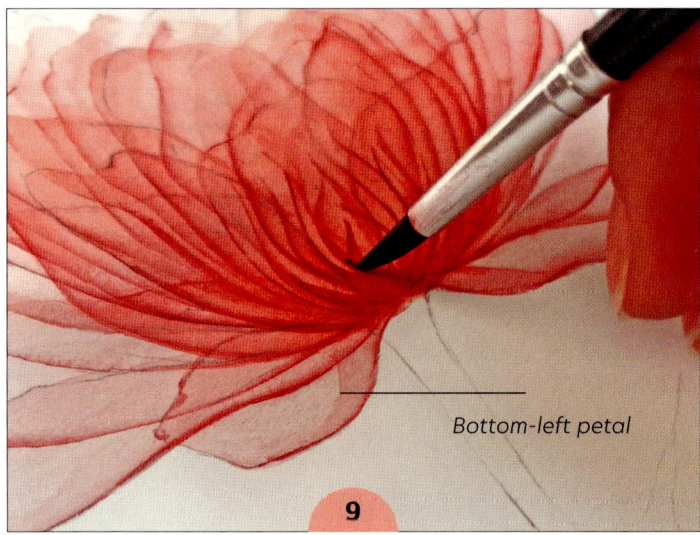

Bottom-left petal

9

Bottom-front petals. Paint in these lower petals in pairs as before, starting from the petals closest to the centre of the flower then working outwards. Again, make sure to allow each set of petals to dry completely before continuing to paint the next pair.

Inner petals. To imitate the look of a peony's tiny inner petals, paint C-shaped strokes in the middle of the flower using the tip of a no. 4 brush and the dark pink mix. Soften the edges from the inner side with a clean, damp brush. To finish the main flower, paint in the small bottom-left petal in the same way as before – a glaze of light pink, followed by outlines in the medium pink then dark pink. Note that, as this petal is more in the foreground, to suggest its more front-facing perspective I've outlined both sides of the petal.

10

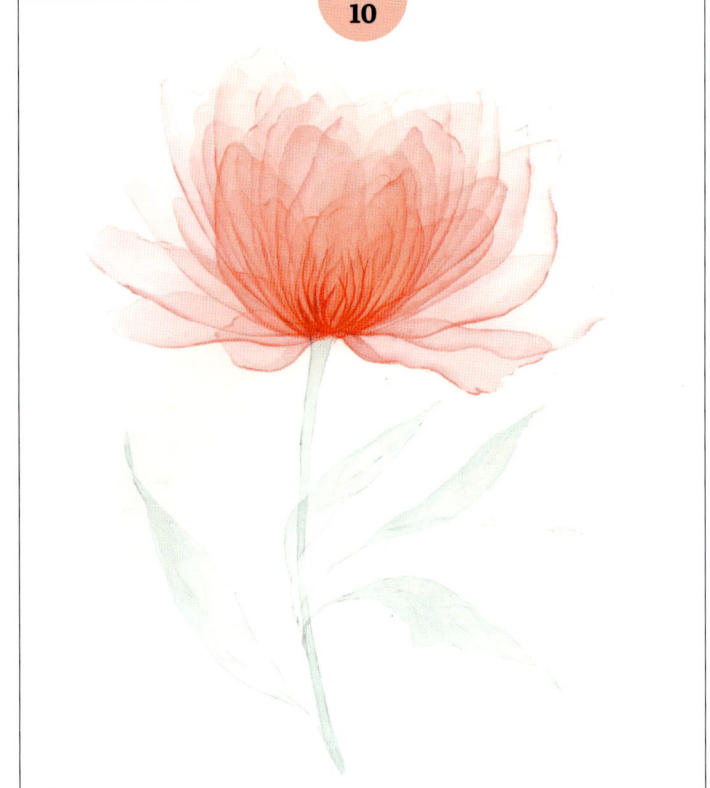

Stem and leaves. Make up the two green mixes, referring to the swatches and their details on page 96. As with the pink mixes, prepare the dark mix first then use this to create the light green mix. Using the no. 4 brush, wet the stem with clean water then glaze in the light green mix along the stem only. Leave to dry completely. Wet the first layer of leaves with clean water then glaze in the light green mix, using the same brush. Again, leave the painting to dry completely.

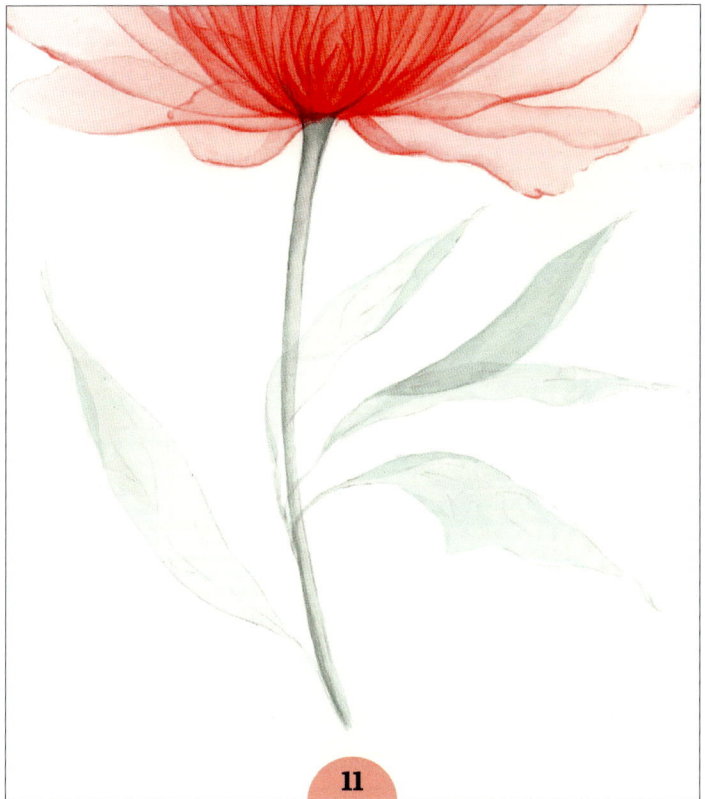

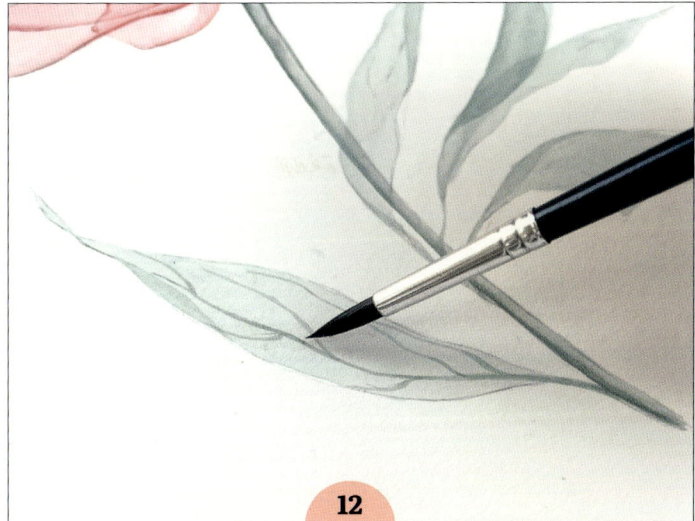

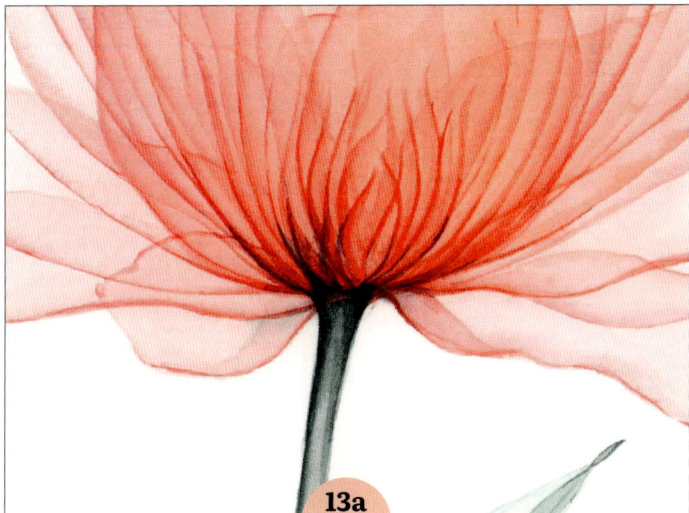

11 Stem and leaves: details. To suggest some of the leaves are folded over, and using the sketched lines established in step 1 as a guide, paint in the folded areas of the leaves with the light green mix and no. 4 brush. Using only the tip of the same brush and the dark green mix, outline both sides of the stem and where the flower connects to the stem. Soften the edges with a clean, damp brush.

12 Stem and leaves: details continued. With the tip of the no. 4 brush, paint veins inside the leaves with the light green mix.

13 Final details. With the dark green mix and no. 4 brush, add dark outlines to some of the inner petals where they meet the stem (**13a**), and to the edges of the leaves and where they branch off the stem (**13b**). These add more contrast and complexity to the painting, and draw the viewer's eye to the intricate greenery.

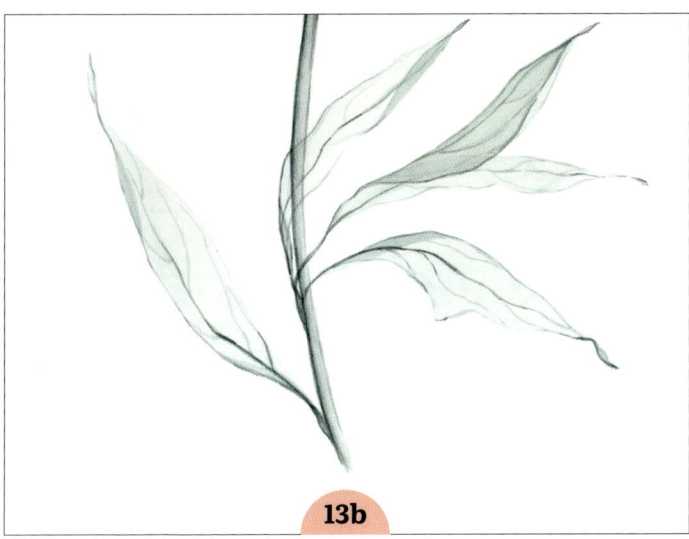

Peony *Gallery*

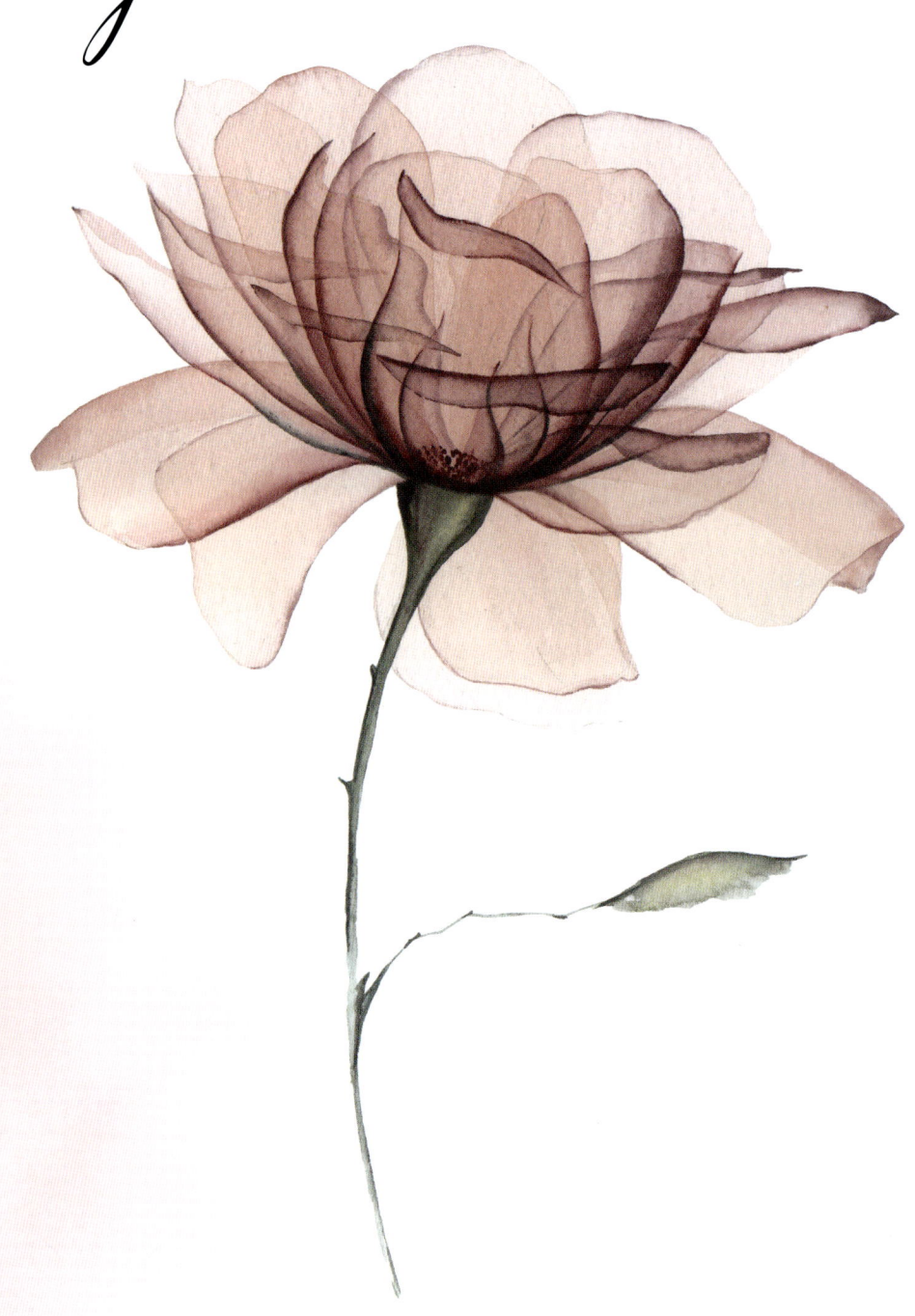

Right

'Dusty Pink Rose'

22 x 30cm (8½ x 12in)

Paint: *Madder Lake Deep, Phthalo Green, Burnt Sienna.*

You can use the same technique for painting the peony to paint multi-petalled flowers like roses. The flowers on this page are a good example of how different a pink colour can look depending on whether it is warm and muted (as it is here) or cold and vibrant (as seen opposite).

Opposite

'Tender Peony'

28 x 36cm (11 x 14¼in)

Paint: *Quinacridone Rose, Payne's Gray, Sepia.*

I used the same technique as in the project but used only Quinacridone Rose for the petals, without including an extra hue.

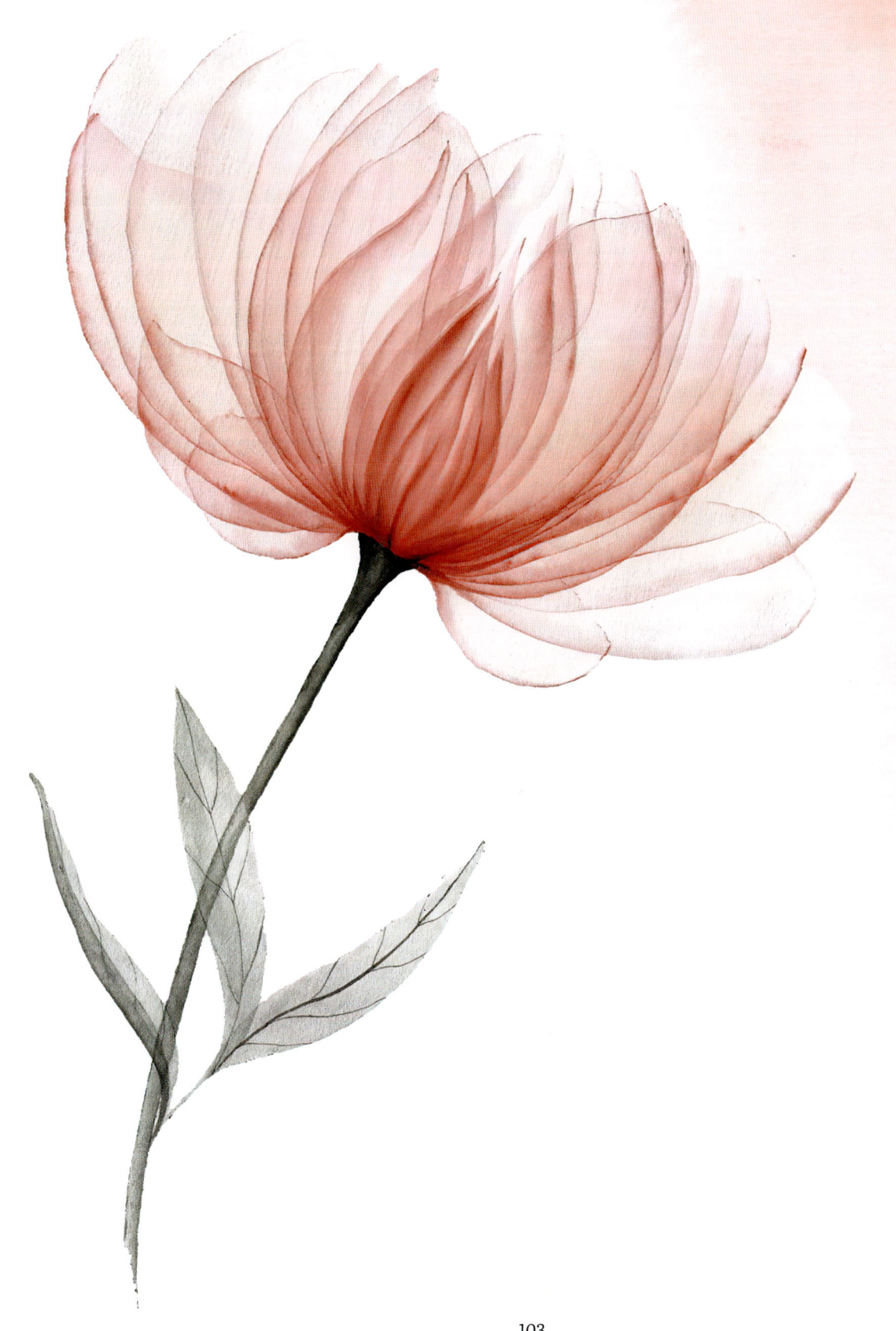

Project Six:

Rose

With the previous flower, we were able to count petals and visualize their inner structure. How should we paint flowers with dozens of petals, like a rose? If we aim to create a lifelike representation in the transparent technique, it would be too complex. That's why, for this painting, we are going to portray fewer petals and simplify the structure of the flower.

There are several different ways to portray roses with the transparent technique. The process for creating the rose is the same as it was for the peony – we will start with the back petals and, layer by layer, move towards the front ones.

You will need

WATERCOLOUR PAINTS:

Madder Lake Deep, Burnt Sienna, Phthalo Green

MATERIALS AND TOOLS:

22 x 30cm (8½ x 12in) sheet of hot-pressed paper; sharp (or mechanical) HB pencil; putty eraser and soft white eraser; kitchen paper or cloth; no. 4 and no. 6 round synthetic brushes with very fine tips; no. 10 sable brush

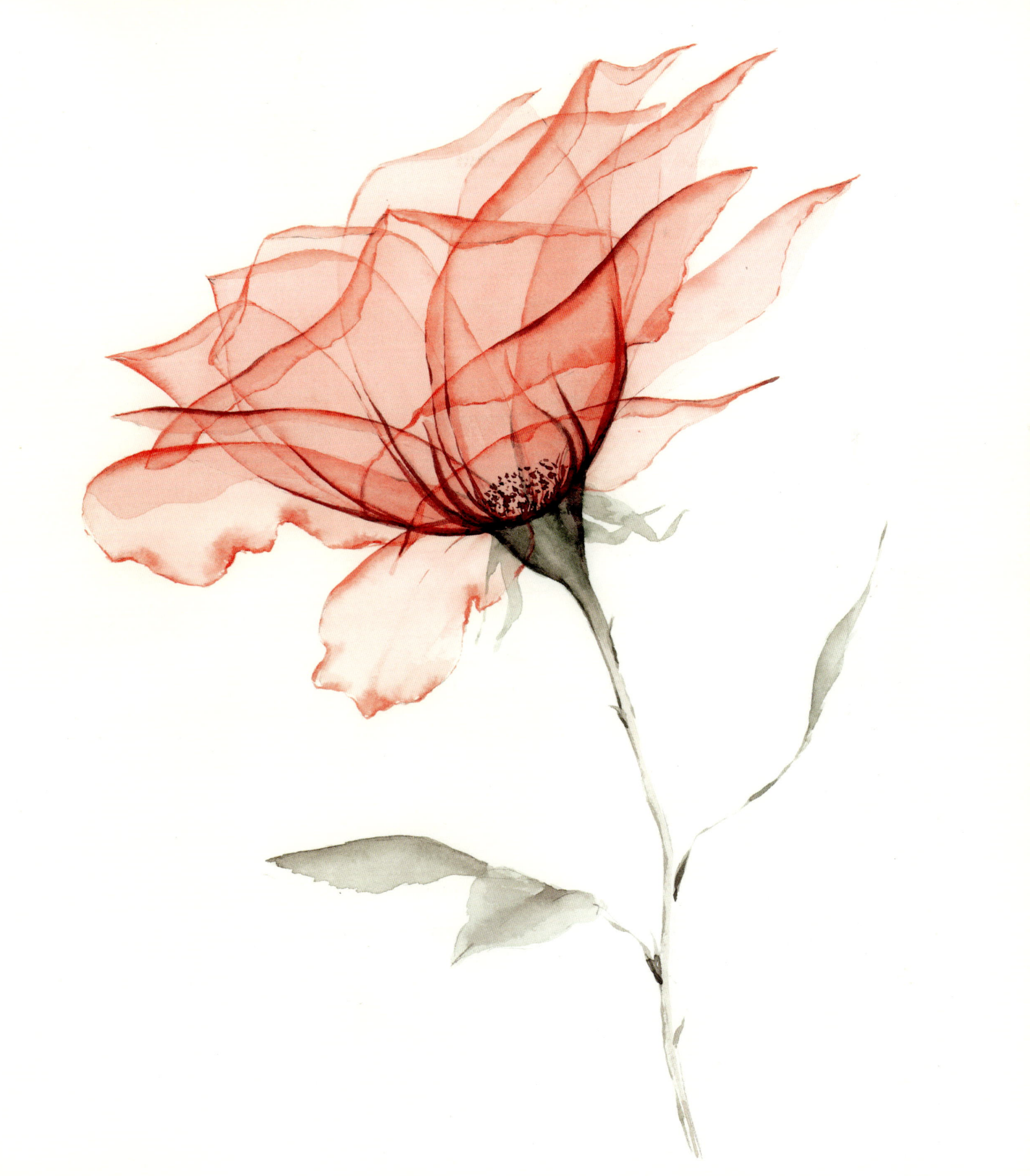

Basic mixes

DARK RED
Madder Lake Deep with
a hint of Burnt Sienna

DARK WARM GREEN
Phthalo Green with a hint
of Madder Lake Deep
and Burnt Sienna

RED-BROWN
Madder Lake Deep with
Phthalo Green and a hint
of Burnt Sienna

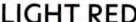

LIGHT RED
As detailed above,
but very diluted

LIGHT WARM GREEN
As detailed above,
but very diluted

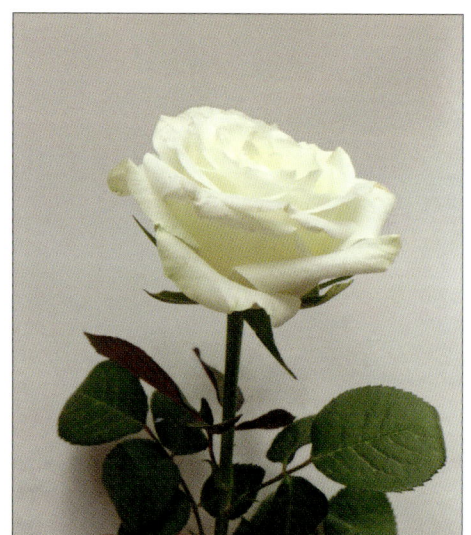

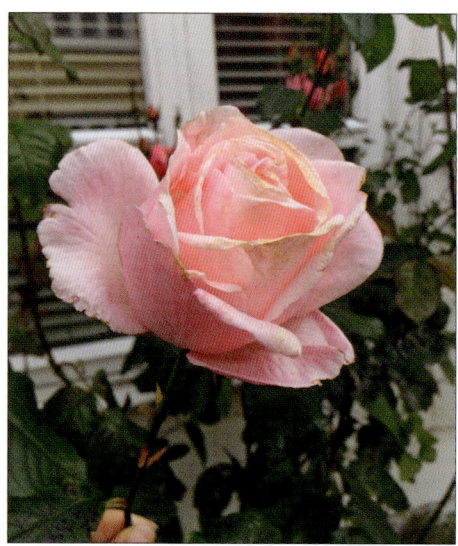

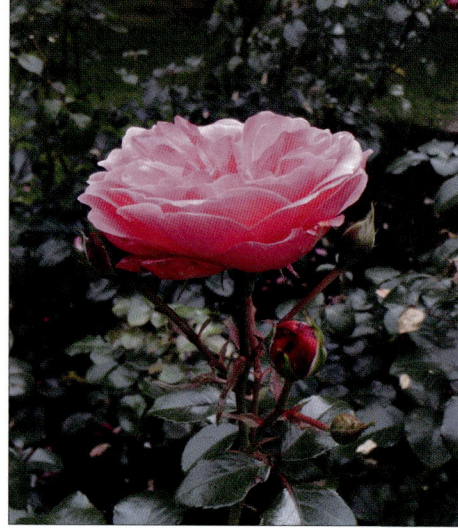

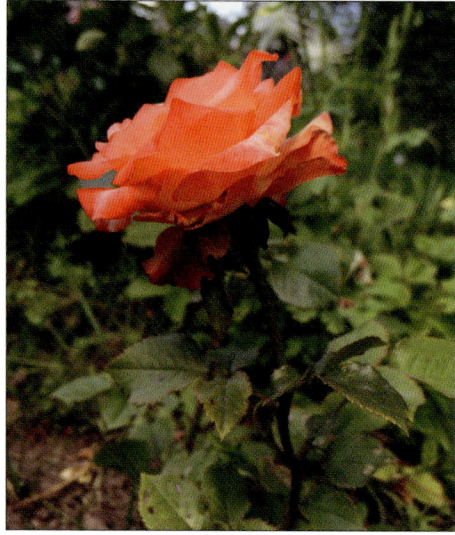

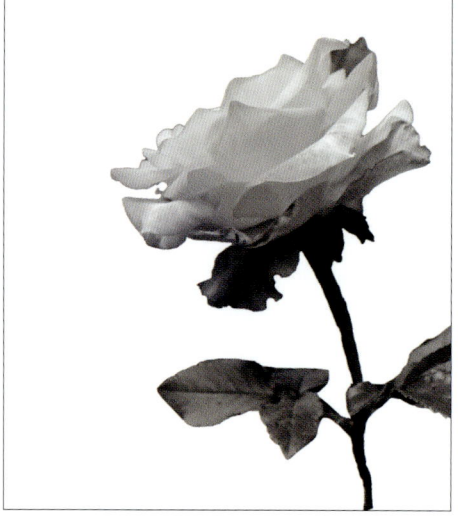

Reference photographs

*Observing roses can be incredibly
inspiring. There are so many different
variations (see the examples above)
that sometimes it is difficult to choose
a flower for reference. I chose this
particular rose for its delicate, folded,
overlapping petals. These features make
it an excellent reference for a transparent
painting technique, as they add
captivating intricacy to the artwork.
Turning the reference image black-and-
white helps identify the value contrasts.*

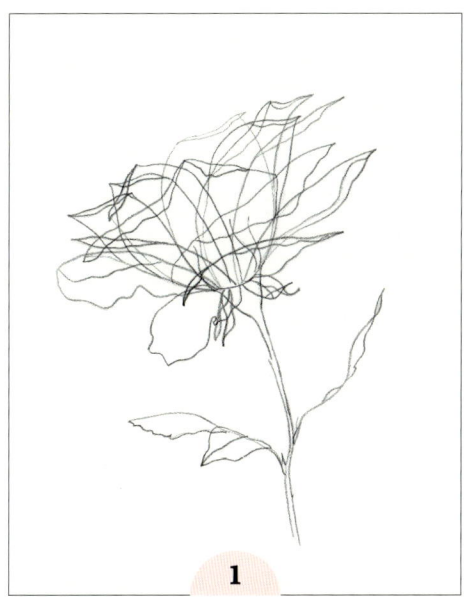

1

Drawing the flower. Using the outline on page 127 or the photo references opposite, draw the rose. If you are using the photo references, know that it's not necessary to draw all the petals; I've just drawn in a few key petals to capture the overall shape of the flower. Note that I've made the stem of the rose thinner than the one in the reference image; drawing a thinner stem adds more delicacy and fragility to the flower.

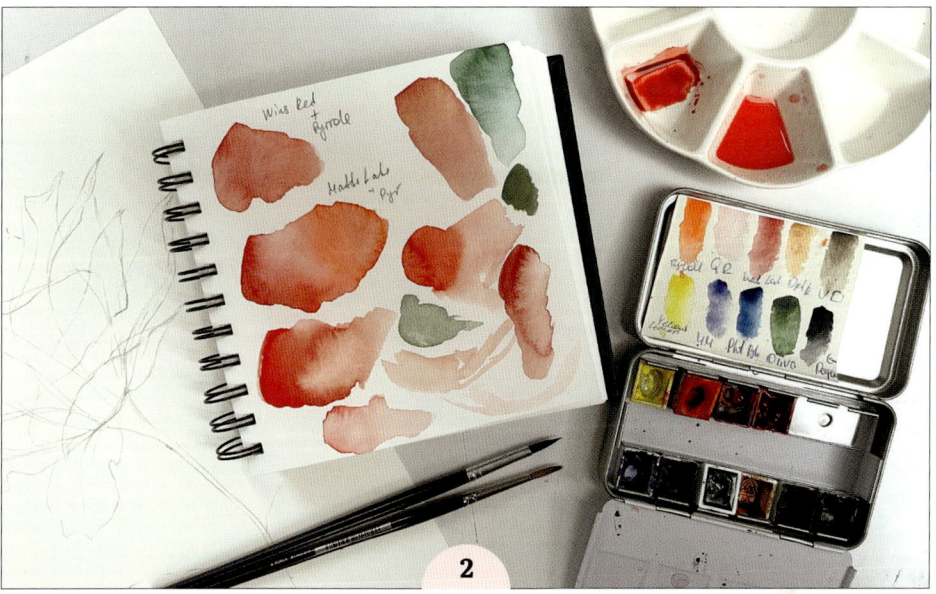

2

Softening the outline and mixing the paints. Once you are happy with the drawing, rub back the lines with a putty eraser, leaving a faint outline. Make up the dark red and light red mixes, referring to the swatches and their details opposite. Start with the dark red mix then, once you are happy with the colour, take a drop of the mixture, place it in a separate well in the palette then dilute it with a large amount of water to create the lighter mix.

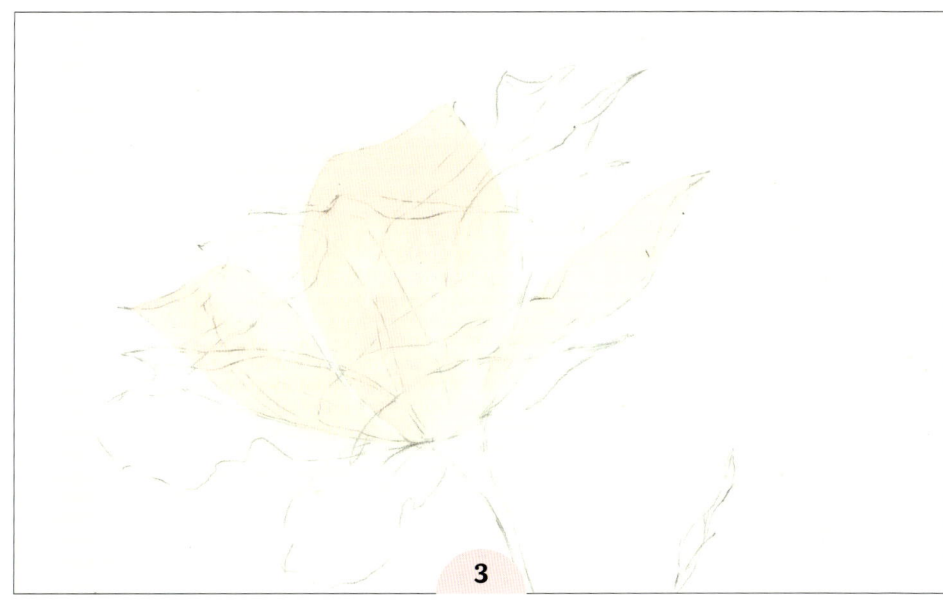

3

The back petals. Using the no. 6 brush and light red mix, glaze the very back outer petals of the rose. Work from top to bottom, distributing the mix evenly on the paper and making sure there are no puddles. Make sure these petals don't overlap each other in the middle of the flower. Leave the painting to dry completely.

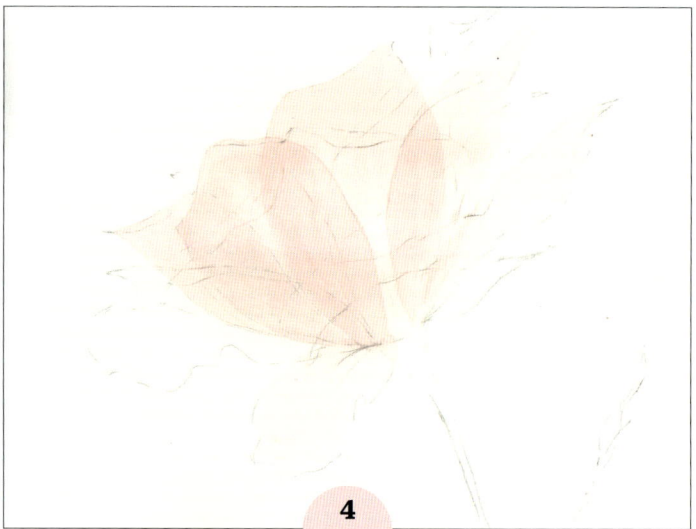

4

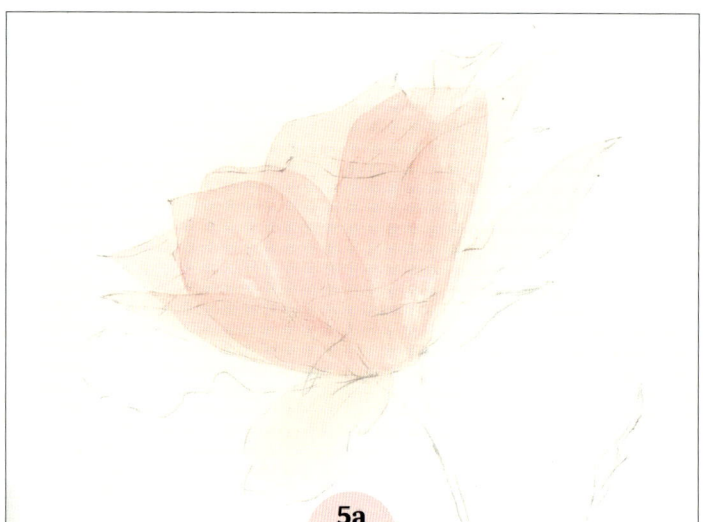

5a

4 Adding more petals. You'll now be working from these back petals towards the front of the rose. Paint the next pair of petals around the middle of the rose the same way as before; these petals will overlap your back petals. Paint in the bottom-left petal also. Leave to painting to dry thoroughly, as before.

5 Adding more petals continued. Paint the back side petals in the same way before, moving from the back towards the front, making sure each set of petals you add don't overlap each other, and letting the painting dry completely after every addition to stop the paints bleeding into each other (**5a**). To speed up this process, you could use a hairdryer. Glaze the folded-over section of the centre-right petal to finish this stage (**5b**).

6 Adding more petals: large front petal. Glaze the large front petal area with the light red mix and the no. 10 sable brush. Make sure that the water is applied evenly on the paper with no puddles. While the glaze is still wet and using the tip of the no. 4 round brush, run the darker red mix along the edges. Soften the dark colour with a clean, damp brush. Leave to dry completely.

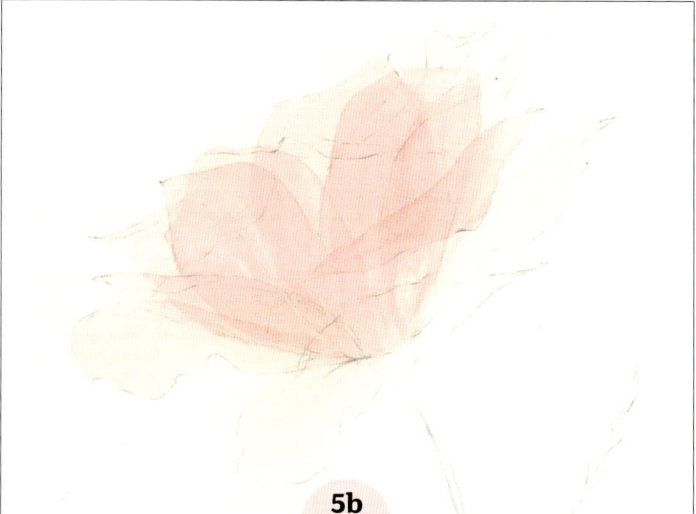

5b

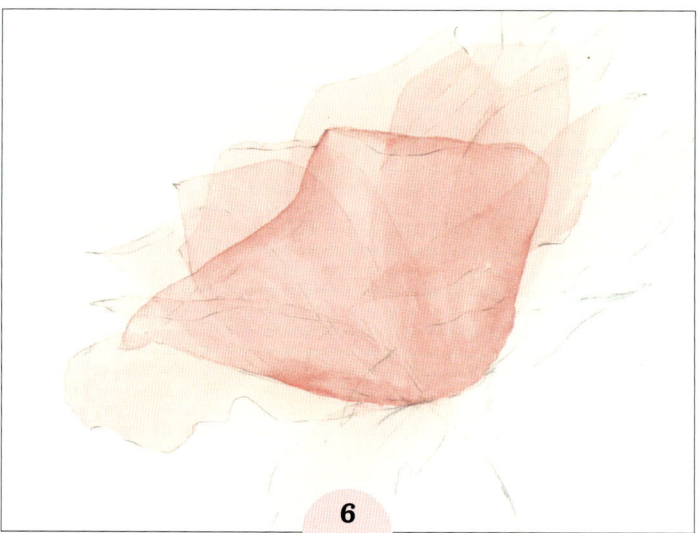

6

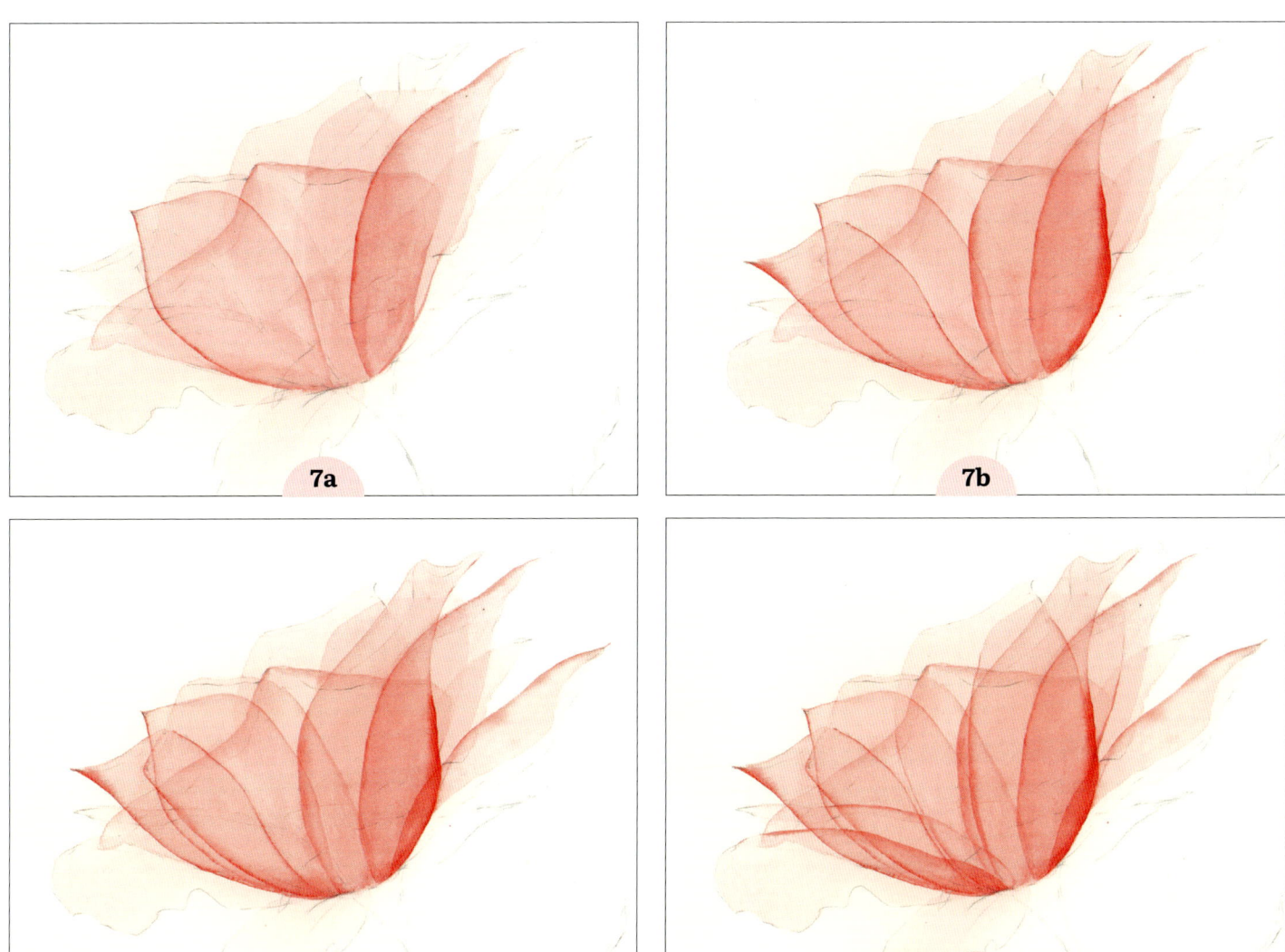

7 **Adding more petals: front petals continued.** Glaze a few more front petals in the same way as described in step 6. With each of these new petals run the dark red mix along the edges, gradually increasing the intensity of colour towards the bottom of the bloom. Note that the petals closer to the centre of the flower have the dark red mix around the most of their edges; the petals that are farther out have the mix only along the top edge. Before starting a new petal, make sure that the previous layer is completely dry.

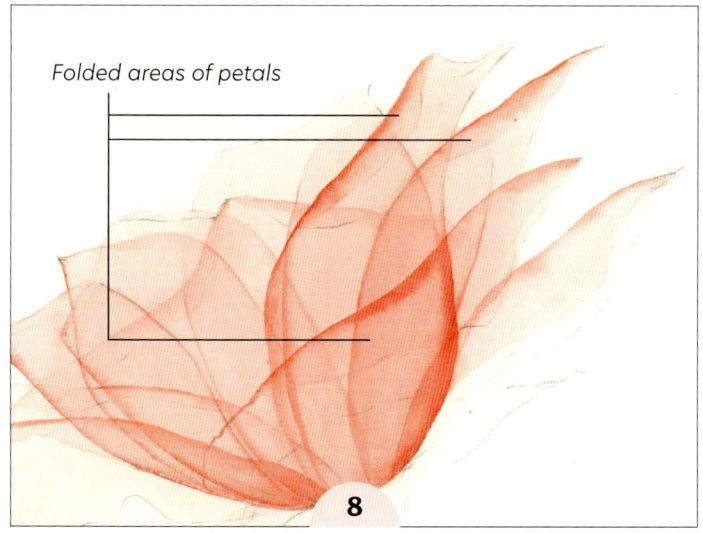

Folded areas of petals

8

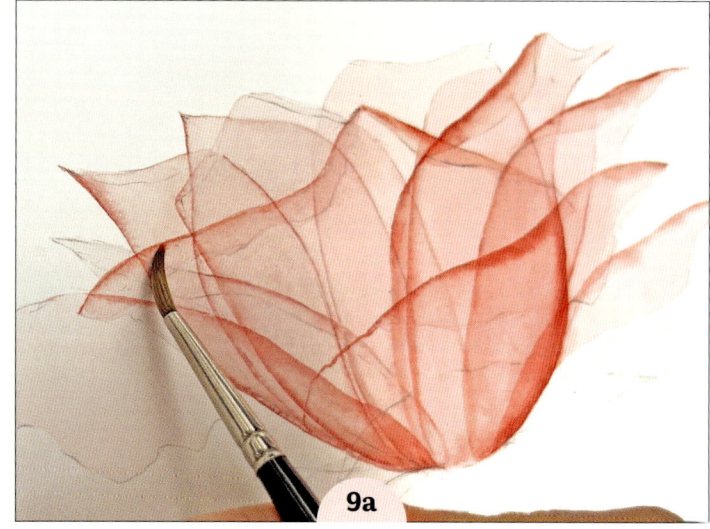

9a

8 Folded-over front petals. Glaze the folded areas with the light red mix using the no. 4 brush. While the paper is still wet, apply the darker red mix along the top of the folded edge then soften the colour with a clean, damp brush. Leave to dry completely.

9 Remaining folded-over petals. Repeat the process with the large front petal (**9a**) then the petals on the left-hand side of the rose (**9b**). Leave to dry completely.

10 Bottom petal. Glaze the bottom petal with the light red mix and no. 6 brush. While the glaze is still wet, and using the tip of the no. 4 brush, run the dark red mix around some of the edges. To suggest folds and a slightly wavy edge around the petal, add drops of the dark red mix in some areas. Soften the dark colour with a clean, damp brush. Leave to dry completely.

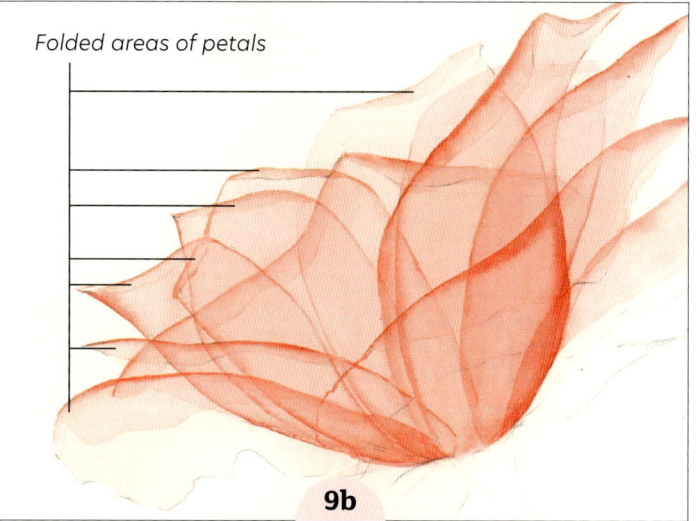

Folded areas of petals

9b

Tip

It is important to portray the way the petals fold over – even along the 'invisible' parts – as this adds to the transparent look of the rose.

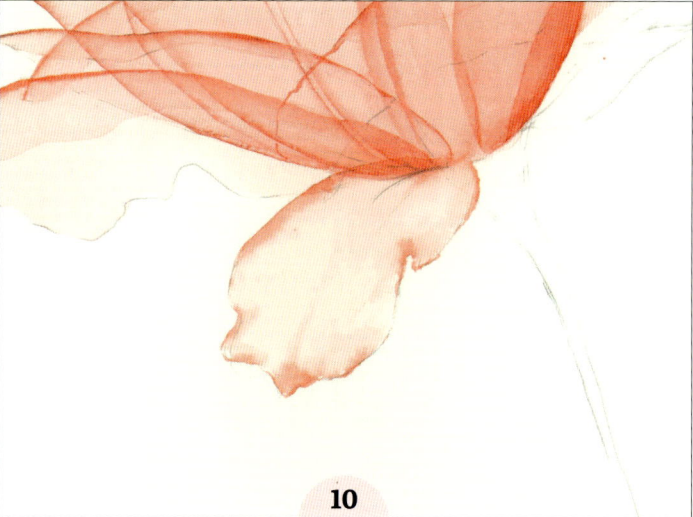

10

110

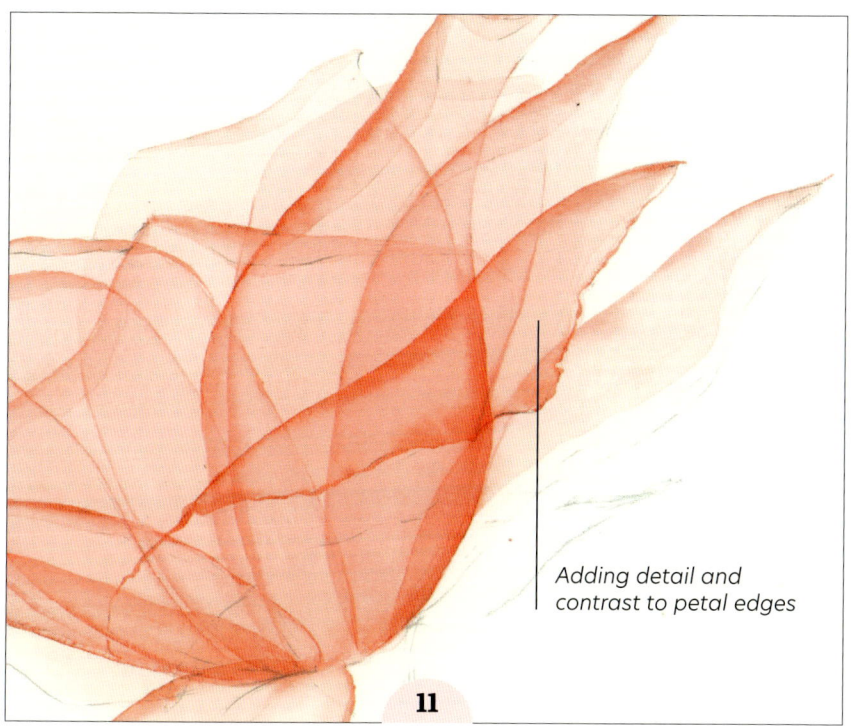

Adding detail and contrast to petal edges

11

11 Finishing the folded edges. Glaze the bent edge of a front petal with water. Make sure that the water is applied evenly on the paper with no puddles. While the glaze is still wet, and using the tip of the no. 4 brush, run the dark red mix around the edges of the petal. Vary pressure on the brush to create a wavy artistic line. Once you're happy with the look of the darker colour, soften it with a clean, damp brush. Leave to dry completely.

Tip

Glazing the petal with only clean water, then adding the dark mix around the edges, keeps the petals light and transparent.

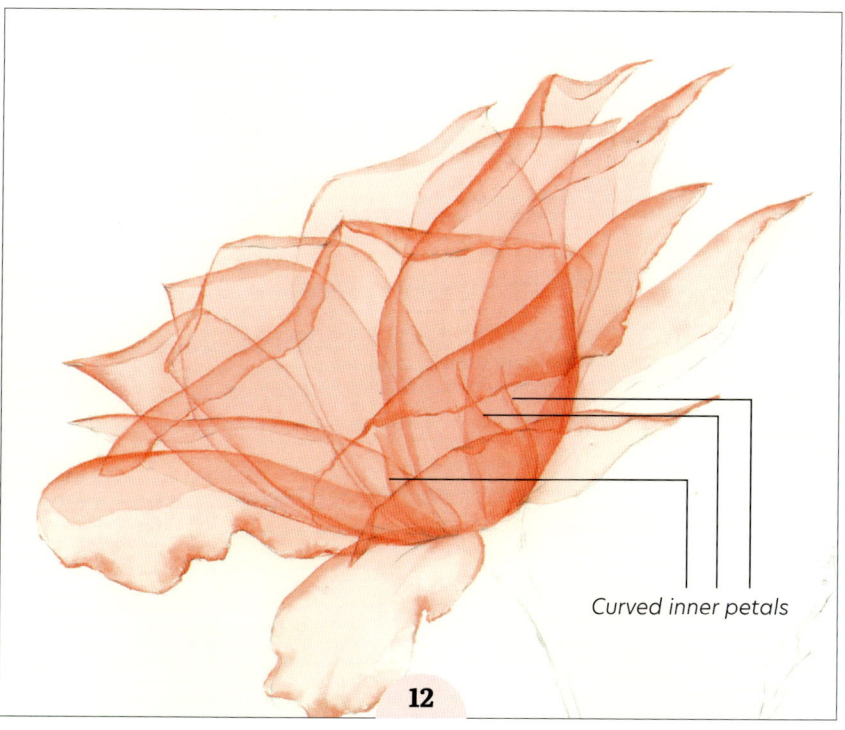

Curved inner petals

12

12 The remaining petals. Use the same techniques described in steps 10 or 11 to add details, contrast and texture to the remaining petals in the rose, switching to one or the other depending on the petal. Work from the bottom up, and make sure to leave the painting to dry completely before moving on to the next petal. To speed up this stage, I used a hairdryer to dry every completed petal. To finish, with the tip of the no. 4 brush and using the dark red mix, paint small C-shaped and backwards C-shaped petals at the base of the rose. These imitate small inner petals. Soften the dark colour with a clean, damp brush, working just inside the folded area.

13 Stem and leaves. Make up the two green mixes, referring to the swatches and their details on page 106. As with the red mixes, start with the darker mix then use this to create the lighter mix. Because I wanted the bloom to be the focal point, I purposefully painted the stem and leaves in a very loose and simple way. Begin to paint your stem by running the light green mix along its length with the no. 6 brush, starting from the receptacle and working downwards. While the paper is still wet and using the tip of the no. 4 brush, run the dark green mix along the edges of the main stem and the leaf stems.

14 Stem and leaves continued. Using the no. 6 brush and the light green mix, paint the leaves. Start with the very left leaf, move to the far right leaf, then finish with the centre-left leaf. Painting the edges with a gentle flicking motion creates the sharp-toothed shape of rose leaves. While the glaze is still wet, add shadows with the same brush and the dark green mix. Note that the shadow in the centre-left leaf starts from the centre top then trails down towards the bottom tip of the leaf; this suggests the slight bend in the leaf, along the centre. Switch to the no. 4 brush then, using only the tip of the brush and the dark green mix once more, paint a few thorns on the stem.

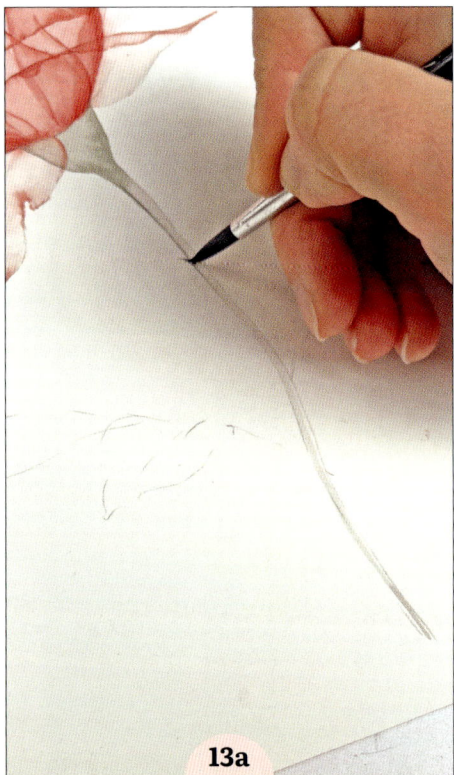

13a

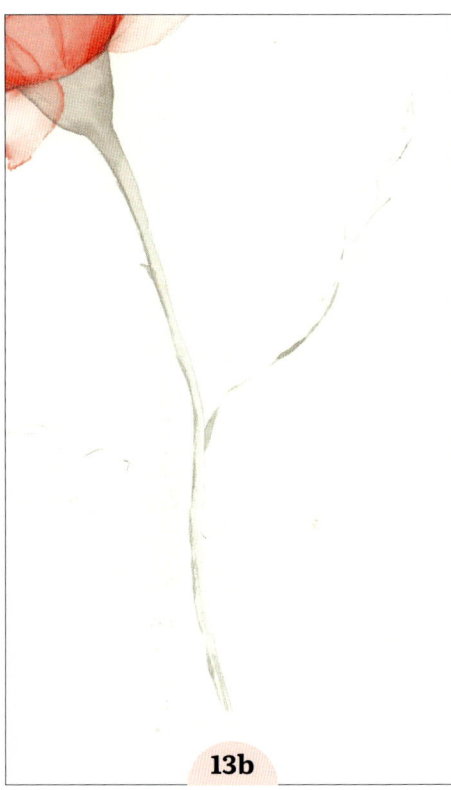

13b

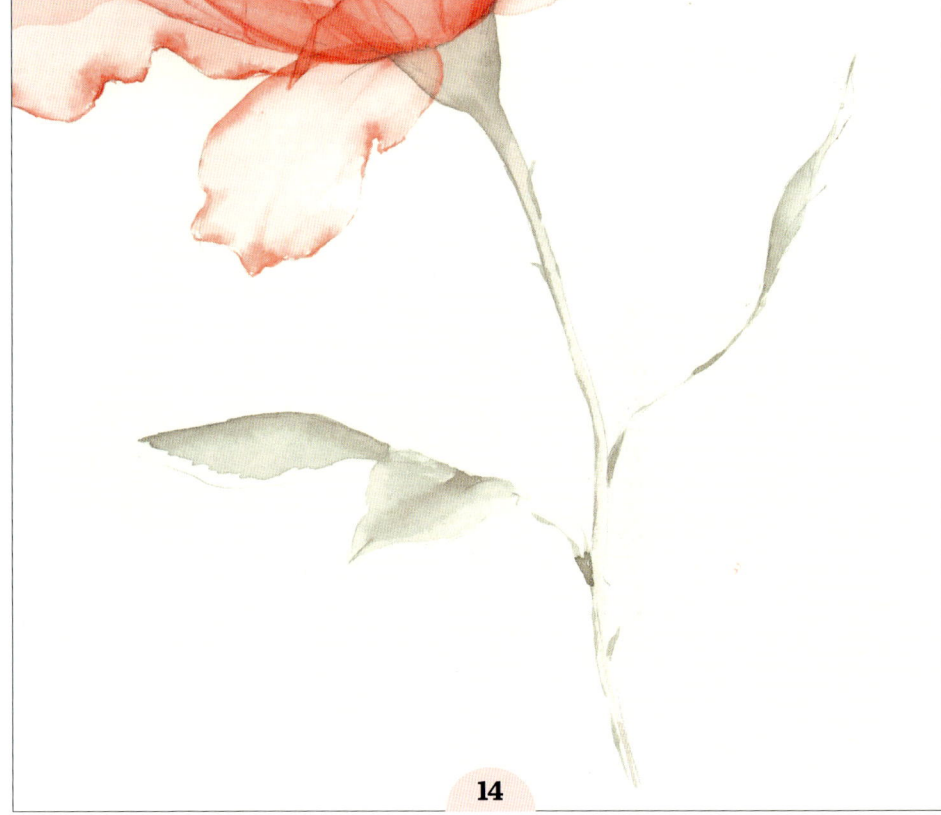

14

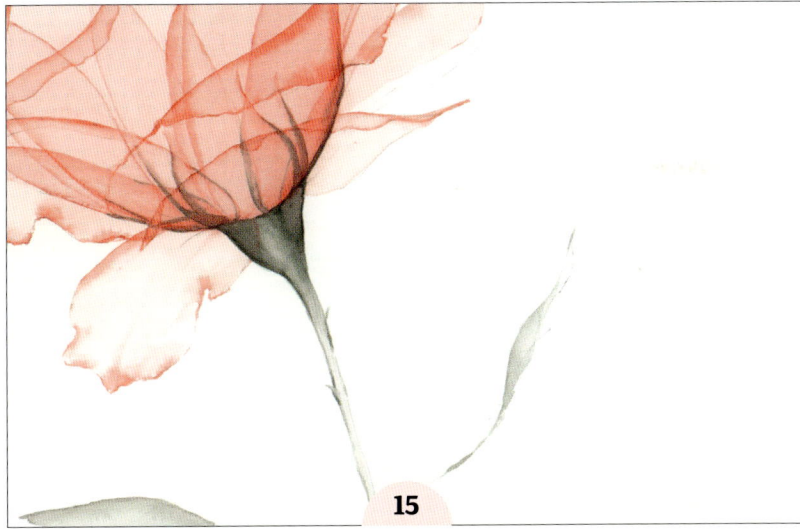

15 **Flower centre and receptacle.** With the tip of the no. 4 brush, run the dark green mix along both sides of the receptacle, working from the top downwards. Soften the edges with a clean, damp brush. With the same brush, apply the dark green mix to the edges of the small inner petals, working from the top downwards and increasing the pressure on the brush while moving to the bottom of the flower.

16 **Shading and stamens.** Create a red-brown colour, referring to the swatch and details on page 106. With this mix and the tip of the damp no. 4 brush, strengthen the top and bottom edges of the front petals as well as the small inner petals. Use the tip of the brush to dot in some of the red-brown mix around the base of the flower to emulate the stamens.

17 **Leaf-like shapes (sepals).** To finish, and with the no. 6 brush and light green mix paint the small sepals under the bud, working from the base of the bud downwards.

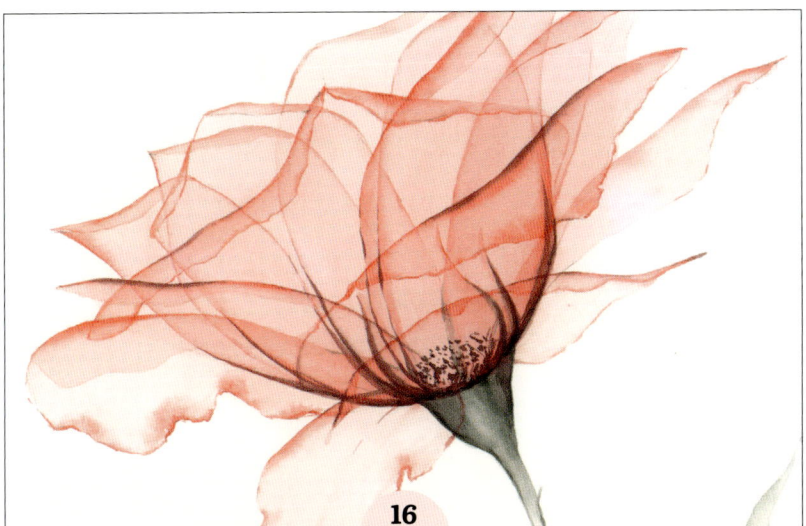

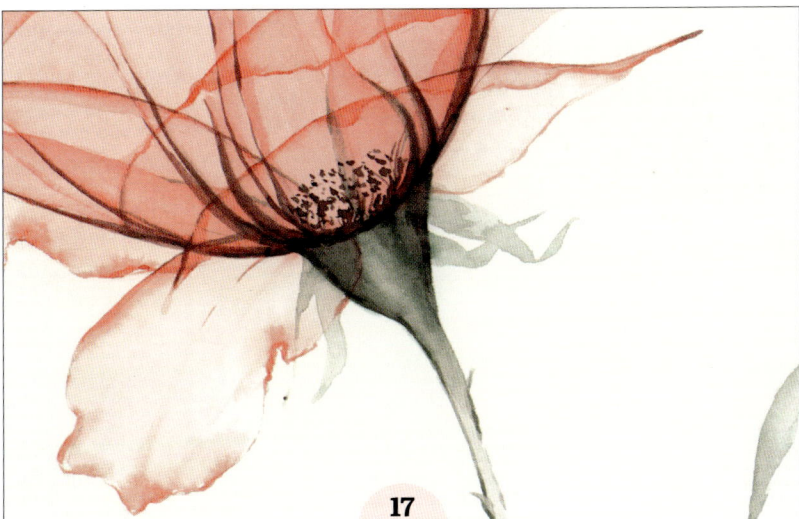

Tip
As you paint a rose, you may find yourself immersed in the process of adding more and more details. Remember that it is important to stop at the right moment and not overdo it.

Rose-inspired
Gallery

Right

'Yellow Rose'

22 x 36cm (8½ x 14¼in)

Paint: *Cadmium Yellow, Burnt Sienna, Phthalo Green, Raw Sienna.*

Yellow is a rather complex colour to paint with the transparent technique, as it has a limited value contrast. You have to start with a very pale yellow mix to have the scope for emphasizing the petals edges with a much stronger mix of yellow.

Opposite, top

'Dusty Purple Rose'

22 x 30cm (8½ x 11¾in)

Paint: *Dusk Violet, Dusk Yellow, Cobalt Green, Sepia.*

I used granulated colours for this rose, but otherwise the technique is the same used in the project.

Opposite, bottom

'Lovely Pink'

22 x 30cm (8½ x 11¾in)

Paint: *Quinacridone Rose, Phthalo Green, Burnt Sienna.*

For this rose, I layered petals on each other almost without adding contrasts to the petals edges. This approach creates a very airy and gentle feeling in the artwork.

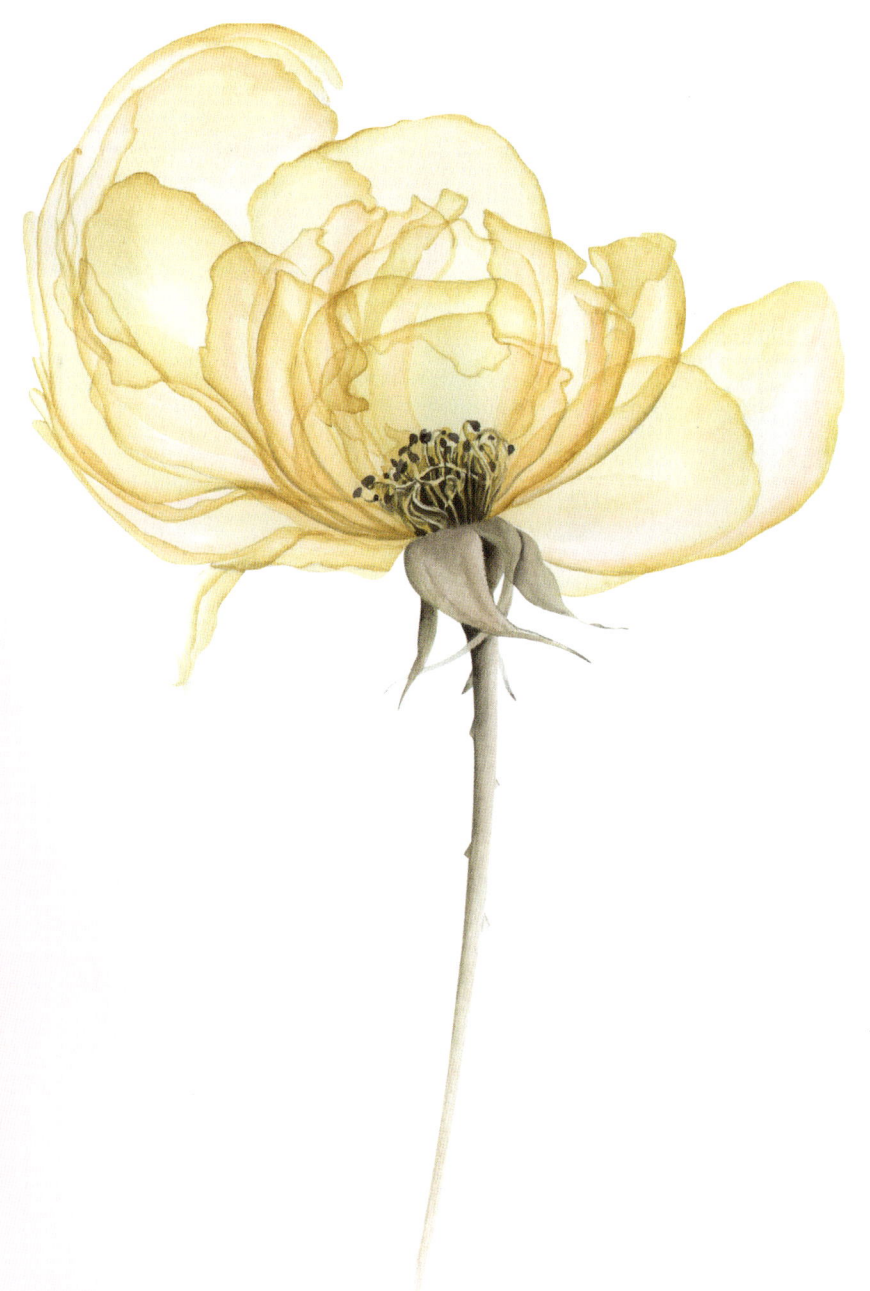

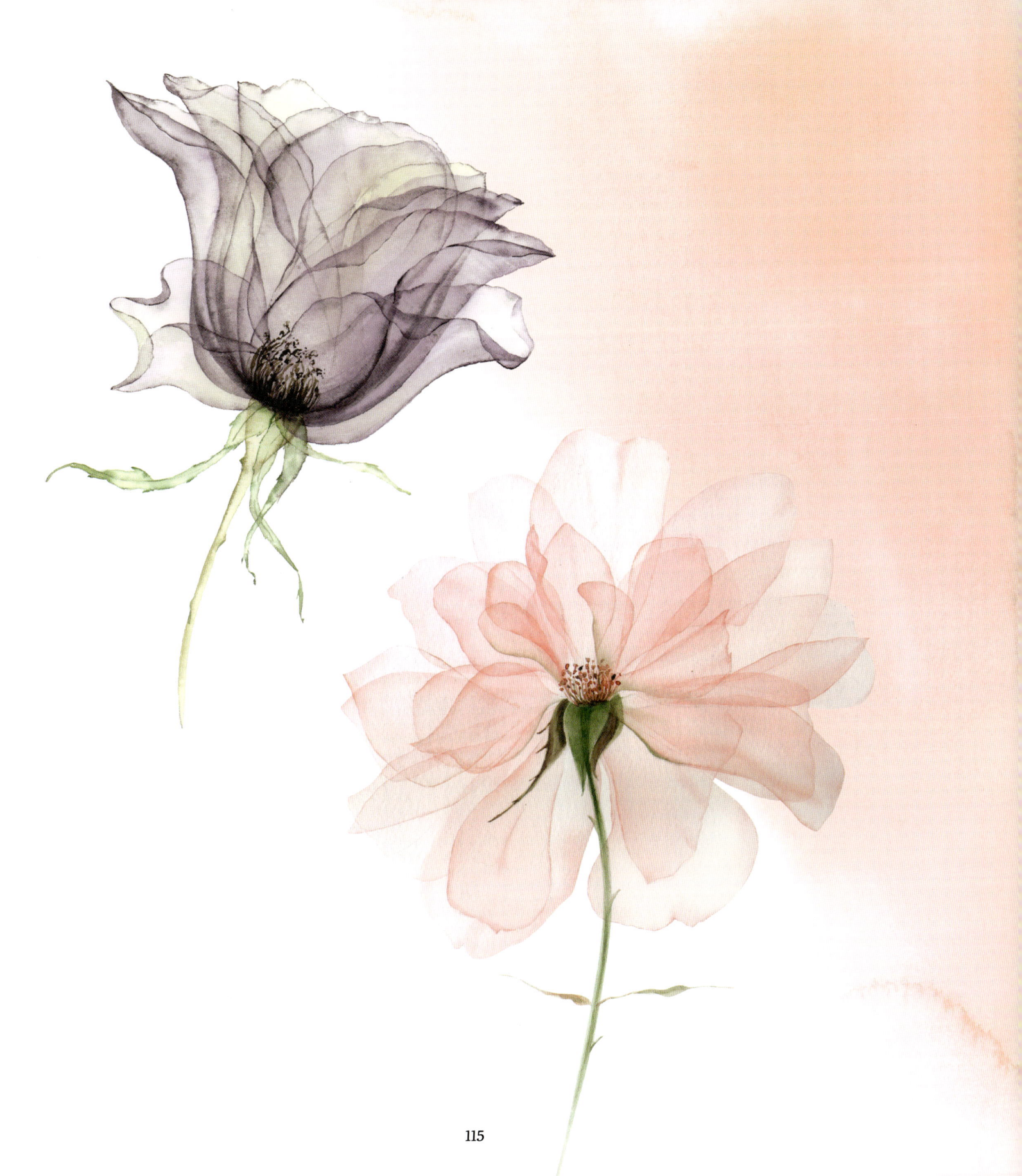

Taking it further

I am open to modern techniques and the fusion of various media, but the constant factor is the presence of flowers. My artworks and illustrations are mostly whimsical floral watercolours in a delicate painting style with a touch of bohemian charm, and my transparent flowers have gained significant popularity – enough that I have been able to license them to numerous companies that produce greeting cards, home decor, kids' apparel and fabrics. I consider myself fortunate to collaborate with many wonderful customers, creating illustrations for them and their products.

Opposite

Despite the various applications, I find it most rewarding to see my flowers framed as wall-art pieces. They can bring a sparkle of romance to minimalistic home décor, or a chic touch to a boho style.

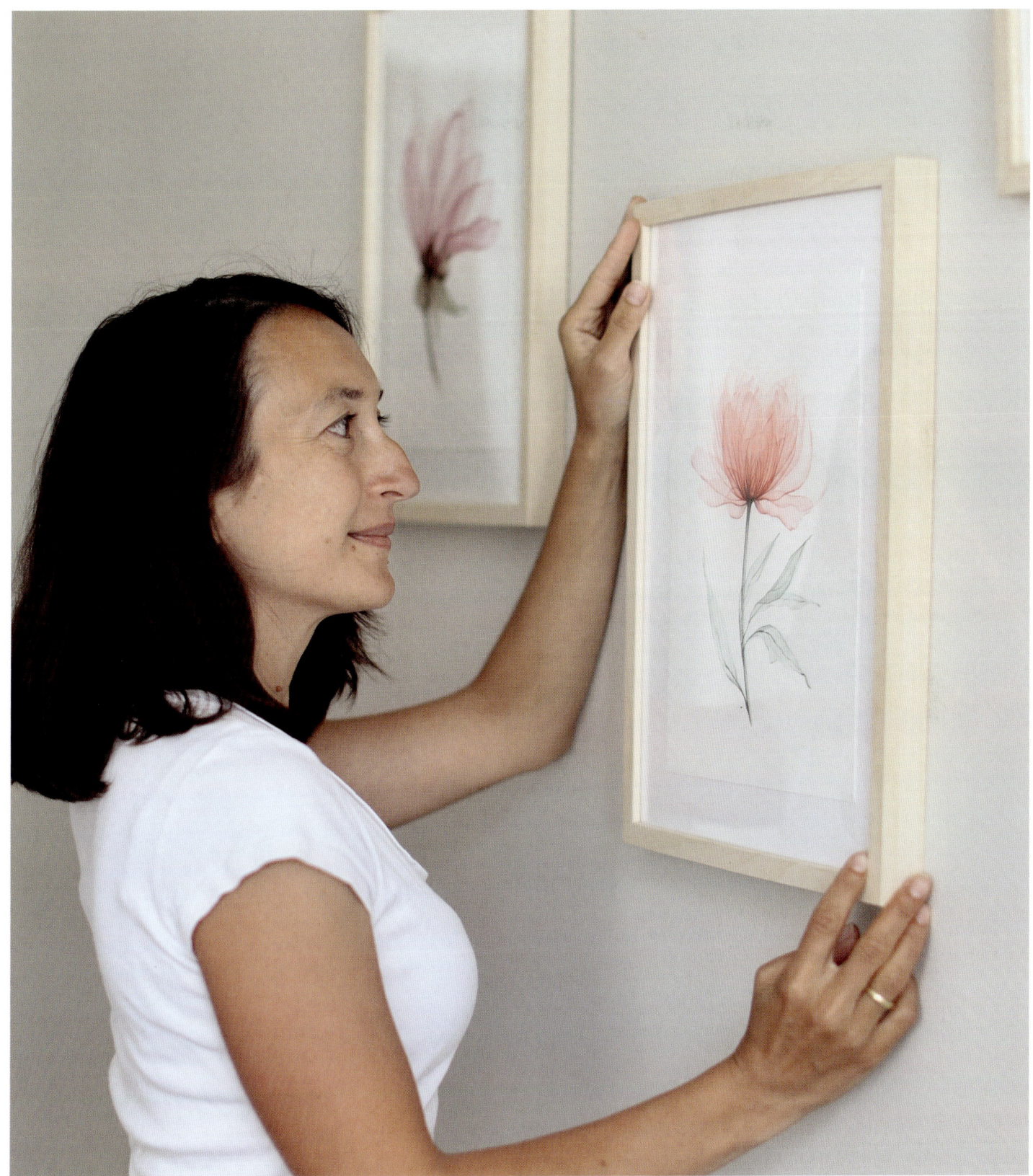

Creating patterns from my illustrations is my second greatest passion after painting. I enjoy the process of working with composition, colours and fashion trends. Naturally, my happiest moments come from seeing my designs brought to life on real products.

When someone mentions that they are an artist, most people envision someone selling artworks in a gallery. Yet, there are so many ways in which art can be incarnated. Just a few years ago, while shopping, I never considered that someone had painted those flowers for that dress's fabric, or the cover of that notebook. Hand-painted designs appear on many of our everyday products, like bed sheets, wallpaper and napkins. Often we take these designs for granted, but countless artists and designers contribute to the beauty and aesthetics that surround us.

In a changing reality where incredible illustrations can be generated in seconds with Artificial Intelligence tools, I continue to believe in the value of hand-painted artworks and designs, as well as the healing influence of mindfully painting something with your own hands.

I create art for a living and I am so grateful for the opportunity to encourage others to be creative. This is the reason I decided to write this book and I am so excited to share it with you. My hope is that this book will inspire you to paint your own favourite flowers in the same transparent technique and that it will boost your confidence in both painting and sharing your art!

Fabrics

Here I'm checking out the colours on fabric samples. It is always exiting to see a printed fabric with your designs for the first time!

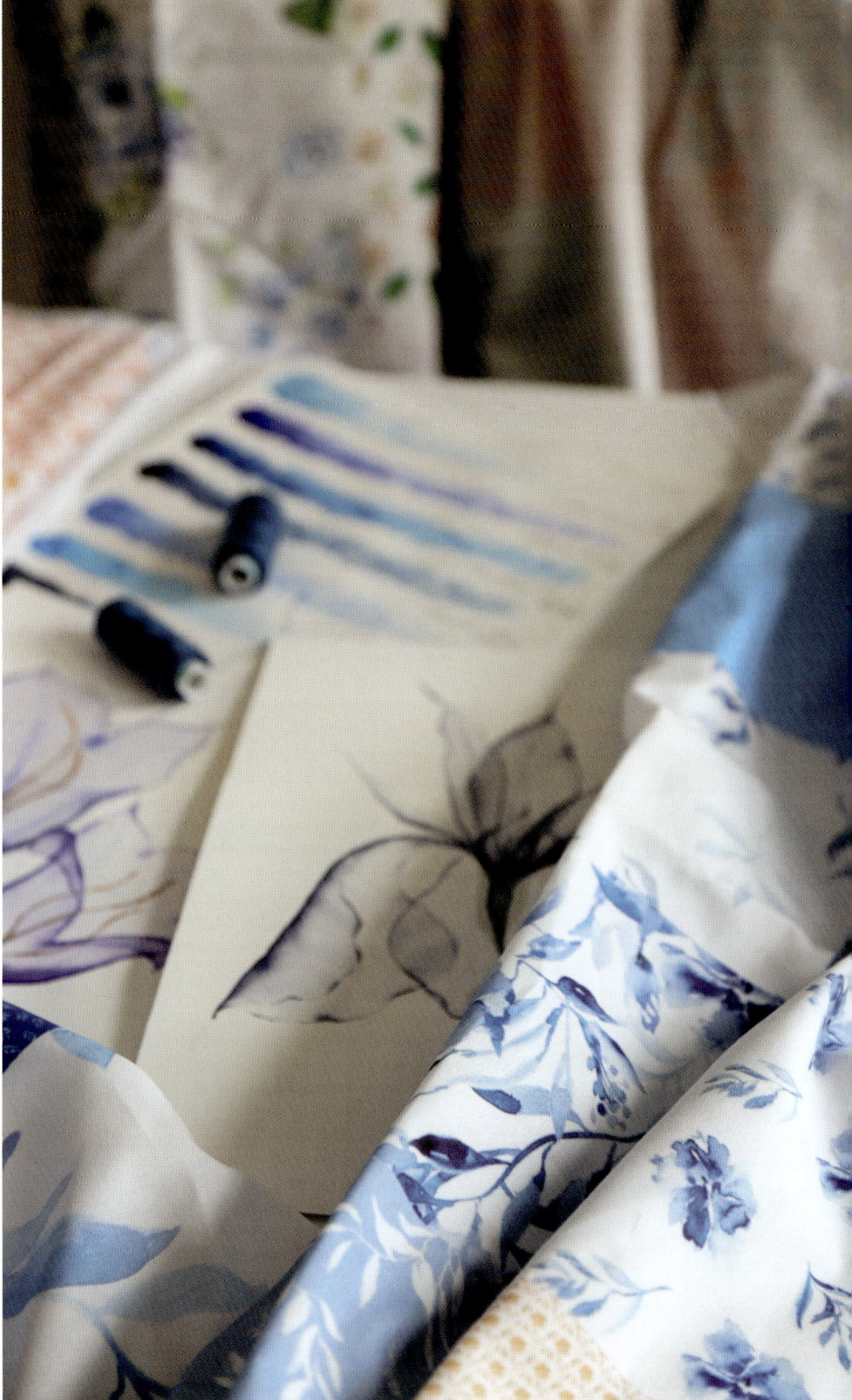

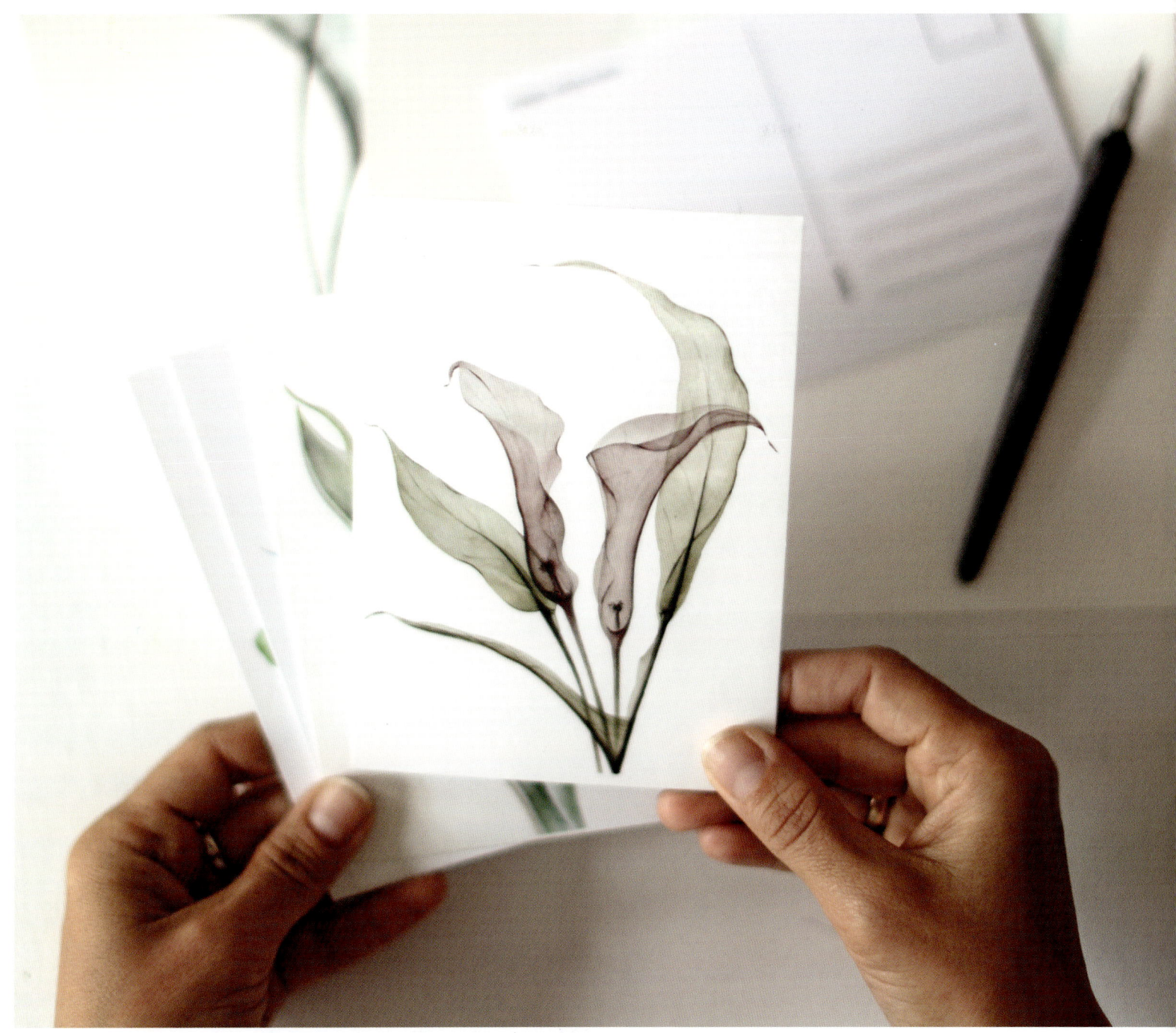

Cards

*Transparent flowers can transform wedding invitations and greeting cards.
I usually add a 'thank you' card to every artwork purchased from my shop, as a
personal touch to my customers.*

Outlines

All of the outlines on the following pages are provided at 100% scale, with no need to enlarge or scale up, to be traced if desired. Note you may need to rotate them when you create your own painting.

While key shapes have been detailed, the more complex flowers (such as the peony) have had their petals simplified to make the transferring process and the initial painting easier. For these complex flowers, you will need to draw in extra petals as you work.

- **Page 121:** Tulip, used on pages 34–43.

- **Page 122:** Eucalyptus, used on pages 46–53.

- **Page 123:** Bellflowers, used on pages 56–65.

- **Page 124:** Magnolia, used on pages 68–77.

- **Page 125:** Iris, used on pages 80–91.

- **Page 126:** Peony, used on pages 94–101.

- **Page 127:** Rose, used on pages 104–113.

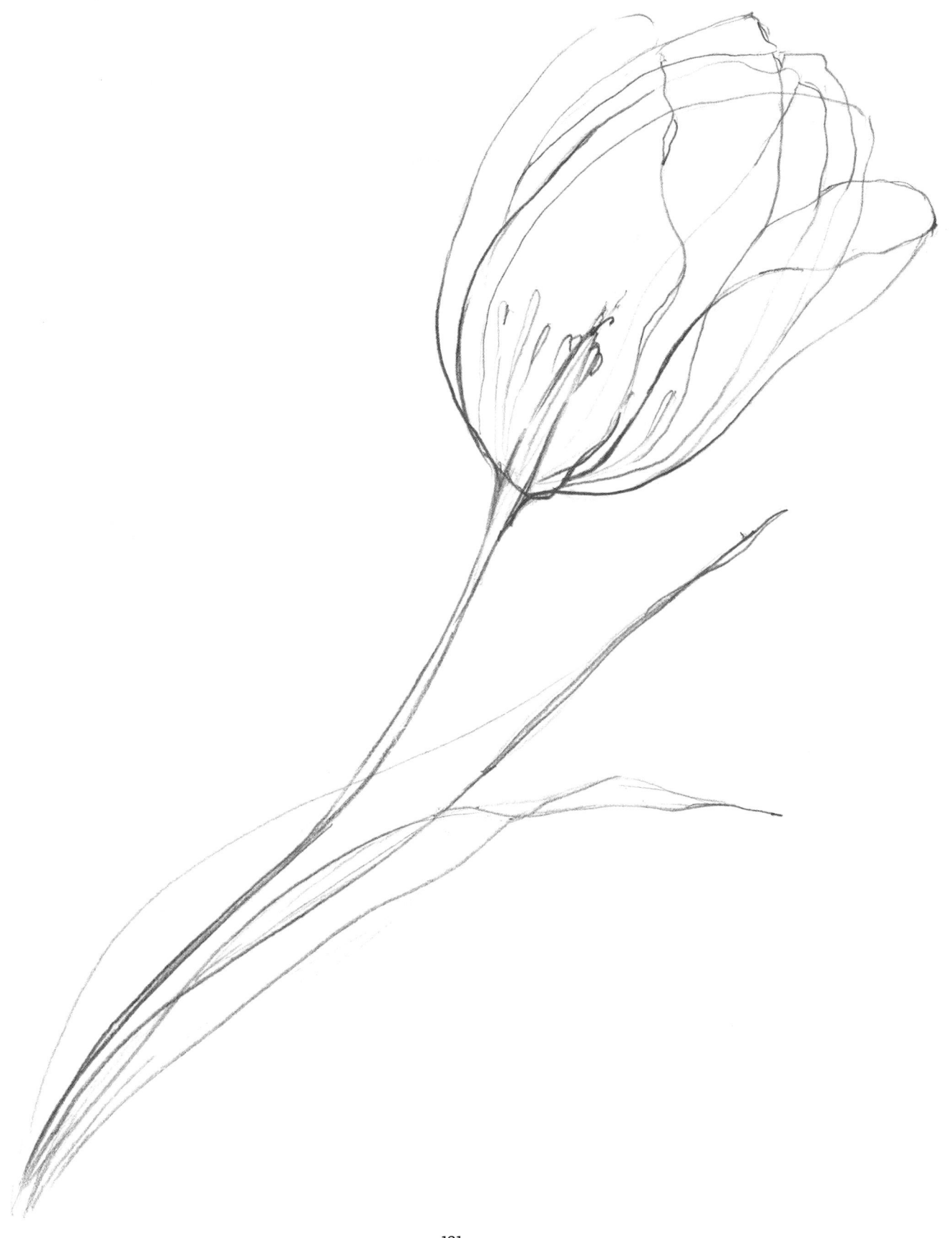

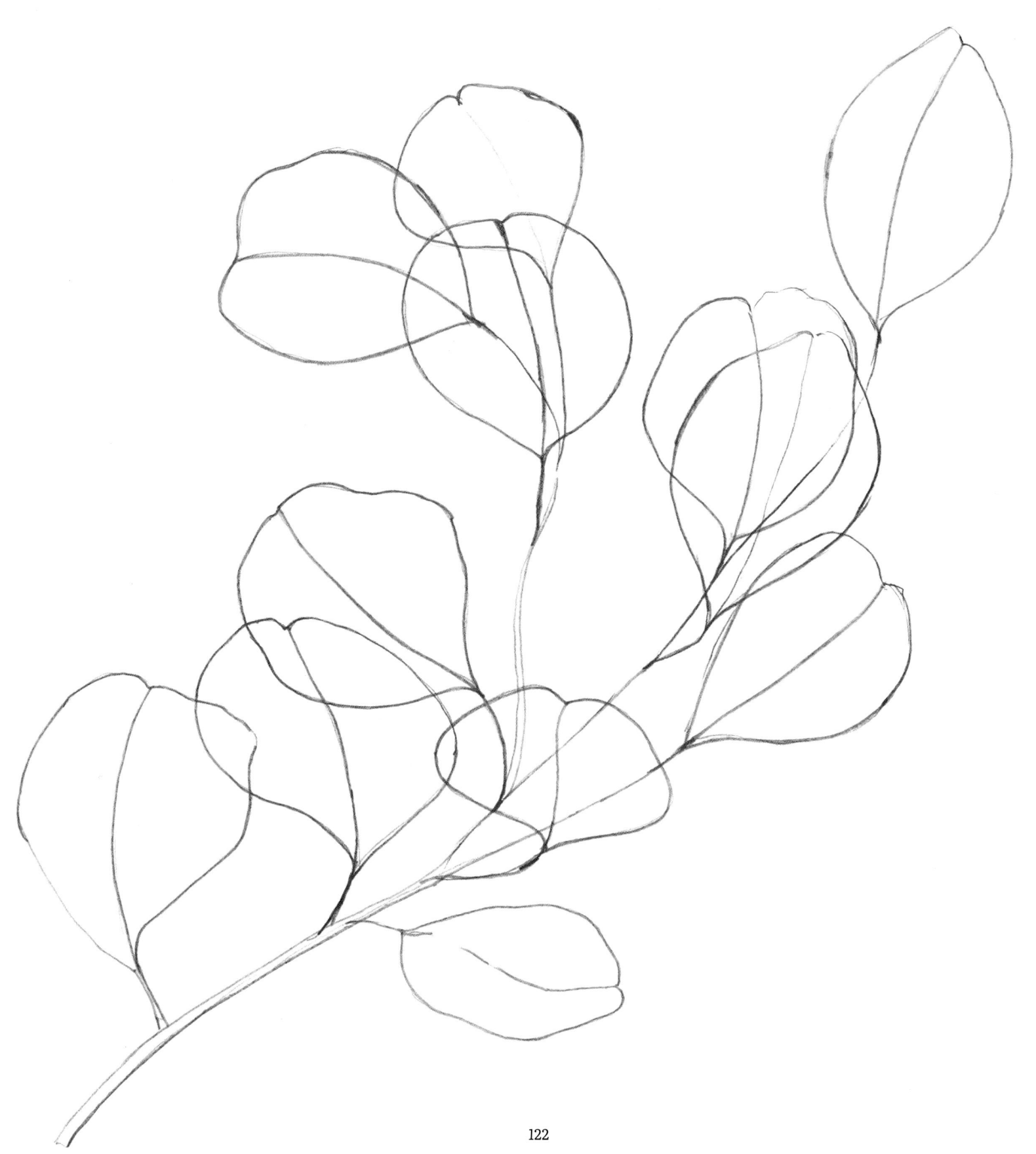

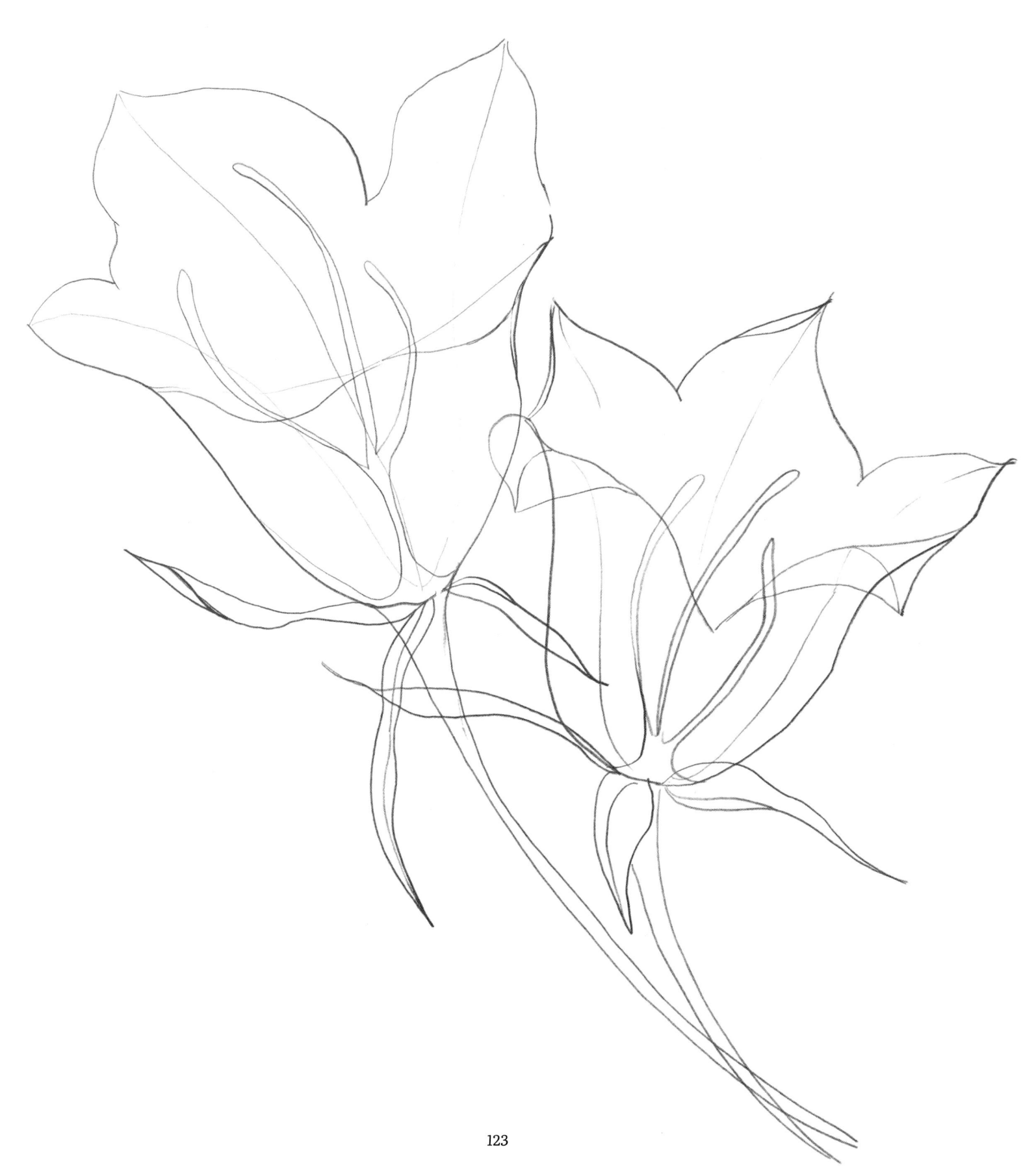

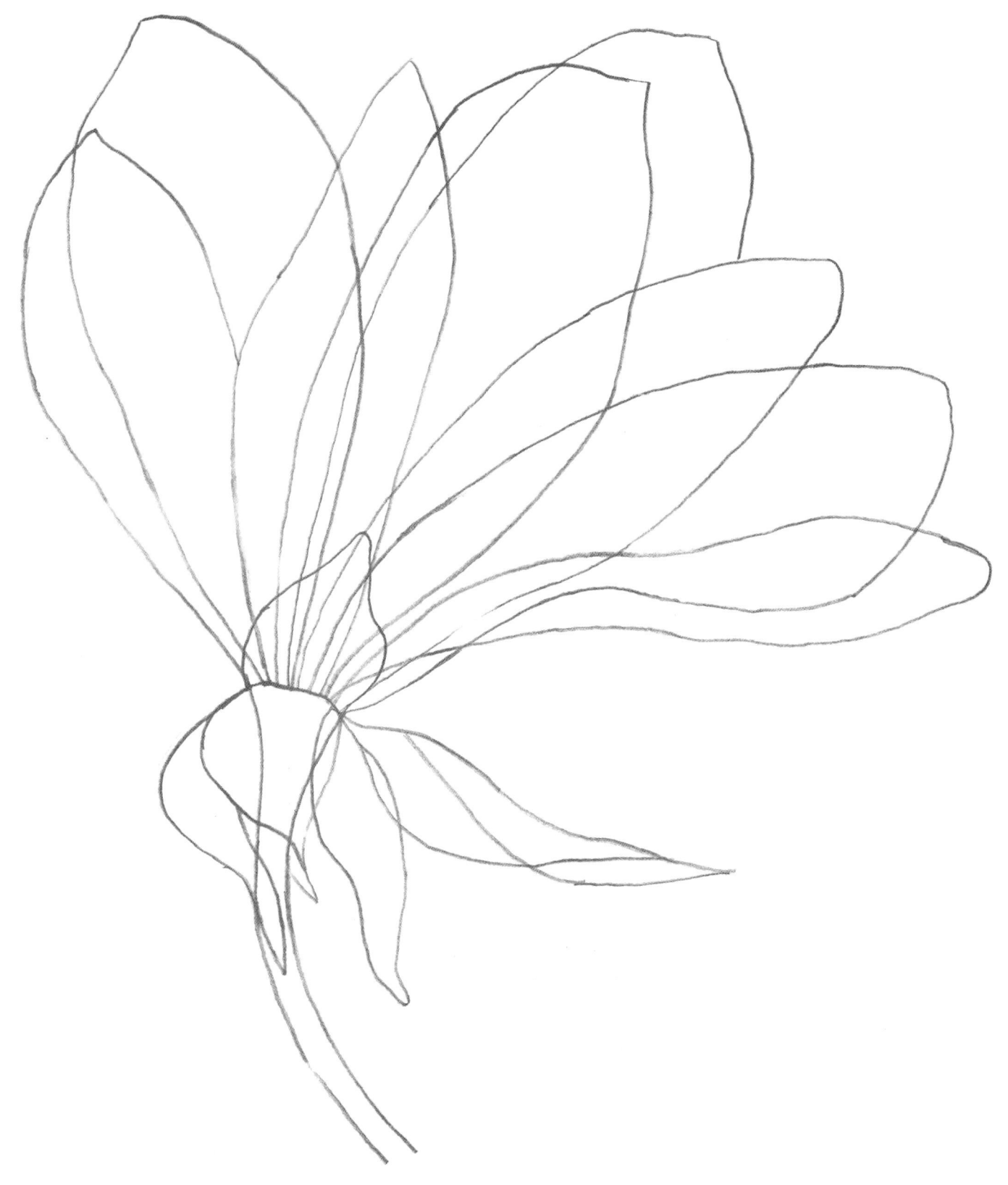

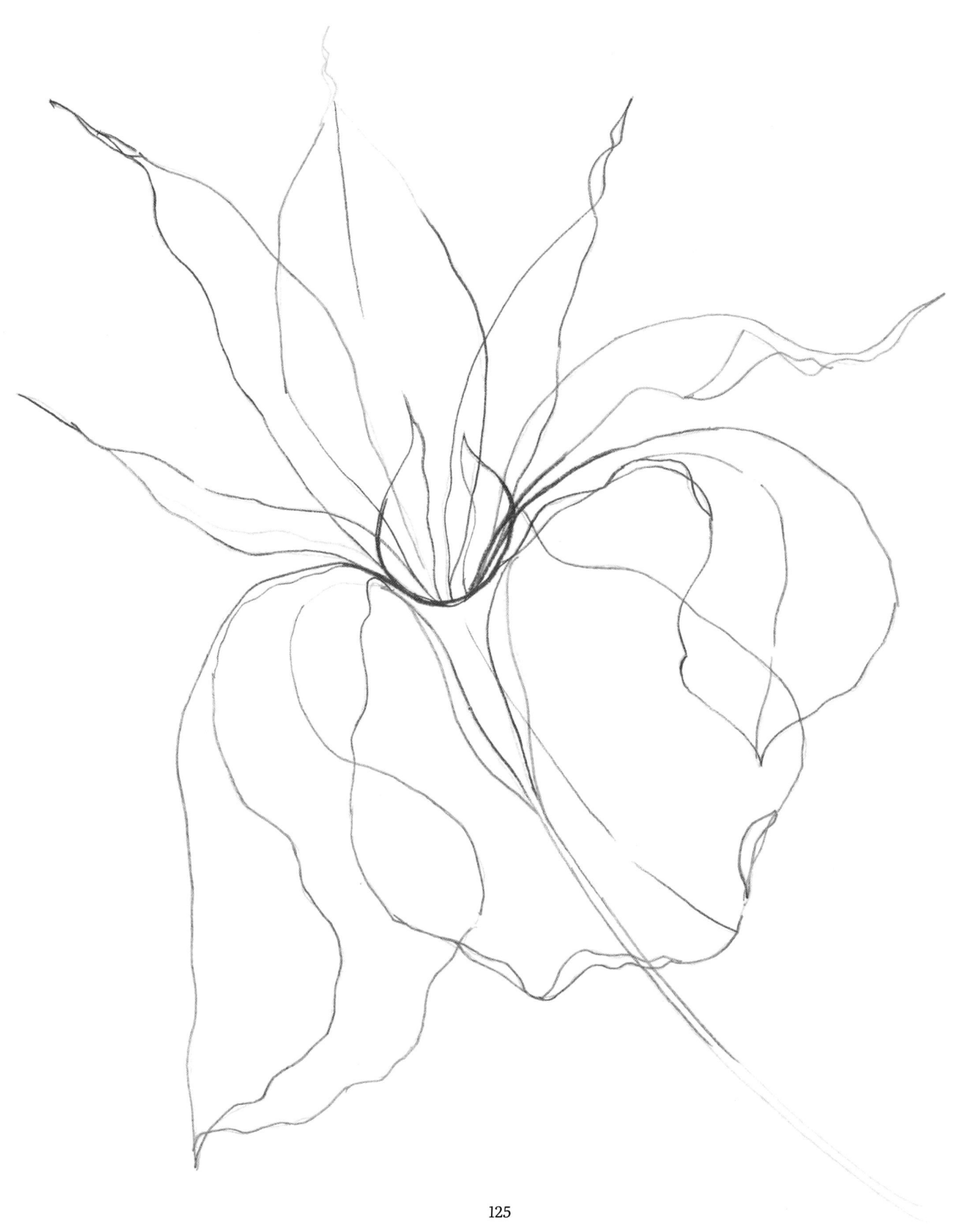

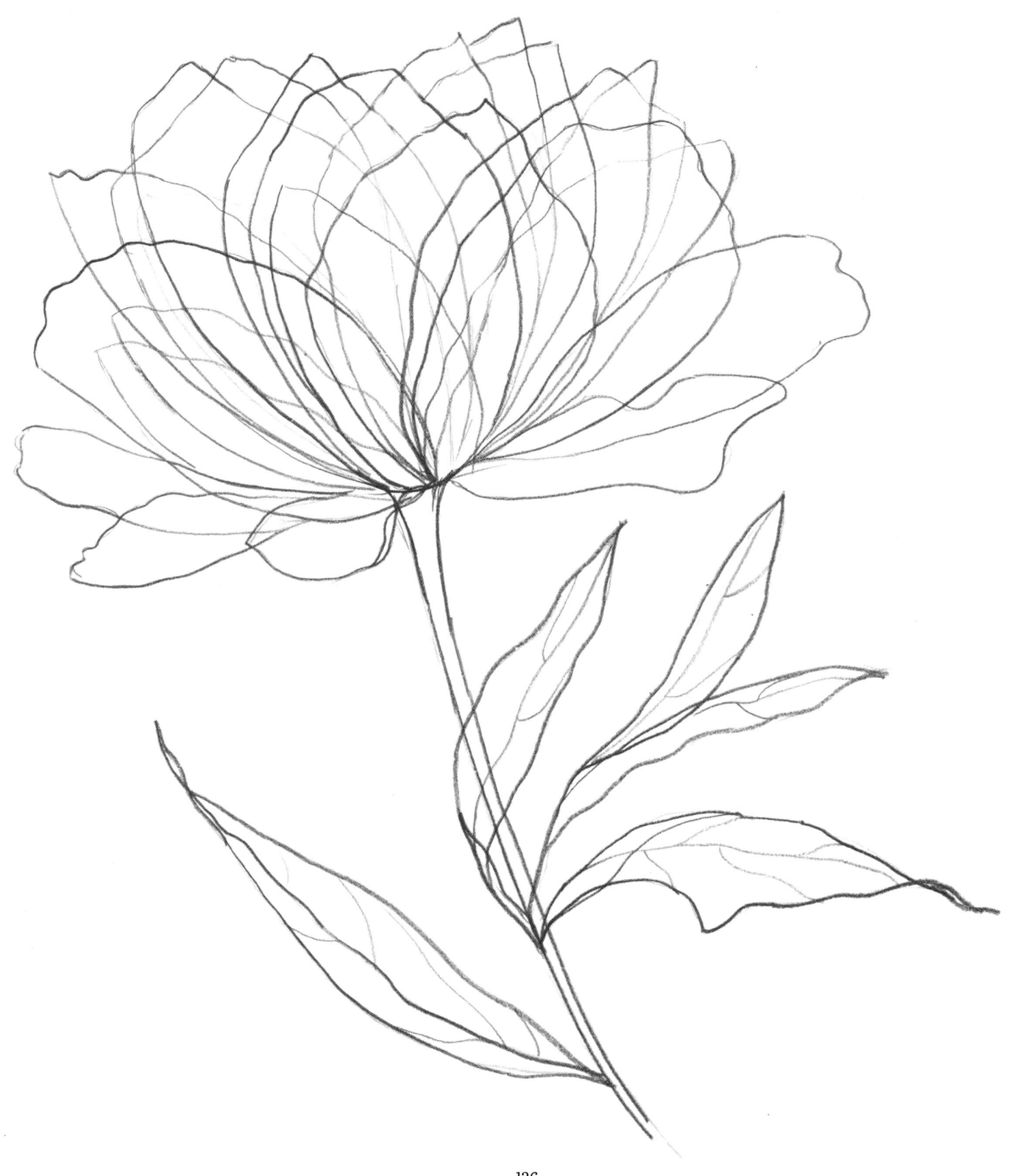

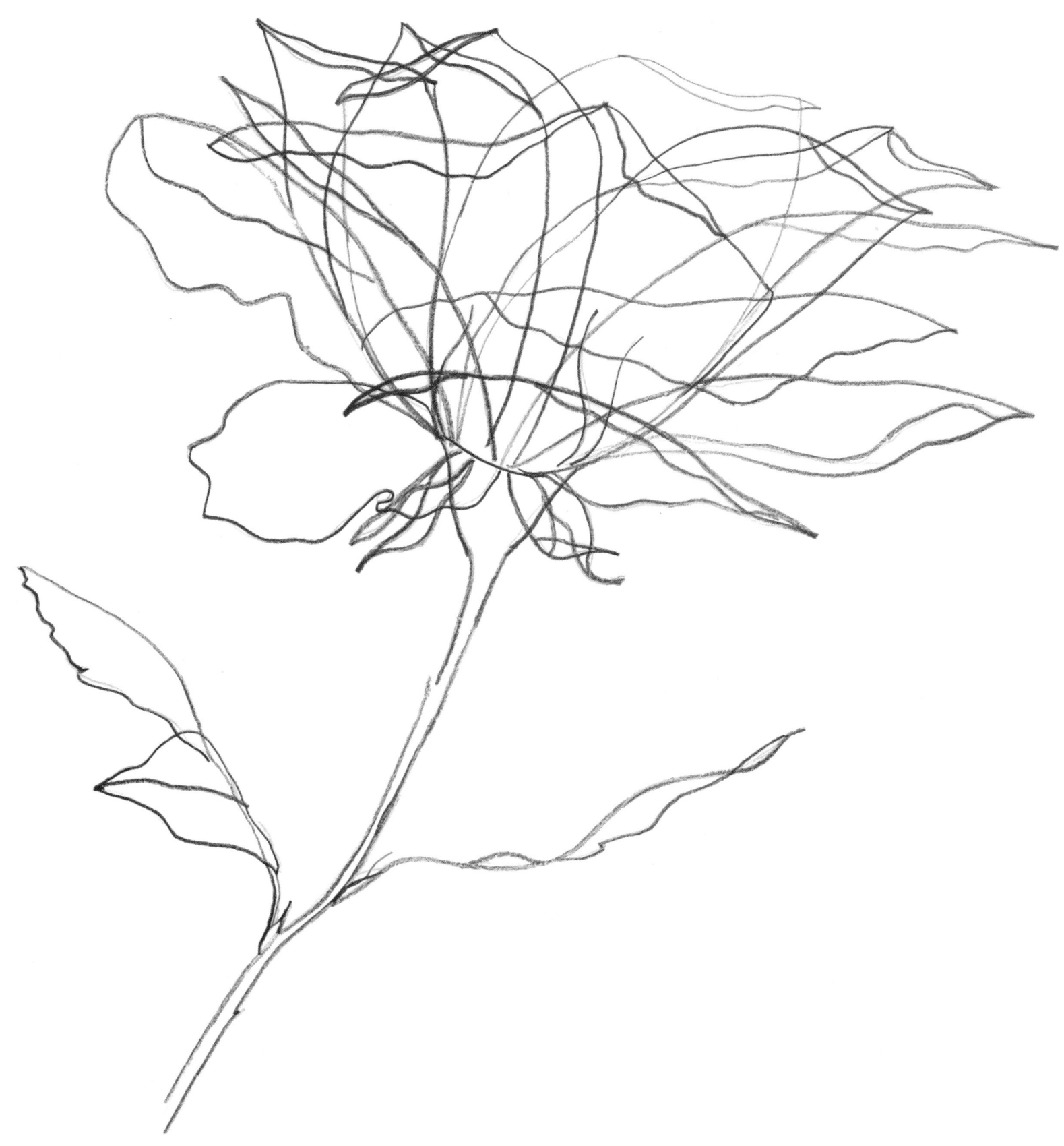

Index

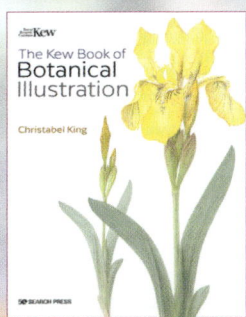
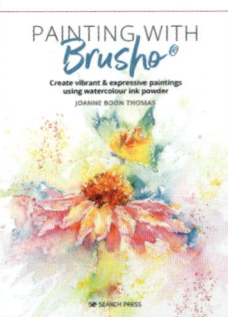
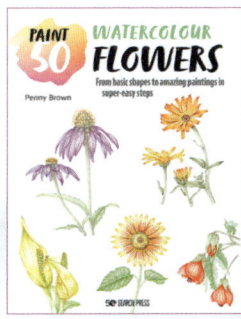
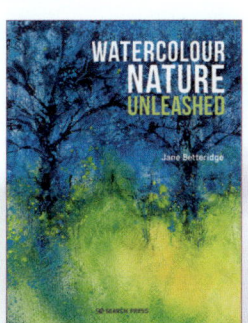
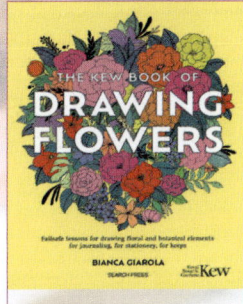
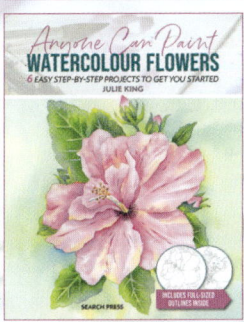
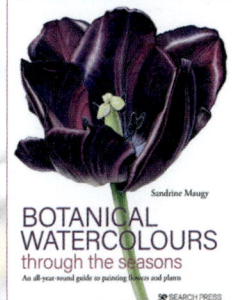
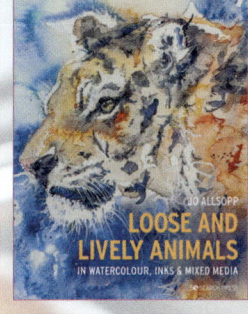
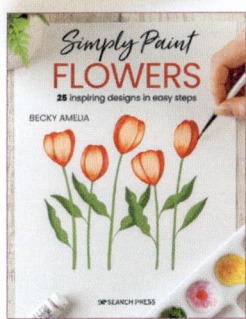
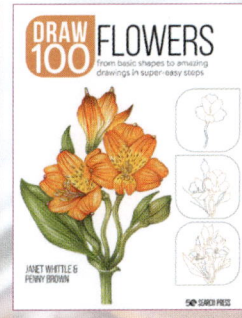
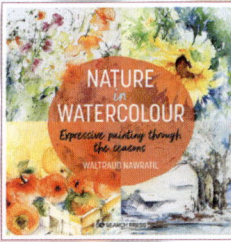
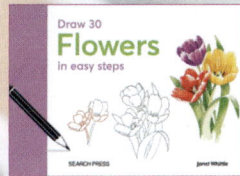

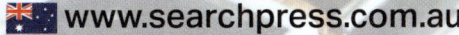

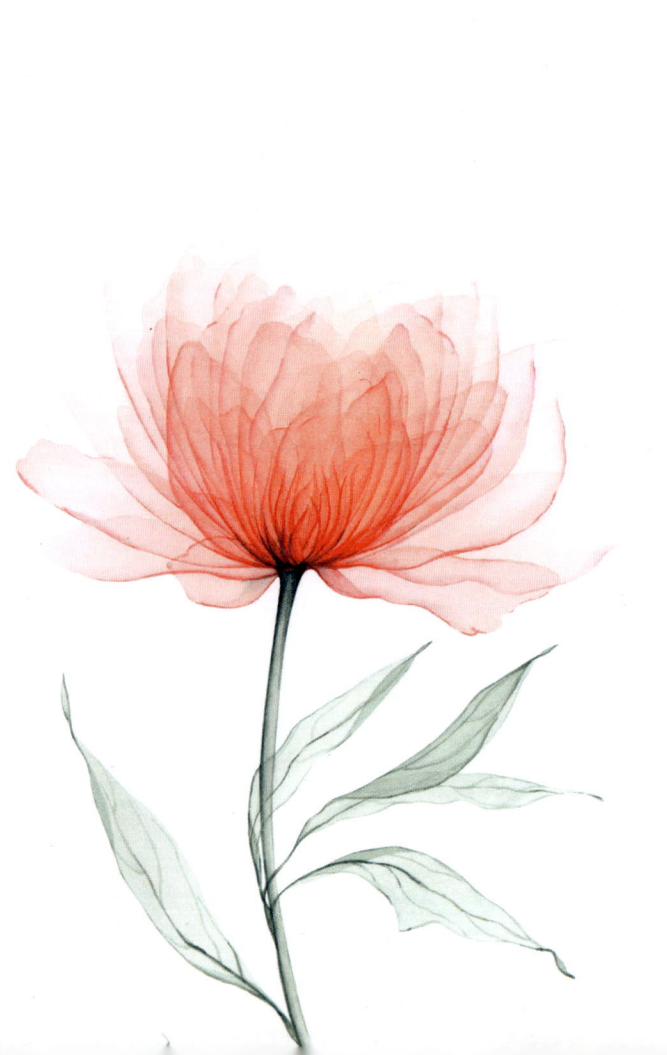